THE POETRY OF OUR WORLD

ALSO BY JEFFERY PAINE

Father India: Westerners Under the Spell of an Ancient Culture

THE POETRY OF OUR WORLD

An International Anthology of Contemporary Poetry

Edited by Jeffery Paine

Perennial
An Imprint of HarperCollins*Publishers*

Permissions, constituting a continuation of this copyright page, appear on pp. 489–94.

A hardcover edition of this book was published in 2000 by HarperCollins Publishers.

THE POETRY OF OUR WORLD. Copyright © 2000 by Jeffery Paine.

HarperCollins books may be purchased for educational, business, or sales promotional use. For information please write: Special Markets Department, HarperCollins Publishers Inc., 10 East 53rd Street, New York, NY 10022.

First Perennial edition published 2001.

Designed by Kyoko Watanabe

The Library of Congress has catalogued the hardcover edition as follows:

The poetry of our world: an international anthology of contemporary
    poetry/edited by Jeffery Paine.—1st ed.
        p.   cm.
    Includes index.
    ISBN 0-06-055369-3
        1. Poetry, Modern—20th century. I. Paine, Jeffery, 1944–   .
PN6101.P57   2000   99-34921
808.81'045—dc21
        ISBN 0-06-095193-1 (pbk.)

07 08 ❖/RRD 10 9 8 7

CONTENTS

PART I
THE ENGLISH-SPEAKING WORLD
Edited by Helen Vendler

PART II
LATIN AMERICA
Edited by Carolyn Forché

PART III
EUROPE
Edited by Joseph Brodsky, Sven Birkerts, and Edward Hirsch

PART IV
AFRICA
Edited by Kwame Anthony Appiah

OF KNOWLEDGE AND PLEASURE GLOBALIZED

A World Tour of the Poetic Moment

A half century ago, or specifically in August 1953, the editors of *The New Republic* decided to assess the state of the art of the arts. *The New Republic* exuded prestige at midcentury, and it had merely to tap with its wand the brightest talents—Stephen Spender, Elizabeth Bowen, Malcolm Cowley, Herbert Read; the list goes on and on—to recruit them for their project. More striking now, than all those bright minds evaluating the artistic world is what "the world" was. With scarcely a qualm, *The New Republic* reduced the globe to five countries: the United States, England, France, Italy, and Germany. The magazine's editors were not entirely ethnomyopic, however, for they sadly reasoned that from South America to the Soviet Union to Red China much of the earth lay squelched under the dictators' boot, where no artistic flowering could bloom. Even without that disclaimer, though, for most literate Americans their country and England and a few other European countries delineated the terrestrial map (or the portion of it that mattered) at midcentury.

A pervasive pessimism hangs, like clouds above, over those *New Republic* essays. Well, why not? World War II had yielded to the Korean War and the Cold War; the nightmarish Hitler had been put to rest, but his cousins Joe Stalin (d. 1953) and Mao Zedong (d. 1976) successfully carried on the manufacture of human misery. (Indeed, *The New Republic* may have shortchanged its pessimism, so innocently oblivious to an environment being grossly fouled and a world population doubling and trebling beyond the resources to feed it.) Those writers are bothered by something quieter, more private, as though criticism bred its own melancholy. The dusk they describe falling on history turns out—reading those essays fifty years later—to be principally a lament for the once-high regard in which art had been held, before being exiled to the sidelines.

In painting, abstraction had thinned the congregation that had once gawked at *Virgin with Child;* so, likewise, had contemporary poetry somehow managed to alienate Byron's and Tennyson's legions of fans. Stephen Spender diagnosed the malady as inbreeding. He lamented how college writing classes standardized or even blinkered would-be poets, who quickly learn which subjects and styles to fasten onto to win approval. As poets traded in the traditional robes of their calling—hero, idealistic lover, or sage—for the more up-to-date uniforms of social misfit, homemaker, or perplexed introvert, did they master to perfection a range of experience but too limited a range? Suppose the critics had obtained a passport to trespass beyond the *cordon sanitaire* of the five "major countries," what surprises undreamed-of would they have found? This anthology addresses, from multiple perspectives and geographies, that question of whether there are further areas of consciousness or experience that a poet may yet explore. What other marriages of history and imagination have transpired in our time, about which the *New Republic* arts inspectors suspected little?

The *New Republic* essays shone with intellectual acuity, humanity, and often humor. Written in the same years as R. P. Blackmur's *Language as Gesture* (1952), Randall Jarrell's *Poetry and the Age* (1953), John Berryman's *The Freedom of the Poet* (pub. posthumously, 1976), and W. H. Auden's *The Dyer's Hand* (1962), this lucid criticism at midcentury surely constellates a silver age of the intellect. Yet their every assumption about what poetry is, about what a poet does, moves in a padding of American perspective or protective European preconceptions. What would happen, though, were all the doors suddenly to blow open?

"A world anthology of poetry—how? Americans have no clue what's transpired even next door, in European poetry." So Joseph Brodsky fretted when we first discussed the possibility of the book now in your hands. "The one percent here who read poetry understands one dot, America, in the landscape. . . . Hmmm. We shall need to include explanation, essays."

Turn Joseph's question upside down, however, and it makes equal sense: How *not* approach the poetry of the world as a whole? Even American poetry cannot be comprehended solely in American terms. Was Walt Whitman the "father" of modern American poetry—or was Charles Baudelaire? In his journal Baudelaire brooded how nothing in modern civilization can justify the continuation of life—which brooding furnishes the starting point for many an American poet. Perhaps nowhere more than in the United States have contemporary poets set about the Baudelairean job of discovering what will justify, what will sustain: They would experience in the cauldron of their own being the anonymous city and mundane home life and their own chaotic urges, and out of them transmute value and meaning. In "Of Modern Poetry," Wallace Stevens already stated the problem:

> The poem of the mind in the act of finding
> What will suffice. It has not always had
> To find: the scene was set; it repeated what
> Was in the script.
>   Then the theatre was changed
> To something else. Its past was a souvenir.
> It has to be living, to learn the speech of the place.
> It has to face the man of the time and to meet
> The women of the time. It has to think about war
> And it has to find what will suffice.

Elsewhere Stevens defined modern poetry as purveying the pleasures of faith in an age of disbelief. Randall Jarrell sounded a kindred defense of the craft: "From Christ to Freud we have believed that, if we know the truth, the truth will set us free: Art is indispensable because so much of this truth can be learned through works of art and through works of art alone."

For the high modern poet, art had become religion (and religion often an inferior sort of art). The poet-priests of modernism—Yeats, Rilke, Eliot, even Stevens—shaped visions that had less in common with Tennyson and Longfellow than with Pascal and Meister Eckhart. But, unlike the Christian philosophers, they were forced to invent their own eccentric terms and individual myths to express their visions and experiences. It could seem a bit much—to have to be both God and worm; to be simultaneously a fallible human mortal, a perfectionist craftsman, and a demiurge—and soon there was a retreat from so Promethean a calling.

In her poem "Poetry," Marianne Moore declared,

> I, too, dislike it: there are things that are important
> beyond all this fiddle.

In contrast to Yeats's and Eliot's high mandarin tone, Ms. Moore, William Carlos Williams, and later poets like A. R. Ammons and John Ashbery assumed that their poetic insights gained in value the less claim they made for them. Contemporary poets who retreat into "domesticity" write fewer poems of genius, perhaps, but many, many of a pleasing competence. If all recent American poetry had been published anonymously, this Anonymous would have written a rambling but great poem. For all together it expands the margins of everyday life; it locates a half beauty in shopping malls and marital discord; it flicks on a lamp in the shadowy gray regions of daily consciousness. The younger generation of American poets has colonized with a sort of meaning the last frontier: the things that, beyond any high-sounding interpretation, just happen to happen.

Marianne Moore, however, lied: She did not dislike poetry at all; to the contrary. Beneath the pose of preoccupation with the accidental and the incidental, many American poets still carry in their backpacks the redemptive assumptions of visionary modernism, though they must never confess this out loud. Not uttering words like "spirit," they have waged regardless a personal battle against a materialist, machine age. Claiming nothing for themselves, they have nonetheless cleared a sphere of subjectivity amid mammoth bureaucracies; forged deeper significance amid an ever-narrower private life; made meaningful order out of a chaotic welter of impressions—that has been the work of the poet in contemporary America. A stated mundane and an unstated hallowedness—with such incongruous strings many recent American bards have strung their lute. Such an unstable coupling—*Heaven and Earth: A Cosmology*, Albert

Goldbarth titled one collection—is that the cosmology for the future? What else, we might wonder, has poetry concerned itself with elsewhere?

American readers will detect a different atmosphere as they enter into the European section of this anthology. The climate may strike them as claustrophobic, the air smoky, and there is a name for that opaqueness: history. Its long tragic years lie like a patina over everything. One does not simply wish them away, those circumscriptions from the past that limit an individual's ability to maneuver in the present. American poets have sounded in many different voices, but never quite the voice that broached Anna Akhmatova as she stood outside the Stalinist prison where her son was locked in.

> I spent seventeen months waiting in line outside the prison in Leningrad. One day somebody in the crowd identified me. Standing behind me was a woman, with lips blue from the cold, who had, of course, never heard me called by name before. Now she startled out of the torpor common to us and asked me in a whisper (everybody whispered there):
> "Can you describe this?"
> And I said: "I can."
> Then something like a smile passed fleetingly over what had once been her face.
>
> (from "Requiem")

Tragedy is daily fare, and Akhmatova is a connoisseur. In the poems reprinted here she evokes the classical European masters of tragedy—Sophocles, the Bible, Dante, Shakespeare—to learn the secret skills that make the unbearable bearable. The Polish poet Zbigniew Herbert also made his argument for "Why the Classics," because without them—without tragic art's antidote to tragic history—all we'll be left with is

> a broken jar
> a small broken soul
> with a great self-pity.

At times history seems the nightmare from which no one awakens. How can there be poetry after the Holocaust? the German philosopher Theodor Adorno asked. How continue to play with beauty and sense; how use language at all, when language helped implement the Final Solution? The Holocaust survivor Paul Celan earned his reputation as Europe's most important postwar poet by navigating a way through the barren rocks, by using broken syntax and shattered grammar to fabricate poetry outside the tainted conventions. In a poem with no title—no such helpful guide-posts here—Celan describes Jews in the camps digging their own graves:

> O einer, o keiner, o niemand, o du:
> Wohin gings, da's nirgendhin ging?
> O du gräbst und ich grab, and ich grab mich dir zu,
> und am Finger erwacht uns der Ring.
> (O one, o none, o no one, o you:/Where led the way
> when nowhere it led?/O you dig and I dig, and I dig
> toward you,/and on our finger the ring awakens.)

Only when history falls like clods on the grave does the longing to escape into a pale pastel light—into ahistorical sensuousness—emerge so fiercely. Twentieth-century European poetry perfects a flushed, heightened sensuality that luxuriates in the pure elements. Come out into the garden—isn't that the way *The Four Quartets* begins?—trying to follow the thrush into a nature artificially heightened beyond nature, where history is momentarily quiet, silenced. In Italy, with its pellucid intoxicated light, Eugenio Montale describes

> bodies languishing in a flowing
> of colors, colors in musics. To vanish,
> then, is the venture of ventures.

And he advises

> . . . let your footstep
> crunch on gravel and stumble
> in tangled seaweed: maybe
> this is the moment, so long awaited,
> that frees you from your journey . . . .

The desire to decamp into pure nature parallels an earlier, Mallarméan tendency to abscond into pure technique, where all social realities attenuate and thin to inconsequence. Consequently Bertolt Brecht could famously object that "to speak of trees is almost a crime/for it is a kind of silence about injustice." The five European poets anthologized here found themselves in the middle of a dark century, knowing too much history and much literary technics, endeavoring to balance one against the other so they might see a tree and still utter a word about injustice.

A man sits on a train, trying to forget Europe. All day long the train's hard benches jolt him, as out the windows he gazes at baobab trees twisting their anguished arms in the drought. As the train skirts small villages, chattering black girls burst from school as birds from a birdcage. "Here I am," he reflects, "trying to forget Europe in the heartland of the Sine [a river in Senegal]."

An American reader, first dipping into African poetry, might wonder about striking or peculiar things there. Why, first of all, does every poet seem to evoke Africa, O Africa? Poets from France or Finland don't apostrophize Europa, though Europe—whose various regions have influenced one another for centuries—is culturally more interconnected than the far-flung African continent with its (until recently) many relatively self-contained traditions. (In his introduction, Anthony Appiah decodes this mantra of "Africa," which issues even from the white South African poet Breyten Breytenbach's lips.) For now the more pressing question is, Could the man on the train forget Europe and have a vision of Africa that is purely African? He did manage to become his country's first president—for he is Senegal's Léopold Sédar Senghor (and the quote is from "All Day Long")—but as for forgetting Europe, even in his poetry, that he could not do. Why not?

The African poets of this anthology, and likewise the ones from Asia, may appear fortunate to have arrived at precisely the right moment, just as the clock was striking dawn. Poets like Senghor can still remember an older Africa vanished or in the process of vanishing, yet with their present-day educations, they are like ambassadors of that older world to modern consciousness, explaining its lost wonders to contemporary readers. In Okot p'Bitek's "The Woman with Whom I Share My Husband," a village housewife complains to her husband, Ocol, about his affair with a modern, Europeanized woman:

> Listen Ocol, my old friend,
> The ways of your ancestors
> Are good,
> Their customs are solid
> . . . .
> I do not understand
> The ways of foreigners
> But I do not despise their customs.
> Why should you despise yours?

More accomplished poets may follow Senghor and p'Bitek, but the combination of old and new knowledges they possessed is not likely, in any later afternoon of time, to come again. P'Bitek and Senghor stood, looking two ways at once, at a crossroads of African history.

They often invoked the Ancestors, which seems fitting. In traditional Africa, as well as in Asia, a sense of one's ancestors loomed large. In Madagascar the travel writer Dervla Murphy encountered wondrous dwellings and inquired to whom they belonged. They were houses for the dead, she learned, on which their descendants spent nine-tenths of their annual income. Most contemporary African and Asian poets, though, no longer knew how to erect the equivalent house in poetry for the ancestral ways. They did wish to honor their forefathers, but that is far from all they wished to do. They also wanted to meet the postcolonial Europeans on their own ground of politics and reclaim that ground; they wanted to measure themselves against Europe's master poets and match them symbol for symbol and irony for irony. Instead of making offerings to the ancestors, many African poets thus ended up borrowing their bardic robes and oral rhythms to express concerns the ancestors never had.

Anthropologists—but usually *not* poets—record some African and Asian people still engaged in the ancestral pastimes of

> hunting for witches,
> exorcising demons,

sacrificing animals to hungry gods,

sanctifying temples,

waiting for messiahs,

scapegoating their sins,

consulting the stars,

flagellating themselves in public,

prohibiting the eating of pork (or dog, or beef, or all
swarming things except locusts, crickets, and
grasshoppers),

wandering on pilgrimage from one dilapidated shrine to
the next,

abstaining from sex on the day of the full moon,

refusing to be in the same room with their wife's elder
sister,

matting their hair with cow dung,

isolating women during menstruation,

seeking salvation by meditating naked in a cave for
several years,

and so on and on.

Of such ancestral doings (this list was compiled by anthropologist Richard Schweder), the poets represented here say hardly a word: They may wish to propitiate their forefathers but, in spite of themselves, are committed to a poetry of modernity in which such propitiation can scarcely occur. Rather than pursue hereditary customs, the "sleepless man" in Antonio Agostinho Neto's "African Poem" dreams of "buying knives and forks to eat with at a table." Certainly when Neto and Senghor and Wole Soyinka sat down at a table to write, it was of streamlined, recent construction, and not so different from where Elizabeth Bishop and Zbigniew Herbert and Pablo Neruda sat, a few chairs down.

Many African and Asian poets—like the Indonesian Chairil Anwar (1922–49), working in a new language and an artificially glued-together country—had no choice but to be modern. Yet modernity cannot mean for poets like Anwar what it meant for, say, Valéry or Eliot. Literary modernism, an aesthetic phenomenon in Europe, often mutated into a political one when exported abroad. A style or technique that was "ideologically neutral" in England or the United States (no one asks whether Wallace Stevens voted Republican or Democrat), once imported into a country in flux such as Anwar's Indonesia or Neto's Angola—because that style approached tradition and apprehended custom differently—could explode like a stick of cultural dynamite.

I remember, a few years back, hearing a poet from a small island country in the Pacific give a reading. The makeshift stage could barely contain her exuberance, she was all energy and daring. She obviously meant to shock: "I was thirteen,/When first I saw a vagina." The forbidden word, like a dotty pornographer past his prime, barely reverberated, though, after a century of such titillations, since *Ubu Roi* shocked Parisian theatergoers by uttering *merde* aloud. After the reading, however, at a party her fellow islanders cast her *déjà-vu* derring-do in a decidedly different light. They told how, when the poet finished her work, instead of rushing it into print she sat in a corner for half a year, suicidal, wondering whether shame dictated burning the manuscript. After her book did appear, supposedly her clan deliberated whether they should *(1)* toss her off a cliff or *(2)* defend her unconditionally (the latter, of course). The poet's work had detonated a bombshell in that remote place, changing forever the way women were thought of and the life they might live there. Some American poets, brooding over their marginality, might covet an island remoteness where poetic words can still change life and merit death.

We know, or assume we know, what makes a writer second rate: An inferior mind is imitating its betters for propagandistic or rhetorical purposes. Some first-class poetic intelligences, though, who exhibited the spark of originality, were still nonetheless not in a position to write to primarily aesthetic considerations. A couple of poets even in this anthology may intrigue us less for their verbal audacity than for how they were caught in between, one foot resting precariously on a crumbling what's-been, the other on an uncertain what-will-be, as they attempted to rhyme more tenable life into existence. Their poetry may sound at times ungainly, measured against a calmly perfected aesthetic standard, in part because their reality is ungainly. When Carolyn Forché first attempted to translate Claribel Alegría, she felt stymied. She could comprehend the Spanish but not whether Alegría was depicting fantasy or reality: She did not know whether a mutilated hand in Alegría's poetry, for instance, was a fact or a metaphor.

"Latin America constantly sends us poets of a different muse," Garcia Lorca once observed, excited that there could be other engines or principles that make poetry run. In Asia, Africa, and Latin America poets are sometimes not only poets but presidents of their country or revolutionaries in prison, high-ranking ambassadors or tribal storytellers. Then the "work of poetry" may shun or postpone its more delicate assignments and perform instead the work of politics, the work of popular entertainment, the work of journalism, or the work of collective memory. When a different muse arrives, it perhaps disappoints our ideas about poetry precisely in order to reveal poetry doing something else in the world.

Finally, is poetry everywhere so dwindling from its former importance that the diagnosis reads: It is dying? Or perhaps already died, one Easter morning. That Easter Sunday, returning from a predawn walk, a troubled soul ventures into his study and decides, the day being what it is, to translate the Gospel According to John afresh. "In the beginning was . . . the Word"? Mere words began it? Faust finds himself "unable to see the word as having supreme value," and so ushers in those modern poets for whom words, mental constructs, cannot adequately embody the mightiness of reality, much less create it. ("For poetry makes nothing happen," wrote W. H. Auden.) In Goethe's play Faust attempts translating Logos as "Mind" and then as "vital force," but at last, demonically, repudiates the Word entirely. "In the beginning was the Act." Faust's mistranslation would soon proliferate into the commonplace assumption that modern lives equal the events that fill them—crammed schedules and too many obligations; knowledge reduced to societal information and scientifically proved data—in which the whisper of poetry is drowned, inaudible.

What Goethe expressed in a symbol, another German would later make explicit in an argument. In The Gay Science (1882) Nietzsche blamed the Americans for introducing a new workaholic rush into society, which was trampling flat all natural and poetic rhythms. "The breathless haste with which they [Americans] work—the distinctive vice of the new world—is already beginning to infect old Europe with its ferocity and is spreading a lack of spirituality like a blanket." "One thinks with a watch in one's hand," Nietzsche lamented, and therefore "just as all forms are visibly perishing by the haste of the workers, the feeling for form itself, *the ear and the eye for the melody of movements are also perishing*" (italics added).

Poetry, in this Nietzschean view, suits a more reflective age of nature rambles and soul examinations, of sinecures and long letters and ample, speculative leisure. A century later the movies are doing more than A. E. Housman can to justify God's ways to man. New gizmos have sprung up, and not only film, but everything from the Internet to psychopharmacology has taken over the entertainment, broadening of mental horizons, or consolation in which poetry once had a dominant market share. Early in this century Yeats already observed that poets play so small a part in the active life that they might be called what the ancients called the dead: spirits apart.

Will Sir Philip Sidney or his millennial heir please step forward to offer a new Defence of Poesie? One defense of the craft, just possibly, may still be feasible, based on the fact that human life is not so endlessly malleable as science fiction writers and futurologists fantasize it. That argument would go something like this. People in America and Argentina still continue to talk, occasionally write something down, and nearly everyone registers a small margin of difference hearing something said funnier or zestier than expected. An amateur enamored of words may still conceivably make a place for him- or herself in that margin of linguistic difference, and make a place for the kinds of utterances that poets from China to Chad have typically made. From Naples to Nepal the old poets' obsession with things like love and death was certainly feverish and now seems passé, and yet— and yet people still fall in love, and still they die. Words need to be uttered at crucial moments, and as for which witnesses may properly utter them, in addition to the priest who is too old-fashioned, the psychiatrist too expensive, and the lawyer too formal, the poet who is too fond may yet have a role to play. When Yeats observed that only two subjects could possibly interest an adult mind (meaning, of course, sex and death), he was indirectly saying he would not be out of a job.

Poets however do not live, or write, solely in the eternal verities of libido and mortality; they are caught up in a particular historical situation, which also needs to be expressed—needs to be domesticated and needs to be made wilder. And if, at present, for reasons noted above, the historically conditioned situation now works against their art, poets may occasionally play hooky from historical determinism. Carl Jung postulated the existence of an autonomous poetic function within the human psyche, which operates separate from the socially conditioned aspects of personality. Practicing poets, too, have made similar declarations of independence. Both Rilke and Eliot saw poetry as almost unrelated to the poor sod who wrote it: Writing poetry, they believed, catalyzed one part of a person, leaving the rest unaffected, leaving drunks, unemployables, and insurance salesmen capable at odd moments of authoring the sublime. Perhaps overstated as a hypothesis, this corner-of-the-brain theory does seem a snapshot of today's poet off writing in a corner, far from the general population preoccupied with more important things. And this very marginality—spirits apart—may be exactly what poetry has to offer in the future.

For if poetry does happen on the periphery, if it is not implicated in political power (as are newspapers) or enmeshed in huge economic bureaucracies (as TV and movies are), it betters its chances to express quaint, eccentric aspects of experience: It can give voice to the angular, the odd, and the private, which the powers-that-be would consign to oblivion or ignore. In an age of mass media, mass marketing—well, mass everything—perhaps only the poet has a vested interest in the individual muttering inconsequentially to himself. By contrast every society, even the most benign, tries to manipulate or influence an individual's thought so that it leads to certain socially preferred kinds of behavior. This chain of control is seen best (or rather worst) in totalitarian states, which police the words in order to police the actions. In China, for example, you had to call Mao Zedong the "Great Chairman Mao" and Zhou Enlai "Beloved Premier Zhou"; to have switched modifiers, and called Zhou "great" instead of "beloved"—treason! In Mao's China undesirable behavior was often condemned as *buxianghua*, "not resembling the words." Poets ran some risk for making the words resemble not what they ideologically should but inching them a little closer toward what actually is and what might be.

Joseph Brodsky knew something about totalitarian states, and imprisoned for his use of words in one, he also knew that poetry was not an entirely innocent pastime. However, winning the Nobel Prize often puts one in a good mood; it had even encouraged Faulkner, then thought of as a recorder of human depravity, to proclaim nobly that man will not merely endure, he will prevail. In his own good mood Brodsky mounted the Nobel platform, and in his last words sounded his defense of poetry for our time: "I am not so sure that man will prevail, as the great man and my fellow American once said, standing, I believe, in this very room; but I am quite positive that a man who reads poetry is harder to prevail upon than one who doesn't."

Only in this sense, Brodsky later elaborated, should we understand "Matthew Arnold's belief that we shall be saved by poetry."

Dear Reader, as you turn this page, you are about to embark on a word-sea of undulating rhythm. Destination: the contemporary world, our strange home. You will set a course through the varieties of aesthetically shaped experience—the crafted evocations of how your fellow passengers found it and resisted; were prevailed upon and prevailed; got blocked here and reimagined it afresh there—to the extent that these experiences are recorded, mimicked, created in poetry. Take your pills along; fair sailing. *Bon voyage.*

In Memoriam

Joseph Brodsky (1940–1996)

Publication of a book should be cause for a little celebration, but here pleasure is mixed with mourning. Our colleague Joseph Brodsky, who helped conceive this work, whose concern for it increased as he approached his fatal heart operation, and who should be here toasting its completion, is sadly more conspicuous by his absence than almost anyone present.

Others who knew him more intimately may better tell of his wonders as a man. Ours was primarily a working relationship, when for some years he was the poetry editor and I the literary editor on the same magazine. Working with Joseph created its own manner of wonder, for possibly never was a human being simultaneously so brilliant, so difficult, and so charming. He was by then writing his essays for the magazine directly in English, an amazing English (insert comparisons to Conrad and Nabokov here), but his prose did pioneer some new linguistic territory where English grammar has never ventured before. As Joseph would make his compelling case for unconventional usage or creative syntax, he would conduct me on a tour of all literature and half of history. As the magazine went to bed, the editorial staff felt like doing the same, exhausted but even more exhilarated by our poetry editor.

Joseph's hand will easily be seen in this anthology, in his introduction to Zbigniew Herbert, in his essay about Akhmatova, but in less tangible ways, in conception and standards, his spirit pervades every corner. He did not live to execute the main task he set himself—writing the essay about European poetry since World War II. To have had Joseph Brodsky

range again, this time across the modern European poetic imagination—
the way he examined his childhood in *Less Than One*, or wrote about
Marcus Aurelius or Robert Frost in *On Grief and Reason*, or about Herbert
and Akhmatova in these pages—that surely would cause any reader to
have his own mental life quickened.

The loss of that essay means that this anthology is less brilliant than it
otherwise might have been. On the other hand, that Joseph did not himself
alone select the European poetry means that the anthology is also less quirky.
After his death the poet Edward Hirsch completed the selections, and he
read, for example, eighteen different translators of Akhmatova before mak-
ing his choice of the best. Joseph might have quickly settled on whichever
translator employed the most formal prosody, even if that translation was,
incidentally, the least readable in English.

Genius comes with a certain price tag. I would have paid it—many
times over, if only I could—and not merely to ransom his unwritten essay
from the ghostly ether. How many times I missed and wished for Joseph's
company while completing this book, for to have had him to discuss it with,
to argue with, and be goaded by—that would have converted all the tedious
chores associated with an anthology into an intellectual adventure.

I glance down at a note he sent, dated January 1996, and one sentence
stands out. "The clarity of my role in our anthology is clouded currently by
humble frame's prospects of being carved up for the 3rd time." Before
Joseph entered the hospital he requested I call him so shortly thereafter
that he could scarcely have had time to recover. He was implying that we
needed to discuss this anthology, but what he was really doing, and doing
elsewhere too I'm sure, was building bridges from there to here. And now
that he is inexplicably not here, those of us who are feel puzzled by a drop
in the intellectual temperature or liveliness, perhaps especially in moments
when we are not specifically remembering him.

• • •

But if pleasure is the principle above, there is a second principle below. That principle, or hypothesis, is that "poetic knowledge" is, or can be, one of the crucial kinds of knowledge of the world. Earlier the critical, informative aspects of this book were likened, metaphorically, to an encyclopedia, and like an encyclopedia they contain much knowledge, some of which a reader may find useful to know, some which he or she won't give a damn about, but all arranged conveniently and accessibly. Indeed, someone wishing to get a quick overview of intellectual life in Japan or South America or Africa might well turn to these pages first. How did a poetic rebirth occur in Maoist China, where every freedom of expression was squelched? Why do some Latin Americans trace their particular form of modernism to a twelfth-century tradition? What do Indians want (at least from their literature)? The answer to hundreds of questions like these, some of which may be difficult to find elsewhere, are easily found here. A peculiar reader might even pick up this book not for the poetry but for the kind of coded information about human beings and their societies that is contained herein.

Helen Vendler is our guide for the English-speaking world; Anthony Appiah, for Africa; Carolyn Forché, Latin America; and a student of Joseph Brodsky's, the critic Sven Birkerts, for Europe. And Asia? Several valiant souls (tact omits mentioning any names) tried to select the poetry and furnish the commentary for all of Asia—and perished in the attempt. Asia is too sprawling; its population outnumbers the rest of the earth's combined. India seems a continent like Europe, and vast Asia, a megacontinent composed of minor ones. Consequently Asian poetry has been apportioned here into five regions, often with two guides—one a poet and the other a critic—navigating us around linguistic barriers and pointing out the historical and literary landmarks necessary for understanding.

Far more people shaped the outcome here than those listed on the book jacket. Edward Dimock, for example, consulted a score of people in both

India and the United States before settling upon A. K. Ramanujan as the Indian poet; Perry Link worked closely with the talented Dutch scholar and translator Maghiel van Crevel in selecting the Chinese poet. Alastair Reid made the valuable suggestion, in order to add range and breadth, to include from each region a sampler of additional poets. Karen Iker, with her bright mind and efficiency, helped with the thankless (but here thanked) job of clearing permissions. A book like this—perhaps every book—needs a few saints hovering somewhere in the vicinity to make sure that all goes well: here they were Saint Terry (Karten), Saint Molly (Friedrich), and Saint Jay (Tolson). The list of the book's helpers and friends, including Amy Albernaz, Megan Barrett, Anne Detrick, Maggie Dietz, and Rochelle Kainer, goes on and on. . . .

But enough preamble. The predinner speaker has droned on overlong. A relief to see the waiters shouldering in, at last, the silver trays, the gleaming plates piled high.

WHAT KIND OF BOOK THIS IS,
ITS (NOT-SO-SECRET) PRINCIPLE,
AND WHO DID WHAT IN IT

The idea seemed simple. One day when Joseph Brodsky and I were surveying (in conversation) the landscape of contemporary poetry, we observed that a certain path through it had never been attempted. Either of us could cite numerous anthologies of poems from many countries in superb translations—Selden Rodman's *One Hundred Modern Poems* (1949) is an early example—but none of these anthologies provided a context for the poems, treating them rather as random isolated treasures washed up on the shore. The worst international anthologies were those that tried to be both representative and comprehensive, because, in order to requestion the whole world's poetry, they were often forced to lower aesthetic standards and include too many questionable poets and tolerate indifferent translations. Joseph complained that he emerged from reading such a bland, respectable hodgepodge thinking that half the poems in it were all penned by the same person, Anonymous's younger brother, under a variety of noms de plume. As we exchanged these observations, the idea for this book stepped in and introduced itself. What about making the poem's shining merit the sole criterion? Why not limit the number of poets included—and not admit the second rate just to fill the quotas—so that a world anthology of poetry, perhaps for the first time, would not merely cover the bases but be primarily a pleasure to read. We agreed: Let's try it.

It seemed simple enough—draw some chalk lines and mark off the boundaries. For the temporal admission requirement, a poet must have written, or continued to write, during the second half of the twentieth century. For the spatial requirement—earthly geography—there would be one poet, we hoped the most interesting, from each of twenty-five different countries. Straightforward, neat, what could be simpler? Yet this anthology, before it was done, would bend its own rules, consume thousands of hours of labor, and turn into the collective work of a fair portion of a generation interested in poetry. (All the critics loitering with intent in these pages were not merely fussing over which poem to choose, of course, but combining their knowledge to create, in this anthology, a kind of "encyclopedia" of the contemporary world as poetry illumines it.)

Whenever the anthology violated its own criteria, it did so only in order to uphold its principle. And that principle was?—The question, in different guises, came up repeatedly. Should poems be chosen because of their historical importance? Select the poets because of their influence or because of their reputation? In each case the answer was no, no, not especially. Every book proceeds by its own morality (or immorality), and here the moral bias in making selections was, as noted above, the pleasure principle. For the sake of greater enjoyment, the admission requirements could be bent a little. Thus not one but two American poets—Robert Lowell and Elizabeth Bishop—are included here because, so Helen Vendler argued, a contemporary anthology in English, addressed to English-language readers, would suffer needless quality damage by omitting either.

As for the demarcating starting year, 1950, well, nothing particularly magical happened during its twelve-month run. This midcentury roadblock is there to bar Yeats, Eliot, Rilke, Stevens, Lorca, Valéry, Cavafy, and our other great familiars, whose inclusion might have left some readers wondering: Haven't I read this book before? Twice, though, the date bar is lifted, to admit César Vallejo (d. 1938 at the age of forty) and Chairil Anwar (d. 1949 at the age of twenty-nine). Despite their abbreviated careers, they are the confrères of more contemporary poets, and they themselves, but for their untimely deaths, might have entered old age as the twentieth century did likewise. The clocks of this anthology are slightly off, ticking to the principle stated above.

PART I

THE ENGLISH-SPEAKING WORLD

GREATEST THINGS FROM LEAST SUGGESTIONS

Helen Vendler

Two books confirmed me in my love of poetry. The first was a book written for young people, *Poetry for You*, by the poet Cecil Day-Lewis. It showed me, for the first time, manuscript drafts of a poem—one of Day-Lewis's own—and made me realize that a poem might begin as an inchoate image, or a stray line, or a fugitive rhythm; it revealed to me that the poet (as Wordsworth said) builds up "greatest things from least suggestions." I found this thrilling, and for several years afterward hunted down evidence of manuscript development, as though by tracking a poem through its multiple stages I could understand what made it into the haunting thing it was. To turn over Dylan Thomas's thirty drafts of "Fern Hill" made me feel that I had been admitted to the heart of creation, and I've never entirely lost that response. To see what has been added, to see what has been canceled, to see what has been accepted but revised—there is no truer way to investigate the aims that a poet is, even unconsciously, pursuing. Day-Lewis disclosed why he had written a given line, why he had omitted another, what he was avoiding, what he was hoping to find: And through those scribbled-in additions and corrections I saw the poem evolve from chaos to order. Later, when I came across the facsimile edition of *The Waste Land* drafts, it seemed entirely natural that such a complex poem should have had a "long foreground"—the phrase is Emerson's, voicing his (correct) speculation that Whitman had been writing for a long time before he burst on the American scene with "Song of Myself."

Though I had no manuscript evidence for most of the poems I read, I

now saw'them less as products than as the result of a process—a process
that had halted at a particular order of words, but that had begun, earlier,
from an undisclosed nucleus. I thought I could often see that nucleus sur-
viving in the final poem—not only when the poet revealed it (as when
Keats mentioned the "stubble plains" as the source of his autumn ode),
but also when I had nothing to go on but conjecture. The unfolding of a
whole from a part still seems to me the most marvelous aspect of poetic
composition.

After Day-Lewis's *Poetry for You,* the second book that meant a great
deal to me was the first volume I ever bought with my own money: Oscar
Williams's *Little Treasury of Modern Poetry.* It introduced me to the great
modernist poets, the ones I had not found at home (since my mother's
knowledge of poetry stopped with Tennyson and Swinburne). Some of the
poets I found irritating (especially Wallace Stevens, who was later to
become my favorite among the moderns), but others I was drawn to
instantly, not least Robert Lowell, who was writing (in "Where the
Rainbow Ends") about my own city of Boston, where

> The Pepperpot, ironic rainbow, spans
> Charles River and its scales of scorched-earth miles.
> I saw my city in the Scales, the pans
> Of judgment rising and descending. Piles
> Of dead leaves char the air—
> And I am a red arrow on this graph
> Of Revelations. Every dove is sold.

"I saw my city in the Scales"—"My city!" I thought. Someone was
writing out of the very life I was living, and as I read other poets—Eliot,
Williams, Cummings, Frost—I found myself experiencing my own cen-
tury in a new and more intense way: "And there I found myself more truly
and more strange" (Stevens). From the first generation of great modernists
I, like so many others, drew intimations of what consciousness might be
in the twentieth century.

The great modernists had made a definitive break with prewar expres-
sion: the Great War had disturbed all social pieties and all social hopes.
Even America did not remain untouched by it; and it seemed as though

the original modernist poets had left little to be done by their successors. Yet a second wave of modernists—who revised, rewrote, and repudiated their predecessors—arrived, especially in America and Ireland, to establish themselves as new masters. And it is these poets who are the subject of this selection.

During the nineteenth and twentieth centuries, inhabitants of the British empire were educated—whatever their mother tongue might have been—in English. In consequence, English poetry now has branches in the Caribbean, in Africa, and in India, for instance, as well as in such Commonwealth countries as Canada, Australia, and New Zealand. Many writers from such countries have spent at least part of their life in either England or the United States, and increasingly the population of both England and America has become diversified by immigration. Such great political changes are bound to affect written production in both prose and verse. In Philip Larkin, we see an Englishman writing after the decline of England as a world power; in Derek Walcott, a St. Lucian educated in a Jamaican university who now divides his time between the United States and the Caribbean; in Seamus Heaney, an Irish poet whose writing reflects the exacerbated political conditions in Northern Ireland. Both Walcott and Heaney have been awarded the Nobel Prize, a sign that poetry in English no longer means "poetry written in England or America."

The majority of poets represented here are American. The proportion would have been different in the nineteenth century; it may change in the twenty-first. But America, as it rose to be a world power, achieved in poetry an upstart confidence that may resemble the confidence felt in England during the Renaissance. In the modernist era, the Muse seemed to choose many Americans: Pound, Eliot, Williams, Stevens, Frost, Moore, Crane. In Great Britain, which lost may poets to the first World War, Owen among them, only Auden and MacDiarmid seemed to be of comparable stature. And after World War II English poetry seemed to decline; Larkin (and, some would add, Geoffrey Hill) were the exceptions, while in the United States a generation of poets arose who have been influential not merely in their own country but in England as well: Lowell, Bishop, Ginsberg, Ashbery, Rich, among others. And there are yet other American poets who, not so visibly influential as those I have named, equal or surpass them in talent: I think particularly of Ammons, Berryman, and Merrill. Since an anthology can reflect only a fraction of the interesting writing now taking poetic form, my own situation, as an American writing about American poetry, may have influenced my choice for inclusion here. A British critic might have chosen otherwise.

The very notion of "poetry" has been in flux since Eliot and Pound boldly chose free verse as their vehicle. And they were, in fact following the experimentation of French and Italian poets, surrealists and futurists, who wrote not only free verse but also prose poems, concrete (shaped) poems that could not be read aloud, and (in the case of Mallarmé) a poem in which the words were scattered on the page like thrown dice. Yet poetry tends to return, having been refreshed by each burst of experimentation, to something closer to the lyrical norm. Since poetry is the art that needs to find, in each generation, a way to use the speech patterns of its era in ways especially concise, patterned, musical, and metaphorical, it is always startlingly fresh. Seamus Heaney has said that when, as a child in school, he saw the word "gnats" in Keats's ode "To Autumn," he knew that what he called such insects was "midges." It is when the young poet-to-be recognizes that poetry has yet to be written in his speech code that he feels he has work to do.

Poetry, in a memorable definition by Hopkins, is "the current language heightened," and the operative word is "current." Unoriginal poets write exactly like the poets they grew up reading, and are consequently, in their own work, one or two generations behind the "current" language. Poets of talent, though, forgetting nothing they found in the poets they grew up reading, use an amalgam of their language and the language they hear around them—in the newspapers, in the streets, on television. Sentences that sound as if they really have issued from a live twentieth-century person are the only ones a current audience can be expected to find believable. Poets may be more imaginative, and possess more words, than their readers; but the readers must recognize the swing of the poet's sentences as coming from their own epoch.

Just as song is what speech would be if we all possessed beautiful voices and had the inventive power to set our speech to a rhythmic melody, so poetry is what speech would be if we all had the gift of metaphorical concision and a compulsion to melody in sentence rhythms. We distinguish poetry from ordinary speech because of the way it is driven by musicality. We distinguish it from the novel and the drama because they are forms in which more than one voice is in play. In lyric poetry only one voice is usually present, and if that voice addresses someone, that someone is typically not present as a silent auditor (as in Browning's dramatic monologues) but absent. A lyric can be addressed to a beloved, or to an ancestor, or to God, but in each case the addressee is not there—is either absent or dead or invisible. A lyric offers its reader a set of shoes to stand in: It intends that when you read it yours should be the predicament, yours the uttering voice. It is a script for performance by you. It offers you access to a privacy we have no way of accessing (except in ourselves) in real life.

The poems below, then, all offer voices speaking in a privacy, as we speak to ourselves when we are alone. As you become that voice, reading the poem silently or aloud, you assume a new identity. This is the way poetry achieves a social effect: you are, for the moment, Elizabeth Bishop at the fish houses, or Robert Lowell at the Shaw Monument, or Philip Larkin watching dancing couples inside a hall. One's vicarious life in poetry is very various. And indeed the function of a successful poem is to admit you to that other life (which is not necessarily the poet's own life). Unsuccessful poems feel "wooden" or "stagey" or "sentimental"; the reader is put off by their unconvincing language. Reading a poem that one has no difficulty entering, one "passes through" the language to the situation of the voice. It is only later that one asks what made the poem so convincing. When you return to the "surface" of the poem, after having been "inside," you are tempted to wonder what skill in the poet enabled that magical passage. At that moment you are on your way to observing and analyzing the components in the writing that made the poem "work."

Each of the poets chosen for this anthology has developed a style of writing that renews what voice sounds like. Because of that renewal, not all poems are easy to "enter": "The poem," said Wallace Stevens, "should resist the intelligence almost successfully." In that remark the deadpan humor lies in Stevens's "almost." That is, all true poems will finally yield to intelligence, but something on the surface—usually, distinctiveness of style—will perhaps make the voice at first disconcerting or difficult. Amazingly, difficult poems get easier with time. Everyone now "understands" *The Waste Land*, but its techniques of style were once so difficult that the poem was even considered a hoax. The poet's temperament finds an objective correlative in the style invented to match that temperament. One would not mistake Ammons's pithy reflectiveness for Ginsberg's dithyrambic explosiveness, Larkin's dry irony for Heaney's earnest richness.

Poets born in the same year in the same country can consequently sound very different from one another, as their attention is drawn by circumstance, temperament, and geographical location to different aspects of feeling. Nonetheless it is helpful to recall something of the era of these poets, and to be aware of the circumstances in which they came of age. The crucial years for a young poet are from twenty to thirty-five. Poets may (and great poets always do) reinvent themselves after thirty-five, stylistically speaking, but by then their life themes are usually clear to them and to their readers.

I want to begin with our poets from the British tradition. Philip Larkin, who came of age during World War II, wrote poetry that drew a powerful response from others, in part because the helplessness Larkin felt before his own temperament mirrored, perhaps, the losses others in England felt in the diminished postwar world. In Larkin's work adventure is ruled out; the stinting miserliness of life seems unchanging; the venues offered by work are crabbed; the erotic life brings more pain and inadequacy than joy. But however widely a lessened England seemed allegorized by Larkin's cramped picture of life, what won him readers was his unyielding style. It forwent the romantic exuberance of the Welsh poet Dylan Thomas, who intoxicated audiences with his powerful readings. Larkin's style spoke for the educated British voice—reticent, wry, self-conscious, self-deprecating, skeptical, but concealing at its heart a passionate disappointment.

No greater contrast could be imagined than that between Larkin and Walcott, though Walcott is Larkin's junior by only eight years. Walcott's style showed a powerful assimilative desire: Educated in British poetry since childhood, he has sounded successively like Yeats, Auden, Crane, Lowell, and Heaney. Yet, warring with the conventionally available styles was the "current language" spoken in St. Lucia, which has entered Walcott's poetry as an alternative rhythm, vocabulary, and sentence structure. The experimental integration and separation of these two available styles constitutes the history of Walcott's verse, from one point of view: from another, his evolution can be measured in his repeated attempts to take the measure of his own personal status. He is a black descended from both European and black ancestors; a St. Lucian, yet educated beyond the island norm; a painter-poet deeply attached to the Caribbean landscape, yet living for much of the year in New England; a rebellious colonial, yet deeply involved, imaginatively, in English poetry. The history of postcolonial literature shows Walcott's predicament to be a widely shared one, yet each postcolonial writer struggles with it in a different way. Walcott has refused to be less literate than his education made him: his *Omeros*, based on *The Iliad*, argues implicitly that the matter of epic is no less available on a Caribbean than on a Greek island. Yet his ease within "high culture" has not led him to forsake entirely the speech patterns of his birthplace. He may publish in New York and London, but his imagination is centered on the Caribbean.

Heaney's poetry could be said to issue from some of the same concerns. Heaney too can be seen as a postcolonial poet inserting into English poetry the predicament of the Northern Irish, who, though living in a British state, are by birth Catholic and therefore members of a minority historically oppressed since the plantation of Ulster. Like Walcott, Heaney was educated in a British system, brought up to know and love English poetry. His early poems show traces of influence from English writers: Wordsworth, Keats, Auden, Wilfred Owen. And like Walcott, Heaney has made various efforts to incorporate into English the characteristics of the speech which he heard about him in childhood. Yet Walcott's poetry is unmarked by any single historic event of his lifetime, while Heaney's writing was ineradicably changed by the civil rights movement in Northern Ireland. In 1969, when Heaney was thirty, British troops were sent into Belfast to control the conflict; in 1972 thirteen unarmed civilians were killed by British soldiers on "Bloody Sunday." After receiving threats Heaney resigned his teaching position at Queen's University and moved his young family from Ulster to the Irish Republic. The violence continued (only in 1995 was a cease-fire tentatively produced), and Heaney's search for adequate means to symbolize its historic origins, its universality in human culture, and its specific nature in Ireland has led him to philology, archaeology (as in his poems about ritually murdered bodies found in both Irish and Scandinavian bogs), allegory (with debts to Eastern European poets), myth (as in his poems about the Irish king Sweeney, who was changed into a bird), and even, like Walcott, to Greek literature (the *Oresteia, Philoctetes*). Yet Heaney is also capable of writing a wholly unpolitical poetry, delicate in perception, marked by visual relish and incorporating metaphysical insight, as in the "squarings"—poems five beats wide and twelve lines long—included here. He has experimented with "thin" lines as against his original Keatsian pentameters; he has written sonnets in a variety of experimental forms; he has done an autobiographical narrative *(Station Island),* translations, even a play. His style, through many reinventions, has remained supple and flexible yet unmistakably his own in its combination of the plain and the rich.

When we turn to the American poets included here, we can see that they tend to fall into three groups. Bishop, Berryman, and Lowell were born between 1911 and 1917. They knew each other well; they came from the middle or upper class and were college-educated; they came to consciousness at a time when the effects of the Depression of 1929 were still evident. But by their thirties they had felt the effect of World War II and the consequent deprovincializing of the United States. Intellectual writers no longer felt (as Frost, Eliot, and even Pound had) that London was the center to which one went to be published and to find an aesthetic community. They could publish in New York or Boston.

The poets of the second group belong to what one might call "the generation of 1926." Between 1926 and 1939 a strong group of poets was born—in 1926 and 1927 alone, Frank O'Hara, Robert Creeley, Robert Bly, A. R. Ammons, Allen Ginsberg, James Merrill, W. D. Snodgrass, John Ashbery, W. S. Merwin, James Wright, and Galway Kinnell. Adrienne Rich in 1929, Gary Snyder in 1930, Sylvia Plath in 1932, and Frank Bidart in 1939 bring the group to a close. These poets came to maturity in the postwar period, when the general patriotism present in intellectuals and writers during World War II went into a decline (through the McCarthy hearings and the Cold War in general), culminating in the disturbances of the sixties, when many poets (Lowell, Ginsberg,

Rich, Bly, Merwin) wrote condemning the U.S. involvement in the Vietnam War. Though the events of the Holocaust had become known in the postwar period, the war in Vietnam, with its atrocities toward civilians, made the guilt of the Holocaust more immediate to Americans.

The poets of my third set were born in the early fifties. They came of age when various movements (against nuclear arms, for integration, for gay rights) were still in process. They witnessed, in rapid succession, the assassinations of John Kennedy (1963), Martin Luther King (1968), and Robert Kennedy (1968), as well as the invasion of Cambodia and the killing of unarmed students at Kent State University by the National Guard (1970). The intellectuals' crisis of confidence in the government, provoked by the 1964 Tonkin Gulf Resolution to amplify the number of troops in Vietnam, reached its apogee in the seventies with the revelations about the My Lai massacre (1971), the publication of the Pentagon Papers (1971), the Watergate hearings (1973), and Nixon's resignation under threat of impeachment (1974). A poet like Rita Dove, born two years before the Supreme Court officially desegregated American schools, grew up in the perplexing moment when, though racism had been theoretically abolished, it was still evidently present, and separatism and integration were disputed alternatives among blacks.

It is of course impossible to connect each poem written by these American poets to the politics, narrowly conceived, of their era. There are many other influences at work in their poetry, not least the presence in their mind of other writers, many of them foreign. Freud is a pervasive influence on Berryman, Lowell, Ginsberg, Merrill, Plath, and Bidart. Bishop draws her many trimeter poems, such as "In the Waiting Room," from the Brazilian poet Carlos Drummond de Andrade (whom she translated). Ashbery would not be the poet he is had he not written on Raymond Roussel. Merrill was influenced by Cavafy; Ginsberg drew his rhythms from the Hebrew psalms and William Blake, and studied Buddhist writings; Plath's best work profited from the example of her husband, Ted Hughes. The younger American poets have been influenced by the presence in their midst of two foreign Nobel Prize–winning poets: Czeslaw Milosz, who has lived in California since the sixties, and Seamus Heaney, who has regularly taught at Harvard since the early eighties. The seriousness with which both Milosz and Heaney have attended to historical events has awakened a deeper historical consciousness in American poets, visible in the work of Jorie Graham and Rita Dove. Yet behind the postwar poets we also feel the presence of the high modernists. These postwar poets were determined to rewrite, correct, and criticize the poetics of the modernist era. Pound's history becomes Lowell's *History;* Eliot's discontinuities (severe, austere, religious) become Ashbery's (genial, disarming, secular); Moore's ethical fables become Bishop's more skeptical narratives; Auden's worldly set forms are borrowed and played with by Merrill.

Modernism was not typically preoccupied with the questions of gender, race, ethnicity, and sexual identity that came to concern younger American poets. During the postwar period an increasing affluence (along with the GI Bill) brought into higher education groups who had not been there in large numbers before the war. After what Lowell called "the tranquilized fifties" (which were already brewing what came to be known as "the sixties"), movements advocating civil rights, feminism, and gay rights arose, to be followed by affirmative action initiatives and other efforts toward greater diversity in education and in the workplace. Poetry became more polarized after the sixties, as writers increasingly defined themselves as feminists, or black writers, or gay poets, or Chicanos. The democratic impulse toward equal opportunity gave rise to an advocacy based on the poet's subject matter (as representative of his or her ethnic or sexual group) rather than on skill in the art. The line between high and low culture became blurred, since the younger poets had their youth mediated by television, movies, sports, and popular music as well as by books and classical music.

The readership of some poets consisted almost entirely of those who resembled them in gender or sexual orientation, but more talented poets continued to attract a wide general readership. Bishop, although a lesbian, refused to allow her poetry to appear in anthologies of women poets, wanting to be recognized simply as a poet. Her poetry tends to address questions of alienation and domesticity provoked by her orphaned status and her life in Brazil, though some poems have lesbian themes, covertly or overtly. Ginsberg, Merrill, and Bidart, all openly gay, have described gay life, but have as often taken up other questions: Ginsberg, American political life and domestic relations; Merrill, travel and art; and Bidart, philosophical issues and forms of asceticism. Graham, who has one Jewish parent, has repeatedly interrogated the Holocaust as emblematic of the processes of history. Plath, whose father was German and whose mother was of Austrian descent, also turned to the Holocaust for metaphors of her father's domination of her spirit.

But the themes of poetry, with their ongoing critique and creation of culture, are something poetry shares with the essays, novels, and plays of the postwar era. What poetry does, by its special interior emphasis, is to show us what the private life of an era is like: to show us the feelings people acknowledge in private, and the meditations that arise as one pursues the roots and implications of such feelings, and the style found to convey such feelings and reflections. Yet a letter could do as much, if it were an eloquent one, and in fact poetry has much in common with a letter. "This is my letter to the world," said Emily Dickinson of her own writing. Something else, then, besides the revelation of the private life concerns lyric, and that something is lyric form.

Lyric form is difficult to define, and impossible to circumscribe, since every good poem constructs an inner form of its own. The form mimics the actions of the mind and heart. If they are vexed, the form must be vexed; if they are indecisive, it must be indecisive; if they are rigid, it must be rigid. In some forms time governs; in others, space. In one, syntax may be the most active agent of form; in another, the adjective may rule; and in yet another, sound dominates. Some forms charm, some horrify. Some are relentless, some are volatile. They represent a gamut of responses available in contemporary life.

The successful invention of form in adequate language leads to new sorts of beauty in lyric. Any new beauty temporarily makes the old beauty look old-fashioned or tasteless or inadequate (in literature as in couture)— just as the old beauty, still the norm in the culture, has a way of making the new beauty look shapeless or vulgar. There is an implicit contest among proposed new forms of beauty, and the poets are sometimes unable to convince even each other: William Carlos Williams hated *The Waste Land* (though he imitated it later in his *Paterson*). It is not to be expected that every reader will respond to all the new forms and new styles in this book, and there will be readers who regret the absence of one or another school of poetry (the Black Mountain poets and Language Poets are not present).

But the poems included here are indicative of the way the wind has been blowing in English-language poetry for the last half century. Though reticence is not dead, a new bluntness of discourse is permitted. Though abstraction toward the universal case is still the chief choice for lyric, socially specified lyric selves are on the rise ("I am black," "I am gay," "I am second-generation Japanese," "I write as a Northern Irish Catholic"). Though shapeliness of form is still prized, large inclusive Whitmanian or Ashberian poems stake a strong claim too. Though the traditional genres (the topographical poem, the sestina, the sonnet sequence) persist, free verse—borrowing from the new media of this century (radio, records, films, television, MTV) have made jump cuts, focus changes, and freeze-frames—predominates. The mixture of specialized discourses to which we are all exposed (found in all its splendor in Ashbery's wayward reveries) acts as a critique to any lyric voice that remains too dully homogeneous. An anthology like this one can make readers in far-flung places aware of just how intellectually and melodically alive the art of poetry in English is now, and has been for the last fifty years.

ROBERT LOWELL

(1917–1977)

Robert Lowell's ancestors—Lowells, Winslows, and Starks—figure in American history from its origins among the Puritans. But Lowell's immediate family—his impatient, literary, and discontented mother and his inconsequential and apologetic father—ensured that their only child found himself longing to be free of those ancestors, yet still obsessed, as his early poems reveal, with his New England ancestry. After an unsuccessful year at Harvard, Lowell transferred to Kenyon College, where he attached himself to Allen Tate, John Crowe Ransom, and Ford Madox Ford. In 1946 he burst on the American literary scene with *Lord Weary's Castle*, a volume of difficult and thundering verse that won the Pulitzer Prize. Lowell's manic-depressive illness had begun to manifest itself in adolescence, and caused repeated hospitalizations and long immersion in psychotherapy (with notable results in the 1960 sequence of poems called *Life Studies*) before his condition was stabilized by lithium in the late sixties. He was married three times, each time to a writer: briefly to the novelist Jean Stafford (a marriage that caused his temporary fling with Roman Catholicism); for more than twenty years to the novelist and essayist Elizabeth "Lizzie" Hardwick, who devoted herself to his well-being through all the attacks of mental illness and who bore him a daughter, Harriet; and, in the last seven years of his life, to the Irish-born journalist and novelist Lady Caroline Blackwood, who bore him a son, Sheridan. All of these figure in his verse.

One volume followed another after *Lord Weary's Castle*, each of them attracting much critical attention, all of them subject to both intense admiration and fierce criticism. Lowell's public actions during World War II (when, after attempting to enlist and being rejected for myopia, he registered as a conscientious objector, wrote a public letter to President Roosevelt, and spent time in New York City's West Street jail with murderers and drug lords) and during the Vietnam War (when he joined the March on Washington and formally refused to attend a dinner at the White House) ensured that his poetry was read not for solely literary reasons. The nakedly autobiographical vignettes of his parents in *Life Studies* were the first accomplished poems to issue from the conversations held between patient and psychoanalyst. Influenced by the Beat poets' free verse, and by Elizabeth Bishop's conversational middle style, Lowell departed from the formal meters of his first book to write a free verse that, by the accumulation of apparently desultory but significant detail, traced the decline and fall of his family and himself. In a symbolic repudiation of Catholicism in "Beyond the Alps," he leaves Rome, "the city of God," in favor of "Paris, our black classic" of worldliness. (In the volume *Imitations* [1961] he published adaptations of lyrics from other languages, both classic and modern—his form of diversion while he was in depression.)

Life Studies was followed by another free-verse volume, *For the Union Dead* (1964), in which the title poem extends the theme of decay not only to Lowell's Boston (he was then teaching at Boston University, where his students included Sylvia Plath and Anne Sexton) but to the whole United States (he mentioned, all as signs of civic decline, the vandalism of constructing a parking garage under Emerson's Boston Common, the dropping of the atomic bomb, and the resistance to desegregation). But no sooner had Lowell's audience accustomed itself to him as a free-verse poet than he published the formal Marvellian poems of *Near the Ocean* (1967), a volume memorializing both marital distress and the conflict in Vietnam, and foreseeing the extinction of society by "small war after small war." He was by then teaching at Harvard University (and was instrumental in bringing Elizabeth Bishop there as a colleague). Encouraged by his newfound mental stability, he poured out an apparently inexhaustible stream of unrhymed journal-sonnets, first as *Notebook 1967–68* (augmented and revised as *Notebook* [1970]), and then rearranged and split in two as *History* and *For Lizzie and Harriet* (both 1973). A final volume of sonnets,

The Dolphin—concerning his third marriage, and also issued in 1973—closed the sonnet series. He returned to free verse in his last volume, *Day by Day* (1977), which, as it sketched his uneasy life in England with Caroline and Sheridan, and the dissolution of his third marriage, was haunted by premonitions of death. He died of a heart attack in a taxi in New York City, after returning from Ireland.

Lowell's courage in breaking and re-forming his mature style was exemplary. He took American verse from the formal patterns of Tate and Ransom into a new era of boldly revolutionary plain speaking; then, in the sonnets, into a torrential new formality. Finally, he invented, in *Day by Day*, a new kind of lyric—wayward, structurally free, intimate, and reticently Horatian—that reflects formally his abandonment of a desire for transcendence and teleological closure in favor of an unforced perception of earthly transience. He was the most influential poet of his generation, and indeed younger poets found it difficult to escape sounding like him. (Among others, Plath, Sexton, Rich, Walcott, and Heaney show that they have felt his power.) His large poetic output has yet to be fully absorbed by critics and the public: There does not yet exist a *Collected Poems* or a collection of letters, though his *Collected Prose* was published in 1987. There are biographies by Ian Hamilton and Paul Mariani.

SAILING HOME FROM RAPALLO
{February 1954}

Your nurse could only speak Italian,
but after twenty minutes I could imagine your final
    week,
and tears ran down my cheeks . . .
When I embarked from Italy with my Mother's body,
the whole shoreline of the *Golfo di Genova*
was breaking into fiery flower.
The crazy yellow and azure sea-sleds
blasting like jack-hammers across
the *spumante*-bubbling wake of our liner,

recalled the clashing colors of my Ford.
Mother traveled first-class in the hold;
her *Risorgimento* black and gold casket
was like Napoleon's at the *Invalides*. . . .

While the passengers were tanning
on the Mediterranean in deck-chairs,
our family cemetery in Dunbarton
lay under the White Mountains
in the sub-zero weather.
The graveyard's soil was changing to stone—
so many of its deaths had been midwinter.
Dour and dark against the blinding snowdrifts,
its black brook and fir trunks were as smooth as masts.
A fence of iron spear-hafts
black-bordered its mostly Colonial grave-slates.
The only "unhistoric" soul to come here
was Father, now buried beneath his recent
unweathered pink-veined slice of marble.
Even the Latin of his Lowell motto:
Occasionem cognosce
seemed too businesslike and pushing here,
where the burning cold illuminated
the hewn inscriptions of Mother's relatives:
twenty or thirty Winslows and Starks.
Frost had given their names a diamond edge. . . .

In the grandiloquent lettering on Mother's coffin,
Lowell had been misspelled *LOVEL*.
The corpse
was wrapped like *panettone* in Italian tinfoil.

HOME AFTER THREE MONTHS AWAY

Gone now the baby's nurse,
a lioness who ruled the roost
and made the Mother cry.
She used to tie
gobbets of porkrind in bowknots of gauze—
three months they hung like soggy toast
on our eight-foot magnolia tree,
and helped the English sparrows
weather a Boston winter.

Three months, three months!
Is Richard now himself again?
Dimpled with exaltation,
my daughter holds her levee in the tub.
Our noses rub,
each of us pats a stringy lock of hair—
they tell me nothing's gone.
Though I am forty-one,
not forty now, the time I put away
was child's-play. After thirteen weeks
my child still dabs her cheeks
to start me shaving. When
we dress her in her sky-blue corduroy,
she changes to a boy,
and floats my shaving brush
and washcloth in the flush. . . .
Dearest, I cannot loiter here
in lather like a polar bear.

Recuperating, I neither spin nor toil.
Three stories down below,
a choreman tends our coffin's length of soil,
and seven horizontal tulips blow.
Just twelve months ago,

these flowers were pedigreed
imported Dutchmen; now no one need
distinguish them from weed.
Bushed by the late spring snow,
they cannot meet
another year's snowballing enervation.
I keep no rank nor station.
Cured, I am frizzled, stale and small.

SKUNK HOUR

{for Elizabeth Bishop}

Nautilus Island's hermit
heiress still lives through winter in her Spartan cottage;
her sheep still graze above the sea.
Her son's a bishop. Her farmer
is first selectman in our village;
she's in her dotage.

Thirsting for
the hierarchic privacy
of Queen Victoria's century,
she buys up all
the eyesores facing her shore,
and lets them fall.

The season's ill—
we've lost our summer millionaire,
who seemed to leap from an L.L. Bean
catalogue. His nine-knot yawl
was auctioned off to lobstermen.
A red fox stain covers Blue Hill.

And now our fairy
decorator brightens his shop for fall;
his fishnet's filled with orange cork,
orange, his cobbler's bench and awl;
there is no money in his work,
he'd rather marry.

One dark night,
my Tudor Ford climbed the hill's skull;
I watched for love-cars. Lights turned down,
they lay together, hull to hull,
where the graveyard shelves on the town. . . .
My mind's not right.

A car radio bleats,
"Love, O careless Love. . . ." I hear
my ill-spirit sob in each blood cell,
as if my hand were at its throat. . . .
I myself am hell;
nobody's here—

only skunks, that search
in the moonlight for a bite to eat.
They march on their soles up Main Street:
white stripes, moonstruck eyes' red fire
under the chalk-dry and spar spire
of the Trinitarian Church.

I stand on top
of our back steps and breathe the rich air—
a mother skunk with her column of kittens
    swills the garbage pail.
She jabs her wedge-head in a cup
of sour cream, drops her ostrich tail,
and will not scare.

FOR THE UNION DEAD

"Relinquunt Omnia Servare Rem Publicam."

The old South Boston Aquarium stands
in a Sahara of snow now. Its broken windows are
    boarded.
The bronze weathervane cod has lost half its scales.
The airy tanks are dry.

Once my nose crawled like a snail on the glass;
my hand tingled
to burst the bubbles
drifting from the noses of the cowed, compliant fish.

My hand draws back. I often sigh still
for the dark downward and vegetating kingdom
of the fish and reptile. One morning last March,
I pressed against the new barbed and galvanized

fence on the Boston Common. Behind their cage,
yellow dinosaur steamshovels were grunting
as they cropped up tons of mush and grass
to gouge their underworld garage.

Parking spaces luxuriate like civic
sandpiles in the heart of Boston.
A girdle of orange, Puritan-pumpkin colored girders
braces the tingling Statehouse,

shaking over the excavations, as it faces Colonel Shaw
and his bell-checked Negro infantry
on St. Gaudens' shaking Civil War relief,
propped by a plank splint against the garage's
    earthquake.

Two months after marching through Boston,
half the regiment was dead;
at the dedication,
William James could almost hear the bronze Negroes
     breathe.

Their monument sticks like a fishbone
in the city's throat.
Its Colonel is as lean
as a compass-needle.

He has an angry wrenlike vigilance,
a greyhound's gentle tautness;
he seems to wince at pleasure,
   and suffocate for privacy.

He is out of bounds now. He rejoices in man's lovely,
peculiar power to choose life and die—
   when he leads his black soldiers to death,
   he cannot bend his back.

On a thousand small town New England greens,
the old white churches hold their air
of sparse, sincere rebellion; frayed flags
   quilt the graveyards of the Grand Army of the Republic.

The stone statues of the abstract Union Soldier
grow slimmer and younger each year—
wasp-waisted, they doze over muskets
and muse through their sideburns. . . .

Shaw's father wanted no monument
except the ditch,
where his son's body was thrown
and lost with his "niggers."

The ditch is nearer.
There are no statues for the last war here;
on Boylston Street, a commercial photograph
shows Hiroshima boiling

over a Mosler Safe, the "Rock of Ages"
that survived the blast. Space is nearer.
When I crouch to my television set,
the drained faces of Negro school-children

> rise like balloons.

Colonel Shaw
is riding on his bubble,
he waits
for the blessed break.

The Aquarium is gone. Everywhere,
giant finned cars nose forward like fish;
a savage servility
slides by on grease.

THE MARCH

{for Dwight MacDonald}

Under the too white marmoreal Lincoln Memorial,
the too tall marmoreal Washington Obelisk,
gazing into the too long reflecting pool,
the reddish trees, the withering autumn sky,
the remorseless, amplified harangues for peace—
lovely to lock arms, to march absurdly locked
(unlocking to keep my wet glasses from slipping)
to see the cigarette match quaking in my fingers,
then to step off like green Union Army recruits
for the first Bull Run, sped by photographers,
the notables, the girls . . . fear, glory, chaos, rout . . .

our green army staggered out on the miles-long
                                  green fields,
met by the other army, the Martian, the ape, the hero,
his new-fangled rifle, his green new steel helmet.

HISTORY

History has to live with what was here,
clutching and close to fumbling all we had—
it is so dull and gruesome how we die,
unlike writing, life never finishes.
Abel was finished; death is not remote,
a flash-in-the-pan electrifies the skeptic,
his cows crowding like skulls against high-voltage wire,
his baby crying all night like a new machine.
As in our Bibles, white-faced, predatory,
the beautiful, mist-drunken hunter's moon ascends—
a child could give it a face: two holes, two holes,
my eyes, my mouth, between them a skull's no-nose—
O there's a terrifying innocence in my face
drenched with the silver salvage of the mornfrost.

WHERE THE RAINBOW ENDS

I saw the sky descending, black and white,
Not blue, on Boston where the winters wore
The skulls to jack-o'-lanterns on the slates,
And Hunger's skin-and-bone retrievers tore
The chickadee and shrike. The thorn tree waits
Its victim tonight
The worms will eat the deadwood to the foot
Of Ararat: the scythers, Time and Death,
Helmed locusts, move upon the tree of breath;
The wild ingrafted olive and the root

Are withered, and a winter drifts to where
The Pepperpot, ironic rainbow, spans
Charles River and its scales of scorched-earth miles.
I saw my city in the Scales, the pans
Of judgment rising and descending. Piles
Of dead leaves char the air—
And I am a red arrow on this graph
Of Revelations. Every dove is sold.
The Chapel's sharp-shinned eagle shifts its hold
On serpent-Time, the rainbow's epitaph.

In Boston serpents whistle at the cold.
The victim climbs the altar steps and sings:
"Hosannah to the lion, lamb, and beast
Who fans the furnace-face of IS with wings:
I breathe the ether of my marriage feast."
At the high altar, gold
And a fair cloth. I kneel and the wings beat
My cheek. What can the dove of Jesus give
You now but wisdom, exile? Stand and live,
The dove has brought an olive branch to eat.

OBIT

Our love will not come back on fortune's wheel—

in the end it gets us, though a man know what he'd
    have:
old cars, old money, old undebased pre-Lyndon
silver, no copper rubbing through . . . old wives;
I could live such a too long time with mine.
In the end, every hypochondriac is his own prophet.
Before the final coming to rest, comes the rest
of all transcendence in a mode of being, hushing
all becoming. I'm for and with myself in my otherness,

in the eternal return of earth's fairer children,
the lily, the rose, the sun on brick at dusk,
the loved, the lover, and their fear of life,
their unconquered flux, insensate oneness,
     painful "It was . . . "
After loving you so much, can I forget
you for eternity, and have no other choice?

FISHNET

Any clear thing that blinds us with surprise,
your wandering silences and bright trouvailles,
dolphin let loose to catch the flashing fish. . . .
saying too little, then too much.
Poets die adolescents, their beat embalms them,
the archetypal voices sing offkey;
the old actor cannot read his friends,
and nevertheless he reads himself aloud,
genius hums the auditorium dead.
The line must terminate.
Yet my heart rises, I know I've gladdened a lifetime
knotting, undoing a fishnet of tarred rope;
the net will hang on the wall when the fish are eaten,
nailed like illegible bronze on the futureless future.

FOR SHERIDAN

We only live between
before we are and what we were.

In the lost negative
you exist,
a smile, a cypher,
an old-fashioned face
in an old-fashioned hat.

Three ages in a flash:
the same child in the same picture,
he, I, you,
chockablock, one stamp
like mother's wedding silver—

gnome, fish, brute cherubic force.

We could see clearly
and all the same things
before the glass was hurt.

Past fifty, we learn with surprise and a sense
of suicidal absolution
that what we intended and failed
could never have happened—
and must be done better.

EPILOGUE

Those blessed structures, plot and rhyme—
why are they no help to me now
I want to make
something imagined, not recalled?
I hear the noise of my own voice:
The painter's vision is not a lens;
it trembles to caress the light.
But sometimes everything I write
with the threadbare art of my eye
seems a snapshot,
lurid, rapid, garish, grouped,
heightened from life,
yet paralyzed by fact.
All's misalliance.
Yet why not say what happened?

Pray for the grace of accuracy
Vermeer gave to the sun's illumination
stealing like the tide across a map
to his girl solid with yearning.
We are poor passing facts,
warned by that to give
each figure in the photograph
his living name.

ELIZABETH BISHOP

(1911–1979)

Elizabeth Bishop was, in effect, orphaned early. Before she was a year old, her father died, and when she was five, her mother had a breakdown that led to insanity and permanent commitment to an asylum. Bishop was raised in Nova Scotia by her maternal grandparents (see the poem "Sestina" for her self-portrait in those years), and later in Massachusetts by an aunt. After graduating from Vassar (in the class commemorated by Mary McCarthy in *The Group*), she lived for some time in Key West, which had a climate favorable for her lifelong asthma, and furnished her first glimpses of the visual appeal of the tropics. While at Vassar, Bishop had been introduced to the poet Marianne Moore by the Vassar librarian, and Moore—with her interest in the natural world and its emblematic and symbolic resonances—proved the ideal mentor for the younger Bishop. In 1946, encouraged by Moore, Bishop published her first book, *North and South*. During a subsequent trip to Brazil, Bishop renewed acquaintance with Lota de Macedo Soares, a wealthy Brazilian whom she had met earlier in New York; Bishop fell ill, was cared for by Soares, and stayed. Bishop's next two books, *A Cold Spring* (1955) and *Questions of Travel* (1965), reflect both life in Brazil and reflections of Nova Scotia. Bishop and Soares lived together for nineteen years, until, under the strain of her own alcoholism and her partner's nervous breakdown ending in suicide, Bishop's life in Brazil came to an end.

After returning to the United States, Bishop taught writing for several years at Harvard, where she met the companion of the latter part of her life, Alice Methfessel. Her time at Harvard overlapped with that of her friend and supporter of several decades, Robert Lowell. Bishop published her last book, *Geography III*, in 1976. After her retirement from Harvard at sixty-five, she taught at the Massachusetts Institute of Technology until her death from a stroke in 1979. Her *Complete Poems* appeared in 1982, the *Collected Prose* in 1984, and *One Art*, her selected letters, in 1994.

Bishop's early poems show the influence of English religious poets—the metaphysicals (especially George Herbert and Thomas Traherne, with their ingeniously formed stanzas) and the Victorian poet Gerard Manley Hopkins (with his "sprung" rhythm). Her Baptist upbringing in her grandparents' house made hymns her introduction to poetry, and elements of religious and metaphysical questioning, together with a nostalgia for an innocence irrecoverable in experience, appear even in her skeptical adult poetry. Her nomadic life raised "questions of travel" as she alternated between a delight in the exotic and a homesickness for the domestic. Similarly she alternated between a guilt over colonial expropriation of the foreign and an exhilaration in the conquest of the unknown.

Bishop's *ars poetica* is expressed in the piece significantly called "Poem," in which she contemplates a small painting done by her granduncle. She first examines it coolly, with the aesthetic distance of one judging its indifferent success; and then exclaims, "Heavens, I recognize the place, I know it!" Both exhilaration and pathos then enter her response, and we find that her poetics is one of intimacy as well as distance. She still judges the painting a minor and unaccomplished one, but its connection with her own memories of Nova Scotia moves her to elegiac celebration and stinted regret:

> Life and memory of it cramped,
> dim, on a piece of Bristol board,
> dim, but how live, how touching in detail
> —the little that we get for free,
> the little of our earthly trust. Not much.

Bishop's reputation has risen steadily since her death, in part because of a rising interest in women's poetry and questions of gender, but also because of her steadfast refusal to take refuge in any philosophical system or religious solution. Her open-eyed realization of both loss (see "One Art") and gain ("Awful but cheerful" is her verdict on experience in "The Bight") is in itself steadying, and her confidence in the resilience of human nature and in the rewarding curiosity of human intelligence argues no need for a further layer of metaphysical reassurance. Her poems typically begin with an unforced and leisured description of a scene or an object—a filling station, a bight, a shore—and then allow a series of human suggestions to arise through the scrim of the scene. The "moral" of the poem—a consideration of "the truth," for instance, at the close of "At the Fishhouses"—emerges so gradually that it seems "natural" rather than prescriptive. In practicing both counted verse (especially the trimeters she borrowed from the Brazilian poet Carlos Drummond de Andrade, whom she had translated) and free verse, Bishop showed herself able to engage freely with both traditional forms and the inventions of modernism. Her discretion of tone and her fineness of vision place her among those poets, such as Herbert and Marvell, to whom urbanity of expression is essential for the full recreation of human feeling modulated by meditative intelligence.

THE FISH

> I caught a tremendous fish
> and held him beside the boat
> half out of water, with my hook
> fast in a corner of his mouth.
> He didn't fight.
> He hadn't fought at all.
> He hung a grunting weight,
> battered and venerable
> and homely. Here and there
> his brown skin hung in strips
> like ancient wallpaper,

and its pattern of darker brown
was like wallpaper:
shapes like full-blown roses
stained and lost through age.
He was speckled with barnacles,
fine rosettes of lime,
and infested
with tiny white sea-lice,
and underneath two or three
rags of green weed hung down.
While his gills were breathing in
the terrible oxygen
—the frightening gills,
fresh and crisp with blood,
that can cut so badly—
I thought of the coarse white flesh
packed in like feathers,
the big bones and the little bones,
the dramatic reds and blacks
of his shiny entrails,
and the pink swim-bladder
like a big peony.
I looked into his eyes
which were far larger than mine
but shallower, and yellowed,
the irises backed and packed
with tarnished tinfoil
seen through the lenses
of old scratched isinglass.
They shifted a little, but not
to return my stare.
—It was more like the tipping
of an object toward the light.
I admired his sullen face,
the mechanism of his jaw,
and then I saw

that from his lower lip
—if you could call it a lip—
grim, wet, and weaponlike,
hung five old pieces of fish line,
or four and a wire leader
with the swivel still attached,
with all their five big hooks
grown firmly in his mouth.
A green line, frayed at the end
where he broke it, two heavier lines,
and a fine black thread
still crimped from the strain and snap
when it broke and he got away.
Like medals with their ribbons
frayed and wavering,
a five-haired beard of wisdom
trailing from his aching jaw.
I stared and stared
and the victory filled up
the little rented boat,
from the pool of bilge
where oil had spread a rainbow
around the rusted engine
to the bailer rusted orange,
the sun-cracked thwarts,
the oarlocks on their strings,
the gunnels—until everything
was rainbow, rainbow, rainbow!
And I let the fish go.

OVER 2,000 ILLUSTRATIONS AND A COMPLETE
   CONCORDANCE

Thus should have been our travels:
serious, engravable.

The Seven Wonders of the World are tired
and a touch familiar, but the other scenes,
innumerable, though equally sad and still,
are foreign. Often the squatting Arab,
or group of Arabs, plotting, probably,
against our Christian Empire,
while one apart, with outstretched arm and hand
points to the Tomb, the Pit, the Sepulcher.
The branches of the date-palms look like files.
The cobbled courtyard, where the Well is dry,
is like a diagram, the brickwork conduits
are vast and obvious, the human figure
far gone in history or theology,
gone with its camel or its faithful horse.
Always the silence, the gesture, the specks of birds
suspended on invisible threads above the Site,
or the smoke rising solemnly, pulled by threads.
Granted a page alone or a page made up
of several scenes arranged in cattycornered rectangles
or circles set on stippled gray,
granted a grim lunette,
caught in the toils of an initial letter,
when dwelt upon, they all resolve themselves.
The eye drops, weighted down, through the lines
the burin made, the lines that move apart
like ripples above sand,
dispersing storms, God's spreading fingerprint,
and painfully, finally, that ignite
in watery prismatic white-and-blue.

Entering the Narrows at St. Johns
the touching bleat of goats reached to the ship.
We glimpsed them, reddish, leaping up the cliffs
among the fog-soaked weeds and butter-and-eggs.
And at St. Peter's the wind blew and the sun shone
     madly.

Rapidly, purposefully, the Collegians marched in lines,
crisscrossing the great square with black, like ants.
In Mexico, the dead man lay
in a blue arcade; the dead volcanoes
glistened like Easter lilies.
The jukebox went on playing "Ay, Jalisco!"
And at Volubilis there were beautiful poppies
splitting the mosaics; the fat old guide made eyes.
In Dingle harbor a golden length of evening
the rotting hulks held up their dripping plush.
The Englishwoman poured tea, informing us
that the Duchess was going to have a baby.
And in the brothels of Marrakesh
the little pockmarked prostitutes
balanced their tea-trays on their heads
and did their belly-dances; flung themselves
naked and giggling against our knees,
asking for cigarettes. It was somewhere near there
I saw what frightened me most of all:
A holy grave, not looking particularly holy,
one of a group under a keyhole-arched stone baldaquin
open to every wind from the pink desert.
An open, gritty, marble trough, carved solid
with exhortation, yellowed
as scattered cattle-teeth;
half-filled with dust, not even the dust
of the poor prophet paynim who once lay there.
In a smart burnoose Khadour looked on amused.

Everything only connected by "and" and "and."
Open the book. (The gilt rubs off the edges
of the pages and pollinates the fingertips.)
Open the heavy book. Why couldn't we have seen
this old Nativity while we were at it?
—the dark ajar, the rocks breaking with light,
an undisturbed, unbreathing flame,

colorless, sparkless, freely fed on straw,
and, lulled within, a family with pets,
—and looked and looked our infant sight away.

THE BIGHT

{On my birthday}

At low tide like this how sheer the water is.
White, crumbling ribs of marl protrude and glare
and the boats are dry, the pilings dry as matches.
Absorbing, rather than being absorbed,
the water in the bight doesn't wet anything,
the color of the gas flame turned as low as possible.
One can smell it turning to gas; if one were Baudelaire
one could probably hear it turning to marimba music.
The little ocher dredge at work off the end of the dock
already plays the dry perfectly off-beat claves.
The birds are outsize. Pelicans crash
into this peculiar gas unnecessarily hard,
it seems to me, like pickaxes,
rarely coming up with anything to show for it,
and going off with humorous elbowings.
Black-and-white man-of-war birds soar
on impalpable drafts
and open their tails like scissors on the curves
or tense them like wishbones, till they tremble.
The frowsy sponge boats keep coming in
with the obliging air of retrievers,
bristling with jackstraw gaffs and hooks
and decorated with bobbles of sponges.
There is a fence of chicken wire along the dock
where, glinting like little plowshares,
the blue-gray shark tails are hung up to dry
for the Chinese-restaurant trade.
Some of the little white boats are still piled up

against each other, or lie on their sides, stove in,
and not yet salvaged, if they ever will be, from the last
    bad storm,
like torn-open, unanswered letters.
The bight is littered with old correspondences.
Click. Click. Goes the dredge,
and brings up a dripping jawful of marl.
All the untidy activity continues,
awful but cheerful.

AT THE FISHHOUSES

Although it is a cold evening,
down by one of the fishhouses
an old man sits netting,
his net, in the gloaming almost invisible
a dark purple-brown,
and his shuttle worn and polished,
The air smells so strong of codfish
it makes one's nose run and one's eyes water.
The five fishhouses have steeply peaked roofs
and narrow, cleated gangplanks slant up
to storerooms in the gables
for the wheelbarrows to be pushed up and down on.
All is silver: the heavy surface of the sea,
swelling slowly as if considering spilling over,
is opaque, but the silver of the benches,
the lobster pots, and masts, scattered
among the wild jagged rocks,
is of an apparent translucence
like the small old buildings with an emerald moss
growing on their shoreward walls.
The big fish tubs are completely lined
with layers of beautiful herring scales
and the wheelbarrows are similarly plastered

with creamy iridescent coats of mail,
with small iridescent flies crawling on them.
Up on the little slope behind the houses,
set in the sparse bright sprinkle of grass,
is an ancient wooden capstan,
cracked, with two long bleached handles
and some melancholy stains, like dried blood,
where the ironwork has rusted.
The old man accepts a Lucky Strike.
He was a friend of my grandfather.
We talk of the decline in the population
and of codfish and herring
while he waits for a herring boat to come in.
There are sequins on his vest and on his thumb.
He has scraped the scales, the principal beauty,
from the unnumbered fish with that black old knife,
the blade of which is almost worn away.

Down at the water's edge, at the place
where they haul up the boats, up the long ramp
descending into the water, thin silver
tree trunks are laid horizontally
across the gray stones, down and down
at intervals of four or five feet.

Cold dark deep and absolutely clear,
element bearable to no mortal,
to fish and seals . . . One seal particularly
I have seen here evening after evening.
He was curious about me. He was interested in music;
like me a believer in total immersion,
so I used to sing him Baptist hymns.
I also sang "A Mighty Fortress Is Our God."
He stood up in the water and regarded me
steadily, moving his head a little.
Then he would disappear, then suddenly emerge

almost in the same spot, with a sort of shrug
as if it were against his better judgment.
Cold dark deep and absolutely clear,
the clear gray icy water . . . Back, behind us,
the dignified tall firs begin.
Bluish, associating with their shadows,
a million Christmas trees stand
waiting for Christmas. The water seems suspended
above the rounded gray and blue-gray stones.
I have seen it over and over, the same sea, the same,
slightly, indifferently swinging above the stones,
above the stones and then the world.
If you should dip your hand in,
your wrist would ache immediately,
your bones would begin to ache and your hand would
    burn
as if the water were a transmutation of fire
that feeds on stones and burns with a dark gray flame.
If you tasted it, it would first taste bitter,
then briny, then surely burn your tongue.
It is like what we imagine knowledge to be:
dark, salt, clear, moving, utterly free,
drawn from the cold hard mouth
of the world, derived from the rocky breasts
forever, flowing and drawn, and since
our knowledge is historical, flowing, and flown.

BRAZIL, JANUARY 1, 1502

> . . . embroidered nature . . . tapestried landscape.
> *Landscape into Art*, by Sir Kenneth Clark

Januaries, Nature greets our eyes
exactly as she must have greeted theirs:
every square inch filling in with foliage—

big leaves, little leaves, and giant leaves,
blue, blue-green, and olive,
with occasional lighter veins and edges,
or a satin underleaf turned over;
monster ferns
in silver-gray relief,
and flowers, too, like giant water lilies
up in the air—up, rather, in the leaves—
purple, yellow, two yellows, pink,
rust red and greenish white;
solid but airy; fresh as if just finished
and taken off the frame.

A blue-white sky, a simple web,
backing for feathery detail:
brief arcs, a pale-green broken wheel,
a few palms, swarthy, squat, but delicate;
and perching there in profile, beaks agape,
the big symbolic birds keep quiet,
each showing only half his puffed and padded,
pure-colored or spotted breast.
Still in the foreground there is Sin:
five sooty dragons near some massy rocks.
The rocks are worked with lichens, gray moonbursts
splattered and overlapping,
threatened from underneath by moss
in lovely hell-green flames,
attacked above
by scaling-ladder vines, oblique and neat,
"one leaf yes and one leaf no" (in Portuguese).
The lizards scarcely breathe; all eyes
are on the smaller, female one, back-to,
her wicked tail straight up and over,
red as a red-hot wire.

Just so the Christians, hard as nails,
tiny as nails, and glinting,
in creaking armor, came and found it all,
not unfamiliar:
no lovers' walks, no bowers,
no cherries to be picked, no lute music,
but corresponding, nevertheless,
to an old dream of wealth and luxury
already out of style when they left home—
wealth, plus a brand-new pleasure.
Directly after Mass, humming perhaps
L'Homme armé or some such tune,
they ripped away into the hanging fabric,
each out to catch an Indian for himself—
those maddening little women who kept calling,
calling to each other (or had the birds waked up?)
and retreating, always retreating, behind it.

SESTINA

September rain falls on the house.
In the failing light, the old grandmother
sits in the kitchen with the child
beside the Little Marvel Stove,
reading the jokes from the almanac,
laughing and talking to hide her tears.

She thinks that her equinotical tears
and the rain that beats on the roof of the house
were both foretold by the almanac,
but only known to a grandmother.
The iron kettle sings on the stove.
She cuts some bread and says to the child,

It's time for tea now; but the child
is watching the teakettle's small hard tears
dance like mad on the hot black stove,
the way the rain must dance on the house.
Tidying up, the old grandmother
hangs up the clever almanac

on its string. Birdlike, the almanac
hovers half open above the child,
hovers above the old grandmother
and her teacup full of dark brown tears.
She shivers and says she thinks the house
feels chilly, and puts more wood in the stove.

It was to be, says the Marvel Stove.
I know what I know, says the almanac.
With crayons the child draws a rigid house
and a winding pathway. Then the child
puts in a man with buttons like tears
and shows it proudly to the grandmother.

But secretly, while the grandmother
busies herself about the stove,
the little moons fall down like tears
from between the pages of the almanac
into the flower bed the child
has carefully placed in the front of the house.

Time to plant tears, says the almanac.
The grandmother sings to the marvelous stove
and the child draws another inscrutable house.

FILLING STATION

Oh, but it is dirty!
—this little filling station,
oil-soaked, oil-permeated

to a disturbing, over-all
black translucency.
Be careful with that match!

Father wears a dirty,
oil-soaked monkey suit
that cuts him under the arms,
and several quick and saucy
and greasy sons assist him
(it's a family filling station),
all quite thoroughly dirty.

Do they live in the station?
It has a cement porch
behind the pumps, and on it
a set of crushed and grease-
impregnated wickerwork;
on the wicker sofa
a dirty dog, quite comfy.

Some comic books provide
the only note of color—
of certain color. They lie
upon a big dim doily
draping a taboret
(part of the set), beside
a big hirsute begonia.

Why the extraneous plant?
Why the taboret?
Why, oh why, the doily?
(Embroidered in daisy stitch
with marguerites, I think,
and heavy with gray crochet.)

Somebody embroidered the doily.
Somebody waters the plant,
or oils it, maybe. Somebody
arranges the rows of cans
so that they softly say:
ESSO—SO—SO—SO
to high-strung automobiles.
Somebody loves us all.

IN THE WAITING ROOM

In Worcester, Massachusetts,
I went with Aunt Consuelo
to keep her dentist's appointment
and sat and waited for her
in the dentist's waiting room.
It was winter. It got dark
early. The waiting room
was full of grown-up people,
arctics and overcoats,
lamps and magazines.
My aunt was inside
what seemed like a long time
and while I waited I read
the *National Geographic*
(I could read) and carefully
studied the photographs:
the inside of a volcano,
black, and full of ashes;
then it was spilling over
in rivulets of fire.
Osa and Martin Johnson
dressed in riding breeches,
laced boots, and pith helmets.
A dead man slung on a pole

—"Long Pig," the caption said.
Babies with pointed heads
wound round and round with string;
black, naked women with necks
wound round and round with wire
like the necks of light bulbs.
Their breasts were horrifying.
I read it right straight through.
I was too shy to stop.
And then I looked at the cover:
the yellow margins, the date.

Suddenly, from inside,
came an *oh!* of pain
—Aunt Consuelo's voice—
not very loud or long.
I wasn't at all surprised;
even then I knew she was
a foolish, timid woman.
I might have been embarrassed,
but wasn't. What took me
completely by surprise
was that it was *me:*
my voice, in my mouth.
Without thinking at all
I was my foolish aunt,
I—we—were falling, falling,
our eyes glued to the cover
of the *National Geographic,*
February, 1918.

I said to myself: three days
and you'll be seven years old.
I was saying it to stop
the sensation of falling off
the round, turning world

into cold, blue-black space.
But I felt: you are an *I,*
you are an *Elizabeth,*
you are one of *them.*
Why should you be one, too?
I scarcely dared to look
to see what it was I was.
I gave a sidelong glance
—I couldn't look any higher—
at shadowy gray knees,
trousers and skirts and boots
and different pairs of hands
lying under the lamps.
I knew that nothing stranger
had ever happened, that nothing
stranger could ever happen.
Why should I be my aunt,
or me, or anyone?
What similarities—
boots, hands, the family voice
I felt in my throat, or even
the *National Geographic*
and those awful hanging breasts—
held us all together
or made us all just one?
How—I didn't know any
word for it—how "unlikely" . . .
How had I come to be here,
like them, and overhear
a cry of pain that could have
got loud and worse but hadn't?

The waiting room was bright
and too hot. It was sliding
beneath a big black wave,
another, and another.

Then I was back in it.
The War was on. Outside,
in Worcester, Massachusetts,
were night and slush and cold,
and it was still the fifth
of February, 1918.

POEM

About the size of an old-style dollar bill,
American or Canadian,
mostly the same whites, gray greens, and steel grays
—this little painting (a sketch for a larger one?)
has never earned any money in its life.
Useless and free, it has spent seventy years
as a minor family relic
handed along collaterally to owners
who looked at it sometimes, or didn't bother to.

It must be Nova Scotia; only there
does one see gabled wooden houses
painted that awful shade of brown.
The other houses, the bits that show, are white.
Elm trees, low hills, a thin church steeple
—that gray-blue wisp—or is it? In the foreground
a water meadow with some tiny cows,
two brushstrokes each, but confidently cows;
two minuscule white geese in the blue water,
back-to-back, feeding, and a slanting stick.
Up closer, a wild iris, white and yellow,
fresh-squiggled from the tube.
The air is fresh and cold; cold early spring
clear as gray glass; a half inch of blue sky
below the steel-gray storm clouds.

(They were the artist's specialty.)
A specklike bird is flying to the left.
Or is it a flyspeck looking like a bird?

Heavens, I recognize the place, I know it!
It's behind—I can almost remember the farmer's name.
His barn backed on that meadow. There it is,
titanium white, one dab. The hint of steeple,
filaments of brush-hairs, barely there,
must be the Presbyterian church.
Would that be Miss Gillespie's house?
Those particular geese and cows
are naturally before my time.

A sketch done in an hour, "in one breath,"
once taken from a trunk and handed over.
*Would you like this? I'll probably never
have room to hang these things again.
Your Uncle George, no, mine, my Uncle George,
he'd be your great-uncle, left them all with Mother
when he went back to England.
You know, he was quite famous, an R.A. . . .*

I never knew him. We both knew this place,
apparently, this literal small backwater,
looked at it long enough to memorize it,
our years apart. How strange. And it's still loved,
or its memory is (it must have changed a lot).
Our visions coincided—"visions" is
too serious a word—our looks, two looks:
art "copying from life" and life itself,
life and the memory of it so compressed
they've turned into each other. Which is which?
Life and memory of it cramped,
dim, on a piece of Bristol board,
dim, but how live, how touching in detail

—the little that we get for free,
the little of our earthly trust. Not much.
About the size of our abidance
along with theirs: the munching cows,
the iris, crisp and shivering, the water
still standing from spring freshets,
the yet-to-be-dismantled elms, the geese.

ONE ART

The art of losing isn't hard to master;
so many things seem filled with the intent
to be lost that their loss is no disaster.

Lose something every day. Accept the fluster
of lost door keys, the hour badly spent.
The art of losing isn't hard to master.

Then practice losing farther, losing faster:
places, and names, and where it was you meant
to travel. None of these will bring disaster.

I lost my mother's watch. And look! my last, or
next-to-last, of three loved houses went.
The art of losing isn't hard to master.

I lost two cities, lovely ones. And, vaster,
some realms I owned, two rivers, a continent.
I miss them, but it wasn't a disaster.

—Even losing you (the joking voice, a gesture
I love) I shan't have lied. It's evident
the art of losing's not too hard to master
though it may look like *(Write it!)* like disaster.

4

PHILIP LARKIN

(1922–1985)

Philip Larkin spent his working life as the librarian of the Hull University Library, and carried on a powerful writing life interspersed with writer's block. He was born in Coventry of a mother to whom he was deeply attached and a father with fascist sympathies, whose eccentric political views influenced his son's curmudgeonly impatience with modern life. Larkin read English at St. John's College, Oxford, and there wrote many of the poems that appear in his first book, *The North Ship* (1945, revised 1966). He turned to fiction, writing two experimental novels, *Jill* (1946) and *A Girl in Winter* (1947), but then gave up narrative. His second book of poetry, appearing ten years after his first, was called, after its title poem, *The Less Deceived*. In it Larkin is unmistakably himself, sounding the rueful spectatorial note with which he would become identified. Nine years later he published *The Whitsun Weddings* (1964), the title gesturing toward the communal life Larkin both envied and despised; and finally, in 1974, there appeared *High Windows*, a collection of poems of deliberate finish and almost complete despair, which did not lack, however, Larkin's characteristically black humor. The *Collected Poems* (1988) regrettably prints poems in chronological order and includes poems Larkin discarded, thereby extinguishing the highly ordered and intended coherence of each separate volume issued in Larkin's lifetime. One must still return to the single volumes to see Larkin as he wished to be remembered.

Larkin edited, in 1973, *The Oxford Book of Twentieth-Century Verse*, which firmly repudiated the international modernist tradition represented by Pound and Eliot, and instead drew a line of modernism descending from Hardy. Hardy was claimed as their ancestor by the poets who made up a postwar cluster later called "The Movement"—a group that included Larkin, Donald Davie, and Thom Gunn. They disapproved of the rhetorical excesses (and easy popular success) of poets such as Dylan Thomas (whose voice, said Larkin, had "a rich fraudulence that sets you chuckling even before—perhaps I should say even after—the adjectival combination-punching begins"). They also disapproved of the overt political rhetoric of the young Auden, Spender, and Day-Lewis. By contrast, the Movement poets depended, for their poetic effects, on concision, indirection, irony, and understatement. The danger of such poetry was that it would damp itself down excessively; but Larkin's gift for enclosing heartbreak in a cool, chiseled, and even comic style made him the best-known, and best, of the group. In 1983 Larkin published a collection of his interviews and essays called *Required Writing: Miscellaneous Pieces 1955–1982*, in which he defines himself by sketching poets whose "sudden sincerities" (Andrew Marvell), or dour slapstick (Ogden Nash), or "authority of sadness" (Stevie Smith), or "spinal cord of thought" (Thomas Hardy), or "constant flickering between solemn and comic" (John Betjeman) appeal to him.

The speaker of a Larkin poem is almost always someone standing outside the communal life of fellow human beings. The unpartnered boy watching through a window as others dance ("Why be out here?/But then, why be in there?"); the tourist in an empty church ("It pleases me to stand in silence here"); the childless man returning to his old school; the loveless person aging alone ("I work all day and get half-drunk at night"); the cuckolded lover, masturbating ("Love again: wanking at ten past three"), are some of his solitaries. The solace found in solitude is its privileged access to bitter truth; the communal life of the herd is seen as premised on denial, lies, self-deception. And a second solace derived from solitude is the moment of vision giving rise to art; often, a Larkin poem will end with a sudden, exalted, and even terrifying openness:

Rather than words comes the thought of high
    windows:
The sun-comprehending glass,
And beyond it, the deep blue air, that shows
Nothing, and is nowhere, and is endless.

It has been argued that Larkin is the voice of the postwar decline of England. But ascribing a temperamental depression as profound as Larkin's to political change is an unprovable venture. If it were nostalgia for empire that caused his bitterness, his values should square with those of empire, but his poetry is profoundly subversive of the institutional exhortations of family, church, school, and work. Its instant resonance in England and abroad suggests (as Larkin said of Ogden Nash) that "he is saying a lot of things that a lot of people are willing to pay to see said, . . . He is [one of] those humorists who make you laugh at things not because they are funny but because laughing at them makes it easier to stand them." Larkin, too, by so savagely and ironically delineating the compromises of life in the finished mastery of his lines, makes life easier to bear, or at least to reflect on.

DAYS

What are days for?
Days are where we live.
They come, they wake us
Time and time over.
They are to be happy in:
Where can we live but days?

Ah, solving that question
Brings the priest and the doctor
In their long coats
Running over the fields.

COUNTING

Thinking in terms of one
Is easily done—
One room, one bed, one chair,
One person there,
Makes perfect sense; one set
Of wishes can be met,
One coffin filled.
But counting up to two
Is harder to do;
For one must be denied
Before it's tried.

HOME IS SO SAD

Home is so sad. It stays as it was left,
Shaped to the comfort of the last to go
As if to win them back. Instead, bereft
Of anyone to please, it withers so,
Having no heart to put aside the theft

And turn again to what it started as,
A joyous shot at how things ought to be,
Long fallen wide. You can see how it was:
Look at the pictures and the cutlery.
The music in the piano stool. That vase.

AFTERNOONS

Summer is fading:
The leaves fall in ones and twos
From trees bordering
The new recreation ground.
In the hollows of afternoons
Young mothers assemble
At swing and sandpit
Setting free their children.

Behind them, at intervals,
Stand husbands in skilled trades,
An estateful of washing,
And the albums, lettered
Our Wedding, lying
Near the television:
Before them, the wind
Is ruining their courting-places
(But the lovers are all in school),
And their children, so intent on
Finding more unripe acorns,
Expect to be taken home.
Their beauty has thickened.
Something is pushing them
To the side of their own lives.

TALKING IN BED

Talking in bed ought to be easiest,
Lying together there goes back so far,
An emblem of two people being honest.

Yet more and more time passes silently.
Outside, the wind's incomplete unrest
Builds and disperses clouds in the sky,

And dark towns heap up on the horizon.
None of this cares for us. Nothing shows why
At this unique distance from isolation

It becomes still more difficult to find
Words at once true and kind,
Or not untrue and not unkind.

DOCKERY AND SON

"Dockery was junior to you,
Wasn't he?" said the Dean. "His son's here now."
Death-suited, visitant, I nod. "And do
You keep in touch with—" Or remember how
Black-gowned, unbreakfasted, and still half-tight
We used to stand before that desk, to give
"Our version" of "these incidents last night?"
I try the door of where I used to live:

Locked. The lawn spreads dazzlingly wide.
A known bell chimes. I catch my train, ignored.
Canal and clouds and colleges subside
Slowly from view. But Dockery, good Lord,
Anyone up today must have been born
In '43, when I was twenty-one.
If he was younger, did he get this son
At nineteen, twenty? Was he that withdrawn

High-collared public-schoolboy, sharing rooms
With Cartwright who was killed? Well, it just shows
How much . . . How little . . . Yawning, I suppose
I fell asleep, waking at the fumes
And furnace-glares of Sheffield, where I changed,
And ate an awful pie, and walked along
The platform to its end to see the ranged
Joining and parting lines reflect a strong

Unhindered moon. To have no son, no wife,
No house or land still seemed quite natural.
Only a numbness registered the shock
Of finding out how much had gone of life,
How widely from the others. Dockery, now:
Only nineteen, he must have taken stock
Of what he wanted, and been capable
Of . . . No, that's not the difference: rather, how

Convinced he was he should be added to!
Why did he think adding meant increase?
To me it was dilution. Where do these
Innate assumptions come from? Not from what
We think truest, or most want to do:
Those warp tight-shut, like doors. They're more a style
Our lives bring with them: habit for a while,
Suddenly they harden into all we've got

And how we got it; looked back on, they rear
Like sand-clouds, thick and close, embodying
For Dockery a son, for me nothing,
Nothing with all a son's harsh patronage.
Life is first boredom, then fear.
Whether or not we use it, it goes,
And leaves what something hidden from us chose,
And age, and then the only end of age.

THIS BE THE VERSE

They fuck you up, your mum and dad.
    They may not mean to, but they do.
They fill you with the faults they had
And add some extra, just for you.

But they were fucked up in their turn
    By fools in old-style hats and coats,
Who half the time were soppy-stern
And half at one another's throats.

Man hands on misery to man.
    It deepens like a coastal shelf.
Get out as early as you can,
And don't have any kids yourself.

AUBADE

I work all day, and get half-drunk at night.
Waking at four to soundless dark, I stare.
In time the curtain-edges will grow light.
Till then I see what's really always there:
Unresting death, a whole day nearer now,
Making all thought impossible but how
And where and when I shall myself die.
Arid interrogation: yet the dread
Of dying, and being dead,
Flashes afresh to hold and horrify.

The mind blanks at the glare. Not in remorse
—The mood not done, the love not given, time
Torn off unused—nor wretchedly because
An only life can take so long to climb
Clear of its wrong beginnings, and may never;
But at the total emptiness for ever,

The sure extinction that we travel to
And shall be lost in always. Not to be here,
Not to be anywhere,
And soon; nothing more terrible, nothing more true.

This is a special way of being afraid
No trick dispels. Religion used to try,
That vast moth-eaten musical brocade
Created to pretend we never die,
And specious stuff that says *No rational being*
Can fear a thing it will not feel, not seeing
That this is what we fear—no sight, no sound,
No touch or taste or smell, nothing to think with,
Nothing to love or link with,
The anaesthetic from which none come round.

And so it stays just on the edge of vision,
A small unfocused blur, a standing chill
That slows each impulse down to indecision.
Most things may never happen: this one will,
And realisation of it rages out
In furnace-fear when we are caught without
People or drink. Courage is no good:
It means not scaring others. Being brave
Lets no one off the grave.
Death is no different whined at than withstood.

Slowly light strengthens, and the room takes shape.
It stands plain as a wardrobe, what we know,
Have always known, know that we can't escape,
Yet can't accept. One side will have to go.
Meanwhile telephones crouch, getting ready to ring
In locked-up offices, and all the uncaring
Intricate rented world begins to rouse.
The sky is white as clay, with no sun.
Work has to be done.
Postmen like doctors go from house to house.

LOVE AGAIN

Love again: wanking at ten past three
(Surely he's taken her home by now?),
The bedroom hot as a bakery,
The drink gone dead, without showing how
To meet tomorrow, and afterwards,
And the usual pain, like dysentery.

Someone else feeling her breasts and cunt,
Someone else drowned in that lash-wide stare,
And me supposed to be ignorant,
Or find it funny, or not to care,
Even . . . but why put it into words?
Isolate rather this element

That spreads through other lives like a tree
And sways them on in a sort of sense
And say why it never worked for me.
Something to do with violence
A long way back, and wrong rewards,
And arrogant eternity.

HIGH WINDOWS

When I see a couple of kids
And guess he's fucking her and she's
Taking pills or wearing a diaphragm,
I know this is paradise

Everyone old has dreamed of all their lives—
Bonds and gestures pushed to one side
Like an outdated combine harvester,
And everyone young going down the long slide

To happiness, endlessly. I wonder if
Anyone looked at me, forty years back,
And thought, *That'll be the life;*
No God any more, or sweating in the dark

About hell and that, or having to hide
What you think of the priest. He
And his lot will all go down the long slide
Like free bloody birds. And immediately

Rather than words comes the thought of high windows;
The sun-comprehending glass,
And beyond it, the deep blue air, that shows
Nothing, and is nowhere, and is endless.

5

SEAMUS HEANEY

(1939–)

Seamus Heaney, who was awarded the 1995 Nobel Prize for Literature, was born in 1939 in County Derry in Northern Ireland, the eldest son of a Catholic farming family. After winning scholarships to boarding school and university (Queen's University in Belfast), he took a teacher-training degree and taught at secondary school, progressing from there to a lectureship at Queen's. While a student, he had begun to write poetry. In 1969 the events of "Bloody Sunday" (when the Belfast police fired on unarmed Catholic civil rights protesters) led to unremitting violence in Ulster. Heaney, who by then had published *Death of a Naturalist* (1966) and *Door into the Dark* (1969), moved in 1970 with his young family to the Republic of Ireland, living in a cottage at Glanmore that had been the gatekeeper's lodge for the Synge estate in Wicklow. (The poem "Exposure" conveys his conflict of conscience in moving south.) He and his wife, Marie, supported the family by her teaching and his freelance writing and broadcasting. In Wicklow, Heaney wrote the poems that became *Wintering Out* (1972) and *North* (1975), the first volume of his maturity, and still his most famous work. After four years in Glanmore, the Heaneys moved to Dublin, and the poet became a professor of English at Carysfort College; his volume *Field Work* (1979) dates from this period. In 1979 he was named to the Boylston Professorship of Rhetoric and Oratory at Harvard University, where he teaches one term each year, spending the rest of the year in Dublin.

Volumes of poetry followed in quick succession: *Station Island* (1984), *The Haw Lantern* (1987), *Seeing Things* (1991), and *The Spirit Level* (1966). He also published a translation of a medieval Irish poem, *Sweeney Astray: A Version from the Irish* (1983) and a version of Sophocles' *Philoctetes,* called *The Cure at Troy* (1990). Heaney's essays and lectures have been collected in three volumes: *Preoccupations* (1980), *The Government of the Tongue* (1988), and *The Redress of Poetry* (1995). His Nobel lecture has been separately published (1996) under the title *Crediting Poetry.*

Heaney's fame has depended on the imaginative richness and intellectual depth of his rendering of the Ireland of the sixties through the nineties, seen through the eyes of an anomalous citizen—a man born in Ulster and belonging to the Catholic minority but highly educated in the British-influenced curriculum of secondary and university training. "Is it any wonder when I thought/I would have second thoughts?" he asked in the poem "Terminus." These "second thoughts" enabled Heaney, while retaining an allegiance to his own origins, to see the full ideological complexity of the North and to view it, as well, in anthropological terms, as part of a geographical belt of violence extending back in time to the middle ages. Joined to his capacity for speculation, Heaney has displayed a remarkable tendency to self-correction, as each book reflects on, and corrects or amplifies, its predecessors. His depth of feeling about both geographical terrain and human suffering has won him a wide readership throughout the world.

Heaney began as a poet of childhood, combining a Wordsworthian and Hardyesque attachment to place with a commitment to local Irish detail in which he was encouraged by the example of Patrick Kavanaugh, a poet of the previous generation. Heaney's early poems show—in their passion for rich sound effects—the influence of both Gerard Manley Hopkins and Dylan Thomas; later, especially in their use of slant rhymes, they show an absorption of Wilfred Owen and W. H. Auden. Heaney has remained a poet using formal patterns, but his poems do not always rhyme: as he went back to early Irish verse via his translation of *Sweeney Astray*, he sought a "thinner" music than the broad Irish pentameter. In one way or another, however, Heaney is always concerned to discover the "binding secret," as he has called it, that will make a poem cohesive, as though its words had grown together by natural affinity.

The two major events affecting Heaney's poetry have been the political conflict in the North of Ireland throughout the seventies and the deaths of his parents in the eighties. The first engendered *North* (with its poems about the medieval bodies of murdered victims found throughout Northern bogs) and many subsequent poems, most recently the war sequence called "Mycenae Wavelengths" in *The Spirit Level* (from which I include the Mycenaean watchman's dawn vision as he waits for the return of Agamemnon from Troy). The second gave rise to many of the poems in *The Haw Lantern* and *Seeing Things*, notably the sequence "Clearances" in memory of Heaney's mother and the poem included here called "Be literal a moment" concerning the death of his father. In seeking a way to treat "the Troubles" in the North without suggesting that they were unique, Heaney looked to other political poets, especially those from Eastern Europe (Osip Mandelstam, Zbigniew Herbert, Czeslaw Milosz, Miroslav Holub) and wrote, in *The Haw Lantern*, a series of allegorical poems from which I have chosen a poem describing a roadblock (a frequent sight on the Irish border) as an allegory of writing.

Heaney's powerful ethical concerns gave his middle poetry a gravity which, in recent years, he has attempted to alleviate by an attention to air and ocean rather than to earth. In writing against the grain, in turning his eyes from the ground and buried bodies toward light, air, desire, the marvelous, Heaney has surprised his readers into a new valuing of his powers.

BOGLAND

For T. P. Flanagan

We have no prairies
To slice a big sun at evening—
Everywhere the sun concedes to
Encroaching horizon,

Is wooed into the cyclops' eye
Of a tarn. Our unfenced country
Is bog that keeps crustling
Between the sights of the sun.

They've taken the skeleton
Of the Great Irish Elk
Out of the peat, set it up,
An astounding crate full of air.

Butter sunk under
More than a hundred years
Was recovered salty and white.
The ground itself is kind, black butter

Melting and opening underfoot,
Missing its last definition
By millions of years.
They'll never dig coal here,

Only the waterlogged trunks
Of great firs, soft as pulp.
Our pioneers keep striking
Inwards and downwards,

Every layer they strip
Seems camped on before.
The bogholes might be Atlantic seepage.
The wet centre is bottomless.

FUNERAL RITES

I

I shouldered a kind of manhood
stepping in to lift the coffins
of dead relations.
They had been laid out

in tainted rooms,
their eyelids glistening,
their dough-white hands
shackled in rosary beads.

Their puffed knuckles
had unwrinkled, the nails
were darkened, the wrists
obediently sloped.

The dulse-brown shroud,
the quilted-satin cribs:
I knelt courteously
admiring it all

as wax melted down
and veined the candles,
the flames hovering
to the women hovering

behind me.
And always, in a corner,
the coffin lid,
its nail-head dressed

with little gleaming crosses.
Dear soapstone masks,
kissing their igloo brows
had to suffice

before the nails were sunk
and the black glacier
of each funeral
pushed away.

II

Now as news comes in
of each neighbourly murder
we pine for ceremony,
customary rhythms:

the temperate footsteps
of a cortege, winding past
each blinded home.
I would restore

the great chambers of Boyne,
prepare a sepulchre
under the cupmarked stones.
Out of side-streets and by-roads

purring family cars
nose into line,
the whole country tunes
to the muffled drumming

of ten thousand engines.
Somnambulant women,
left behind, move
through emptied kitchens

imagining our slow triumph
towards the mounds.
Quiet as a serpent
in its grassy boulevard,

the procession drags its tail
out of the Gap of the North
as its head already enters
the megalithic doorway.

III

When they have put the stone
back in its mouth
we will drive north again
past Strang and Carling fjords,

the cud of memory
allayed for once, arbitration
of the feud placated,
imagining those under the hill

disposed like Gunnar
who lay beautiful
inside his burial mound,
though dead by violence

and unavenged.
Men said that he was chanting
verses about honour
and that four lights burned

in corners of the chamber:
which opened then, as he turned
with a joyful face
to look at the moon.

THE GRAUBALLE MAN

As if he had been poured
in tar, he lies
on a pillow of turf
and seems to weep

the black river of himself.
The grain of his wrists
is like bog oak,
the ball of his heel

like a basalt egg.
His instep has shrunk
cold as a swan's foot
or a wet swamp root.

His hips are the ridge
and purse of a mussel,
his spine an eel arrested
under a glisten of mud.

The head lifts,
the chin is a visor
raised above the vent
of his slashed throat

that has tanned and toughened.
The cured wound
opens inward to a dark
elderberry place.

Who will say 'corpse'
to his vivid cast?
Who will say 'body'
to his opaque repose?

And his rusted hair,
a mat unlikely
as a foetus's.
I first saw his twisted face

in a photograph,
a head and shoulder
out of the peat,
bruised like a forceps baby,

but now he lies
perfected in my memory.
down to the red horn
of his nails.

hung in the scales
with beauty and atrocity:
with the Dying Gaul
too strictly compassed

on his shield,
with the actual weight
of each hooded victim.
slashed and dumped.

THE FIRST KINGDOM

The royal roads were cow paths.
The queen mother hunkered on a stool
and played the harpstrings of milk
into a wooden pail.
With seasoned sticks the nobles
lorded it over the hindquarters of cattle.

Units of measurement were pondered
by the cartful, barrowful and bucketful.
Time was a backward rote of names and mishaps,
bad harvests, fires, unfair settlements,
deaths in floods, murders and miscarriages.

And if my rights to it all came only
by their acclamation, what was it worth?
I blew hot and blew cold.
They were two-faced and accommodating.
And seed, breed and generation still
they are holding on, every bit
as pious and exacting and demeaned.

AN ARTIST

I love the thought of his anger.
His obstinancy against the rock, his coercion
of the substance from green apples.

The way he was a dog barking
at the image of himself barking.
And his hatred of his own embrace
of working as the only thing that worked—
the vulgarity of expecting ever
gratitude or admiration, which
would mean a stealing from him.

The way his fortitude held and hardened
because he did what he knew.
His forehead like a hurled *boule*
travelling unpainted space
behind the apple and behind the mountain.

FROM THE FRONTIER OF WRITING

The tightness and the nilness round that space
when the car stops in the road, the troops inspect
its make and number and, as one bends his face

towards your window, you catch sight of more
on a hill beyond, eyeing with intent
down cradled guns that hold you under cover

and everything is pure interrogation
until a rifle motions and you move
with guarded unconcerned acceleration—

a little emptier, a little spent
as always by that quiver in the self,
subjugated, yes, and obedient.

So you drive on to the frontier of writing
where it happens again. The guns on tripods;
the sergeant with his on-off mike repeating

data about you, waiting for the squawk
of clearance; the marksman training down
out of the sun upon you like a hawk.

And suddenly you're through, arraigned yet freed,
as if you'd passed from behind a waterfall
on the black current of a tarmac road

past armour-plated vehicles, out between
the posted soldiers flowing and receding
like tree shadows into the polished windscreen.

FROM *Squarings*

   II

Roof it again. Batten down. Dig in.
Drink out of tin. Know the scullery cold,
A latch, a door-bar, forged tongs and a grate.

Touch the cross-beam, drive iron in a wall,
Hang a line to verify the plumb
From lintel, coping-stone and chimney-breast.

Relocate the bedrock in the threshold.
Take squarings from the recessed gable pane.
Make your study the unregarded floor.

Sink every impulse like a bolt. Secure
The bastion of sensation. Do not waver
Into language. Do not waver in it.

XXIV

Deserted harbour stillness. Every stone
Clarified and dormant under water,
The harbour wall a masonry of silence.

Fullness. Shimmer. Laden high Atlantic
The moorings barely stirred in, very slight
Clucking of the swell against boat boards.

Perfected vision: cockle minarets
Consigned down there with green-slicked bottle glass,
Shell-debris and a reddened bud of sandstone.

Air and ocean known as antecedents
Of each other. In apposition with
Omnipresence, equilibrium, brim.

XXXIII

Be literal a moment. Recollect
Walking out on what had been emptied out
After he died, turning your back and leaving.

That morning tiles were harder, windows colder,
The raindrops on the pane more scourged, the grass
Barer to the sky, more wind-harrowed,

Or so it seemed. The house that he had planned
"Plain, big, straight, ordinary, you know,"
A paradigm of rigour and correction,

Rebuke to fanciness and shrine to limit,
Stood firmer than ever for its own idea
Like a printed X-ray for the X-rayed body.

XLVII

The visible sea at a distance from the shore
Or beyond the anchoring grounds
Was called the offing.

The emptier it stood, the more compelled
The eye that scanned it.
But once you turned your back on it, your back

Was suddenly all eyes like Argus's.
Then, when you'd look again, the offing felt
Untrespassed still, and yet somehow vacated

As if a lambent troop that exercised
On the borders of your vision had withdrawn
Behind the skyline to manoeuvre and regroup.

HIS DAWN VISION

Cities of grass. Fort walls. The dumbstruck palace.
I'd come to with the night wind on my face,
Agog, alert again, but far, far less

Focused on victory than I should have been—
Still isolated in my old disdain
Of claques who always needed to be seen

And heard as the true Argives. Mouth athletes,
Quoting the oracle and quoting dates,
Petitioning, accusing, taking votes.

No element that should have carried weight
Out of the grievous distance would translate.
Our war stalled in the pre-articulate.

The little violets' heads bowed on their stems,
The pre-dawn gossamers, all dew and scrim
And star-lace, it was more through them

I felt the beating of the huge time-wound
We lived inside. My soul wept in my hand
When I would touch them, my whole being rained

Down on myself, I saw cities of grass,
Valleys of longing, tombs, a wind-swept brightness,
And far-off, in a hilly, ominous place,

Small crowds of people watching as a man
Jumped a fresh earth-wall and another ran
Amorously, it seemed, to strike him down.

6

DEREK WALCOTT

(1930–)

Derek Walcott was born in the Caribbean island of St. Lucia, and received the standard British-centered education then in place since the island had been colonized by England. It is no surprise, then, that Walcott's earliest lyrics showed powerfully the influence of the two most celebrated British poets of the twentieth century—Yeats and Auden. And Yeats's work—coming from an island that had also, until recently, been colonized by the English—offered Walcott a possible model for a poetry that used the colonizer's language for nationalist purposes. But Yeats came from the nationalist sector of the ascendancy, from a class allied by education and culture, if not by politics, with their colonizers, while Walcott was a black descendant of the slave culture of the Caribbean: He could not use English with the same sense of heritage as Yeats.

Walcott founded a theater company in St. Lucia, and began to write plays directly concerned with life on the island. He looked subsequently to the United States for a model of an independent postcolonial literature, and found inspiration in the work of Robert Lowell, whose turbulent sense of history—classical, European, colonial, and postcolonial—was congenial to Walcott's own. Still later Walcott's verse shows the influence of the writing of Seamus Heaney, whose attitude toward political troubles had been formed—unlike that of Yeats—by being one of the Catholic minority in Protestant Ulster. In a bold departure from "standard English," Walcott wrote a long poem in island dialect, "The Schooner Flight," which had a momentum and swing, a powerful originality, hailed by all its readers.

• • •

For some years Walcott has taught courses in the writing of poetry and plays at Boston University, and has produced plays there, both his own and those of others. His midlife poetry began to look at race relations in the United States, notably in *The Gulf* (1970). In the opening of "The Schooner Flight" (1979) included here, he declares "either I'm nobody, or I'm a nation." In *Omeros* (1990), Walcott imaginatively used the Homeric narratives as the basis for a modern long poem. He was awarded the Nobel Prize for Literature in 1992.

NIGHTS IN THE GARDENS OF PORT OF SPAIN

Night, our black summer, simplifies her smells
into a village; she assumes the impenetrable

musk of the Negro, grows secret as sweat,
her alleys odorous with shucked oyster shells,

coals of gold oranges, braziers of melon.
Commerce and tambourines increase her heat.

Hellfire or the whorehouse: crossing Park Street,
a surf of sailors' faces crests, is gone

with the sea's phosphorescence; the *boites de nuit*
twinkle like fireflies in her thick hair.

Blinded by headlamps, deaf to taxi klaxons,
she lifts her face from the cheap, pitch-oil flare

towards white stars, like cities, flashing neon,
burning to be the bitch she will become.

As daylight breaks the Indian turns his tumbril
of hacked, beheaded coconuts towards home.

THE GULF

{for Jack and Barbara Harrison}

I

The airport coffee tastes less of America.
Sour, unshaven, dreading the exertion
of tightening, racked nerves fuelled with liquor,

some smoky, resinous bourbon,
the body, buckling at its casket hole,
a roar like last night's blast racing its engines,

watches the fumes of the exhausted soul
as the trans-Texas jet, screeching, begins
its flight and friends diminish. So, to be aware

of the divine union the soul detaches
itself from created things. "We're in the air,"
the Texan near me grins. All things: these matches

from LBJ's campaign hotel, this rose
given me at dawn in Austin by a child,
this book of fables by Borges, its prose

a stalking, moonlit tiger. What was willed
on innocent, sun-streaked Dallas, the beast's claw
curled round that hairspring rifle is revealed

on every page as lunacy or feral law;
circling that wound we leave Love Field.
Fondled, these objects conjure hotels,
quarrels, new friendships, brown limbs
nakedly moulded as these autumn hills
memory penetrates as the jet climbs

the new clouds over Texas; their home means
an island suburb, forest, mountain water;
they are the simple properties for scenes

whose joy exhausts like grief, scenes where we learn,
exchanging the least gifts, this rose, this napkin,
that those we love are objects we return,

that this lens on the desert's wrinkled skin
has priced our flesh, all that we love in pawn
to that brass ball, that the gifts, multiplying,

clutter and choke the heart, and that I shall
watch love reclaim its things as I lie dying.
My very flesh and blood! Each seems a petal

shrivelling from its core. I watch them burn,
by the nerves' flare I catch their skeletal
candour! Best never to be born,

the great dead cry. Their works shine on our shelves,
by twilight tour their gilded gravestone spines,
and read until the lamplight page revolves

to a white stasis whose detachment shines
like a propeller's rainbowed radiance.
Circling like us; no comfort for their loves!

II

The cold glass darkens. Elizabeth once wrote
that we make glass the image of our pain;
I watch clouds boil past the cold, sweating pane

above the Gulf. All styles yearn to be plain
as life. The face of the loved object under glass
is plainer still. Yet, somehow, at this height,

above this cauldron boiling with its wars,
our old earth, breaking to familiar light,
that cloud-bound mummy with self-healing scars

peeled of her cerements again looks new;
some cratered valley heals itself with sage,
through that grey, fading massacre a blue

lighthearted creek flutes of some siege
to the amnesia of drumming water.
Their cause is crystalline: the divided union

of these detached, divided states, whose slaughter
darkens each summer now, as one by one,
the smoke of bursting ghettos clouds the glass

down every coast where filling station signs
proclaim the Gulf, an air, heavy with gas,
sickens the state, from Newark to New Orleans.

III

Yet the South felt like home. Wrought balconies,
the sluggish river with its tidal drawl,
the tropic air charged with the extremities

of patience, a heat heavy with oil,
canebrakes, that legendary jazz. But fear
thickened my voice, that strange, familiar soil

prickled and barbed the texture of my hair,
my status as a secondary soul.
The Gulf, your gulf, is daily widening,

each blood-red rose warns of that coming night
when there's no rock cleft to go hidin' in
and all the rocks catch fire, when that black might,

their stalking, moonless panthers turn from Him
whose voice they can no more believe, when the black X's
mark their passover with slain seraphim.

IV

The Gulf shines, dull as lead. The coast of Texas
glints like a metal rim. I have no home
as long as summer bubbling to its head

boils for that day when in the Lord God's name
the coals of fire are heaped upon the head
of all whose gospel is the whip and flame,

age after age, the uninstructing dead.

SEA GRAPES

That sail which leans on light,
tired of islands,
a schooner beating up the Caribbean

for home, could be Odysseus,
home-bound on the Aegean;
that father and husband's

longing, under gnarled sour grapes, is
like the adulterer hearing Nausicaa's name
in every gull's outcry.

This brings nobody peace. The ancient war
between obsession and responsibility
will never finish and has been the same

for the sea-wanderer or the one on shore
now wriggling on his sandals to walk home,
since Troy sighed its last flame,

and the blind giant's boulder heaved the trough
from whose groundswell the great hexameters come
to the conclusions of exhausted surf.

The classics can console. But not enough.

FROM "THE DIVIDED CHILD"

CHAPTER 3, II

Ajax,
        lion-coloured stallion from Sealey's stable,
        by day a cart horse, a thoroughbred
        on race days, once a year,
        plunges the thunder of his neck, and sniffs
        above the garbage smells, the scent
        of battle, and the shouting,
        he saith among the kitchen peels, "Aha!"
debased, bored animal,
        its dung cakes pluming, gathers
        the thunder of its flanks, and drags
        its chariot to the next block, where

Berthilia,
> the frog-like, crippled crone,
> a hump on her son's back, is carried
> to her straw mat, her day-long perch,
> Cassandra, with her drone unheeded.
> Her son, Pierre, carries night-soil in buckets,
> she spurs him like a rider,
> horsey-back, horsey-back;
> when he describes his cross he sounds content,
> he is everywhere admired. A model son.

Choiseul,
> surly chauffeur from Clauzel's garage,
> bangs Troy's gate shut!
> It hinges on a scream. His rusty
> common-law wife's. Hands hard as a crank handle,
> he is obsequious, in love with engines.
> They can be reconstructed. Before
> human complications, his horny hands are thumbs.
> Now, seal your eyes, and think of Homer's grief.

Darnley,
> skin freckled like a mango leaf,
> feels the sun's fingers press his lids.
> His half-brother Russell steers him by the hand.
> Seeing him, I practise blindness.
> Homer and Milton in their owl-blind towers,
> I envy him his great affliction. Sunlight
> whitens him like a negative.

Emanuel
> Auguste, out in the harbour, lone Odysseus,
> tattooed ex-merchant sailor, rows alone
> through the rosebloom of dawn to chuckling oars
> measured, dip, pentametrical, reciting
> through narrowed eyes as his blades scissor silk,

"Ah moon/(bend, stroke)
of my delight/(bend, stroke)
that knows no wane.
The moon of heaven/(bend, stroke)
is rising once again,"

defiling past Troy town, his rented oars
remembering what seas, what smoking shores?

FARAH & RAWLINS, temple with
plate-glass front, gutted, but girded by
Ionic columns, before which mincing

Gaga,
the town's transvestite, housemaid's darling,
is window-shopping, swirling his plastic bag,
before his houseboy's roundtrip to Barbados,
most Greek of all, the love that hath no name, and

Helen?
Janie, the town's one clear-complexioned whore,
with two tow-headed children in her tow,
she sleeps with sailors only, her black
hair electrical
as all that trouble over Troy,
rolling broad-beamed she leaves
a plump and pumping vacancy,
"O promise me," as in her satin sea-heave follow
cries of

Ityn!Tin!Tin!
from Philomene, the bird-brained idiot girl,
eyes skittering as the sea-swallow
since her rape,
laying on lust, in her unspeakable tongue,
her silent curse.

Joumard,
 the fowl-thief with his cockerel's strut,
 heads home like Jason, in his fluttering coat
 a smoke-drugged guinea hen,
 the golden fleece,

Kyrie! kyrie! twitter
 a choir of surpliced blackbirds in the pews
 of telephone wires, bringing day to

Ligier,
 reprieved murderer, tangled in his pipe smoke,
 wrestling Laocoon,
 bringing more gold to

Midas,
 Monsieur Auguste Manoir,
 pillar of business and the Church,
 rising to watch the sunlight work for him,
 gilding the wharf's warehouses with his name.

Nessus,
 nicknamed N'homme Maman Migrain
 (your louse's mother's man),
 rises in sackcloth, prophesying
 fire and brimstone on the gilt wooden towers of
 offices, ordures, on
 Peter & Co. to burn like Pompeii, on J.
 Q. Charles's stores, on the teetering scabrous City of
 Refuge, my old grandmother's barracks, where, once

Submarine,
 the seven-foot-high bum boatman,
 loose, lank, and gangling as a frayed cheroot,
 once asking to see a ship's captain, and refused,
 with infinite courtesy bending, inquired,

"So what the hell is your captain?
A fucking microbe?"

Troy town awakens,
in its shirt of fire, but on our street

Uncle Eric
sits in a shadowed corner,
mumbling, hum-eyed,
writing his letters to the world,
his tilted hand scrambling for foothold.

Vaughan,
battling his itch, waits for the rumshop's
New Jerusalem, while Mister

Weekes,
slippered black grocer in gold-rimmed spectacles,
paddles across a rug of yellow sunshine
laid at his feet by the shadows of tall houses,
towards his dark shop,
propelled in his tranced passage by one star:
Garvey's imperial emblem of Africa United,
felt slippers muttering in Barbadian brogue,
and, entering his shop,
is mantled like a cleric
in a soutane of onion smells, saltfish, and garlic,
salt-flaked Newfoundland cod hacked by a cleaver
on a scarred counter where a bent halfpenny
shows Edward VII, Defender of the Faith, Emperor
of India,
next to a Lincoln penny, IN GOD WE TRUST
"and in God one, b'Christ," thinks Mr. Weekes,
opening his Bible near the paradise plums,
arm crooked all day over a window open
at the New Jerusalem, for Coloured People Only.
At Exodus.

Xodus, bearing back the saxophonist,
    Yes, whose ramshorn is his dented saxophone,
    bearing back to the green grasses of Guinea,

Zandoli,
    nicknamed The Lizard,
    rodent exterminator, mosquito murderer,
    equipment slung over a phthisic shoulder,
    safariing from Mary Ann Street's cafe,
    wiping a gum-bright grin, out for the week's
        assault on
    roaches, midges, jiggers, rodents, bugs, and larvae,
    singing, refumigating
    Jerusalem, for Coloured People Only.

    These dead, these derelicts,
    that alphabet of the emaciated,
    they were the stars of my mythology.

1 ADIOS, CARENAGE

In idle August, while the sea soft,
and leaves of brown islands stick to the rim
of this Caribbean, I blow out the light
by the dreamless face of Maria Concepcion
to ship as a seaman on the schooner *Flight*.
Out in the yard turning grey in the dawn,
I stood like a stone and nothing else move
but the cold sea rippling like galvanize
and the nail holes of stars in the sky roof,
till a wind start to interfere with the trees.
I pass me dry neighbour sweeping she yard
as I went downhill, and I nearly said:

"Sweep soft, you witch, 'cause she don't sleep hard,"
but the bitch look through me like I was dead.
A route taxi pull up, park-lights still on.
The driver size up my bags with a grin:
"This time, Shabine, like you really gone!"
I ain't answer the ass, I simply pile in
the back seat and watch the sky burn
above Laventille pink as the gown
in which the woman I left was sleeping,
and I look in the rearview and see a man
exactly like me, and the man was weeping,
for the houses, the streets, that whole fucking island.

Christ have mercy on all sleeping things!
From that dog rotting down Wrightson Road
to when I was a dog on these streets;
if loving these islands must be my load,
out of corruption my soul takes wings,
But they had started to poison my soul
with their big house, big car, big-time bohbohl,
coolie, nigger, Syrian, and French Creole,
so I leave it for them and their carnival—
I taking a sea-bath, I gone down the road.
I know these islands from Monos to Nassau,
a rusty head sailor with sea-green eyes
that they nickname Shabine, the patois for
any red nigger, and I, Shabine, saw
when these slums of empire was paradise.
I'm just a red nigger who love the sea,
I had a sound colonial education,
I have Dutch, nigger, and English in me,
and either I'm nobody, or I'm a nation.

—from "The Schooner Flight"

THE SEASON OF PHANTASMAL PEACE

Then all the nations of birds lifted together
the huge net of the shadows of this earth
in multitudinous dialects, twittering tongues,
stitching and crossing it. They lifted up
the shadows of long pines down trackless slopes,
the shadows of glass-faced towers down evening streets,
the shadow of a frail plant on a city sill—
the net rising soundless as night, the birds' cries
        soundless, until
there was no longer dusk, or season, decline, or weather,
only this passage of phantasmal light
that not the narrowest shadow dared to sever.

And men could not see, looking up, what the wild geese
        drew,
what the ospreys trailed behind them in silvery ropes
that flashed in the icy sunlight; they could not hear
battalions of starlings waging peaceful cries,
bearing the net higher, covering this world
like the vines of an orchard, or a mother drawing
the trembling gauze over the trembling eyes
of a child fluttering to sleep;
                                it was the light
that you will see at evening on the side of a hill
in yellow October, and no one hearing knew
what change had brought into the raven's cawing,
the killdeer's screech, the ember-circling chough
such an immense, soundless, and high concern
for the fields and cities where the birds belong,
except it was their seasonal passing, Love,
made seasonless, or, from the high privilege of their
        birth,
something brighter than pity for the wingless ones

below them who shared dark holes in windows and in
     houses
and higher they lifted the net with soundless voices
above all change, betrayals of falling suns,
and this season lasted one moment, like the pause
between dusk and darkness, between fury and peace,
but, for such as our earth is now, it lasted long.

FROM *Midsummer*

XLI

The camps hold their distance—brown chestnuts and
     grey smoke
that coils like barbed wire. The profit in guilt continues.
Brown pigeons goose-step, squirrels pile up acorns like
     little shoes,
and moss, voiceless as smoke, hushes the peeled bodies
like abandoned kindling. In the clear pools, fat
trout rising to lures bubble in umlauts.
Forty years gone, in my island childhood, I felt that
the gift of poetry had made me one of the chosen,
that all experience was kindling to the fire of the Muse.
Now I see her in autumn on that pine bench where she
     sits,
their nut-brown ideal, in gold plaits and *lederhosen,*
the blood drops of poppies embroidered on her white
     bodice,
the spirit of autumn to every Hans and Fritz
whose gaze raked the stubble fields when the smoky cries
of rooks were nearly human. They placed their cause in
her cornsilk crown, her cornflower iris,
winnower of chaff for whom the swastikas flash
in skeletal harvests. But had I known then

that the fronds of my island were harrows, its sand the
    ash
of the distant camps, would I have broken my pen
because this century's pastorals were being written
by the chimneys of Dachau, of Auschwitz, of
    Sachsenhausen?

TOMORROW, TOMORROW

I remember the cities I have never seen
exactly. Silver-veined Venice, Leningrad
with its toffee-twisted minarets. Paris. Soon
the Impressionists will be making sunshine out of shade.
Oh! and the uncoiling cobra alleys of Hyderabad.

To have loved one horizon is insularity;
it blindfolds vision, it narrows experience.
The spirit is willing, but the mind is dirty.
The flesh wastes itself under crumb-sprinkled lines,
widening the *Weltanschauung* with magazines.

A world's outside the door, but how upsetting
to stand by your bags on a cold step at dawn
roses the brickwork and before you start regretting,
your taxi's coming with one beep of its horn,
sidling to the curb like a hearse—so you get in.

7

A Sampling of Other English-Language Poets

A. R. Ammons (United States)

Easter Morning

I have a life that did not become,
that turned aside and stopped,
astonished:
I hold it in me like a pregnancy or
as on my lap a child
not to grow or grow old but dwell on

it is his grave I most
frequently return and return
to ask what is wrong, what was
wrong, to see it all by
the light of a different necessity
but the grave will not heal
and the child,
stirring, must share my grave
with me, an old man having
gotten by on what was left

when I go back to my home country in these
fresh far-away days, it's convenient to visit
everybody, aunts and uncles, those who used to say,
look how he's shooting up, and the
trinket aunts who always had a little
something in their pocketbooks, cinnamon bark
or a penny or nickel, and uncles who
were the rumored fathers of cousins
who whispered of them as of great, if
troubled, presences, and school
teachers, just about everybody older
(and some younger) collected in one place
waiting, particularly, but not for
me, mother and father there, too, and others
close, close as burrowing
under skin, all in the graveyard
assembled, done for, the world they
used to wield, have trouble and joy
in, gone

the child in me that could not become
was not ready for others to go,
to go on into change, blessings and
horrors, but stands there by the road
where the mishap occurred, crying out for
help, come and fix this or we
can't get by, but the great ones who
were to return, they could not or did
not hear and went on in a flurry and
now, I say in the graveyard, here
lies the flurry, now it can't come
back with help or helpful asides, now
we all buy the bitter
incompletions, pick up the knots of
horror, silently raving, and go on
crashing into empty ends not

completions, not rondures the fullness
has come into and spent itself from

I stand on the stump
of a child, whether myself
or my little brother who died, and
yell as far as I can, I cannot leave this place, for
for me it is the dearest and the worst,
it is life nearest to life which is
life lost: it is my place where
I must stand and fail,
calling attention with tears
to the branches not lofting
boughs into space, to the barren
air that holds the world that was my world

though the incompletions
(& completions) burn out
standing in the flash high-burn
momentary structure of ash, still it
is a picture-book, letter-perfect
Easter morning: I have been for a walk:
the wind is tranquil: the brook
works without flashing in an abundant
tranquility: the birds are lively with
voice: I saw something I had
never seen before: two great birds,
maybe eagles, blackwinged, whitenecked
and -headed, came from the south oaring
the great wings steadily; they went
directly over me, high up, and kept on
due north: but then one bird,
the one behind, veered a little to the
left and the other bird kept on seeming
not to notice for a minute: the first
began to circle as if looking for

something, coasting, resting its wings
on the down side of some of the circles:
the other bird came back and they both
circled, looking perhaps for a draft;
they turned a few more times, possibly
rising—at least, clearly resting—
then flew on falling into distance till
they broke across the local bush and
trees: it was a sight of bountiful
majesty and integrity: the having
patterns and routes, breaking
from them to explore other patterns or
better ways to routes, and then the
return: a dance sacred as the sap in
the trees, permanent in its descriptions
as the ripples round the brook's
ripplestone: fresh as this particular
flood of burn breaking across us now
from the sun.

JOHN ASHBERY (UNITED STATES)

SOONEST MENDED

Barely tolerated, living on the margin
In our technological society, we were always having to be
    rescued
On the brink of destruction, like heroines in *Orlando
    Furioso*
Before it was time to start all over again.
There would be thunder in the bushes, a rustling of
    coils,
And Angelica, in the Ingres painting, was considering
The colorful but small monster near her toe, as though
    wondering whether forgetting

The whole thing might not, in the end, be the only
    solution.
And then there always came a time when
Happy Hooligan in his rusted green automobile
Came plowing down the course, just to make sure
    everything was O.K.,
Only by that time we were in another chapter and
    confused
About how to receive this latest piece of information.
Was it information? Weren't we rather acting this out
For someone else's benefit, thoughts in a mind
With room enough and to spare for our little problems
    (so they began to seem),
Only our daily quandary about food and the rent and
    bills to be paid?
To reduce all this to a small variant,
To step free at last, minuscule on the gigantic plateau—
This was our ambition: to be small and clear and free.
Alas, the summer's energy wanes quickly.
A moment and it is gone. And no longer
May we make the necessary arrangements, simply as they
    are.
Our star was brighter perhaps when it had water in it.
Now there is no question even of that, but only
Of holding on to the hard earth so as not to get thrown
    off,
With an occasional dream, a vision: a robin flies across
The upper corner of the window, you brush your hair
    away
And cannot quite see, or a would will flash
Against the sweet faces of the other, something like:
This is what you want to hear, so why
Did you think of listening to something else? We are all
    talkers
It is true, but underneath the talk lies
The moving and not wanting to be moved, the loose
Meaning, untidy and simple like a threshing floor.

There were some hazards of the course,

Yet though we knew the course *was* hazards and nothing
    else

It was still a shock when, almost a quarter of a century
    later,

The clarity of the rules dawned on you for the first time.

They were the players, and we who had struggled at the
    game

Were merely spectators, though subject to its
    vicissitudes

And moving with it out of the tearful stadium, borne on
    shoulder, at last.

Night after night this message returns, repeated

In the flickering bulbs of the sky, raised past us, taken
    away from us,

Yet ours over and over until the end that is past truth,

The being of our sentences, in the climate that fostered
    them,

Not ours to own, like a book, but to be with, and
    sometimes

To be without, alone and desperate.

But the fantasy makes it ours, a kind of fence-sitting

Raised to the level of an esthetic ideal. These were
    moments, years,

Solid with reality, faces, nameable events, kisses, heroic
    acts,

But like the friendly beginning of a geometrical
    progression

Not too reassuring, as though meaning could be cast
    aside some day

When it had been outgrown. Better, you said, to stay
    cowering

Like this in the early lessons, since the promise of
    learning

Is a delusion, and I agreed, adding that

Tomorrow would alter the sense of what had already
    been learned.
That the learning process is extended in this way, so that
    from this standpoint
None of us ever graduates from college,
For time is an emulsion, and probably thinking not to
    grow up
Is the brightest kind of maturity for us, right now at any
    rate.
And you see, both of us were right, though nothing
Has somehow come to nothing; the avatars
Of our conforming to the rules and living
Around the home have made—well, in a sense, "good
    citizens" of us,
Brushing the teeth and all that, and learning to accept
The charity of the hard moments as they are doled out,
For this is action, this not being sure, this careless
Preparing, sowing the seeds crooked in the furrow,
Making ready to forget, and always coming back
To the mooring of starting out, that day so long ago.

MARGARET ATWOOD (CANADA)

FOUR SMALL ELEGIES*
(1838, 1977)

I

Beauharnois

The bronze clock brought
with such care over the sea
which ticked like the fat slow heart
of a cedar, of a grandmother,
melted and its hundred years
of time ran over the ice and froze there.

We are fixed by this frozen clock
at the edge of the winter forest.
Ten below zero.
Shouts in a foreign language
come down blue snow.

The women in their thin nightgowns
disappear wordlessly among the trees.
Here and there a shape,
a limp cloth bundle, a child
who could not keep up

---

*After the failure of the uprising in Lower Canada (now Quebec) in 1838, the British army and an assortment of volunteers carried out reprisals against the civilian population around Beauharnois, burning houses and barns and turning the inhabitants out into the snow. No one was allowed to give them shelter and many froze to death. The men were arrested as rebels; those who were not home were presumed to be rebels and their houses were burned.

The volunteers from Glengarry were Scots, most of them in Canada because their houses had also been burned during the Highland Clearances, an aftermath of the British victory at Culloden. Dufferin, Simcoe, and Grey are the names of three counties in Ontario, settled around this period.

lies sprawled face down in a drift
near the trampled clearing.

No one could give them clothes or shelter,
these were the orders.

We didn't hurt them, the man said,
we didn't touch them.

II
Beauharnois, Glengarry

Those whose houses were burned
burned houses. What else ever happens
once you start?

      While the roofs plunged
into the root-filled cellars,
they chased ducks, chickens, anything
they could catch, clubbed their heads
on rocks, spitted them, singed off the feathers
in fires of blazing fences,
ate them in handfuls, charred
and bloody.

Sitting in the snow
in those mended plaids, rubbing their numb feet,
eating soot, still hungry,
they watched the houses die like
sunsets, like their own
houses. Again

those who gave the orders
were already somewhere else,
of course on horseback.

III
Beauharnois

Is the man here, they said,
where is he?

        She didn't know, though
she called to him as they dragged her
out of the stone house by both arms
and fired the bedding.

He was gone somewhere with the other men,
he was not hanged, he came back later,
they lived in a borrowed shack.

A language is not words only,
it is the stories
that are told in it,
the stories that are never told.

He pumped himself for years
after that into her body
which had no feet
since that night, which had no fingers.
His hatred of the words
that had been done became children.

They did the best they could:
she fed them, he told them
one story only.

IV
Dufferin, Simcoe, Grey

This year we are making
nothing but elegies.
Do what you are good at,
our parents always told us,
make what you know.

This is what we are making,
these songs for the dying.
You have to celebrate something.
The nets rot, the boats rot, the farms
revert to thistle, foreigners
and summer people admire the weeds
and the piles of stones dredged from the fields
by men whose teeth were gone by thirty.

But the elegies are new and yellow,
they are not even made, they grow,
they come out everywhere,
in swamps, at the edges of puddles,
all over the acres
of parked cars, they are mournful
but sweet, like flowered hats
in attics we never knew we had.

We gather them, keep them in vases,
water them while our houses wither.

JOHN BERRYMAN (UNITED STATES)

DREAM SONG 14

Life, friends, is boring. We must not say so.
After all, the sky flashes, the great sea yearns,
we ourselves flash and yearn,
and moreover my mother told me as a boy
(repeatedly) 'Ever to confess you're bored
means you have no

Inner Resources.' I conclude now I have no
inner resources, because I am heavy bored.
Peoples bore me,
literature bores me, especially great literature,
Henry bores me, with his plights & gripes
as bad as achilles,

who loves people and valiant art, which bores me.
And the tranquil hills, & gin, look like a drag
and somehow a dog
has taken itself & its tail considerably away
into mountains or sea or sky, leaving
behind: me, wag.

GEOFFREY HILL (ENGLAND)

LV (*Vergine bella*)

Vergine bella—it is here that I require
a canzone of some substance. There are sound
precedents for this, of a plain eloquence
which would be perfect. But—
ought one to say, I am required; or, it is
required of me; or, it is requisite that I should

make such an offering, bring in such a tribute?
And is this real obligation or actual
pressure of expectancy? One cannot purchase
the goodwill of your arduously simple faith
as one would acquire a tobacconist's cum paper shop
or a small convenience store
established by aloof, hardworking Muslims.
Nor is language, now, what it once was
even in—wait a tick—nineteen hundred and forty-
five of the common era, when your blast-scarred face
appeared staring, seemingly in disbelief
shocked beyond recollection, unable to recognize
the might and the tender salutations
that slowly, with innumerable false starts, the ages
had put together for your glory
in words and in the harmonies of stone.
But you have long known and endured all things
since you first suffered the Incarnation:
endless the extortions, endless the dragging
in of your name. *Vergine bella*, as you
are well aware, I here follow
Petrarch, who was your follower,
a sinner devoted to your service.
I ask that you acknowledge the work
as being contributive to your high praise,
even if no-one else shall be reconciled
to a final understanding of it in that light.

PAUL MULDOON (IRELAND)

MILKWEED AND MONARCH

As he knelt by the grave of his mother and father
the taste of dill, or tarragon—
he could barely tell one from the other—

filled his mouth. It seemed as if he might smother.
Why should he be stricken
with grief, not for his mother and father,

but a woman slinking from the fur of a sea-otter
in Portland, Maine, or, yes, Portland, Oregon—
he could barely tell one from the other—

and why should he now savour
the tang of her, her little pickled gherkin,
as he knelt by the grave of his mother and father?

* * *

He looked about. He remembered her palaver
on how both earth and sky would darken—
"You could barely tell one from the other"—

while the Monarch butterflies passed over
in their milkweed-hunger: "A wing-beat, some reckon,
may trigger off the mother and father

of all storms, striking your Irish Cliffs of Moher
with the force of a hurricane."
Then: "Milkweed and Monarch 'invented' each other."

* * *

He looked about. Cow's-parsley in a samovar.
He'd mistaken his mother's name, "Regan," for "Anger":
as he knelt by the grave of his mother and father
he could barely tell one from the other.

LES MURRAY (AUSTRALIA)

COTTON FLANNELETTE

Shake the bed, the blackened child whimpers,
O shake the bed! through beak lips that
never will come unwry. And wearily the iron-
framed mattress, with nodding crockery bulbs,
jinks on its way.
        Her brothers and sister take
shifts with the terrible glued-together baby
when their unsleeping absolute mother
reels out to snatch an hour, back to stop
the rocking and wring pale blue soap-water
over nude bladders and blood-webbed chars.

Even their cranky evasive father
is awed to stand watches rocking the bed.
Lids frogged shut, *O please shake the bed*
her contours whorl and braille tattoos
from where, in her nightdress, she flared
out of hearth-drowse to a marrow shriek
pedalling full tilt firesleeves in mid-air,
        are grainier with repair
than when the doctor, crying *Dear God, woman!*
No one can save that child. Let her go!
spared her the treatments of the day.

Shake the bed. Like: count phone poles, rhyme,
classify realities, band the head, any
iteration that will bring, in the brain's forks,
the melting molecules of relief,
and bring them again.
                    O rock the bed!
Nibble water with bared teeth, make lymph
like arrowroot gruel, as your mother grips you
for weeks in the untrained perfect language,
till the doctor relents. Salves and wraps you
in dressings that will be the fire again,
ripping anguish of agony,
                    and will confirm
the ploughland ridges in your woman's skin
for the sixty more years your family weaves you
on devotion's loom, rick-racking the bed
as you yourself, six years old, instruct them.

SYLVIA PLATH (UNITED STATES)

LADY LAZARUS

I have done it again.
One year in every ten
I manage it—

A sort of walking miracle, my skin
Bright as a Nazi lampshade,
My right foot

A paperweight,
My face a featureless, fine
Jew linen.

Peel off the napkin
O my enemy.
Do I terrify?—

The nose, the eye pits, the full set of teeth?
The sour breath
Will vanish in a day.

Soon, soon the flesh
The grave cave ate will be
At home on me

And I a smiling woman.
I am only thirty.
And like the cat I have nine times to die.

This is Number Three.
What a trash
To annihilate each decade.

What a million filaments.
The peanut-crunching crowd
Shoves in to see

Them unwrap me hand and foot—
The big strip tease.
Gentlemen, ladies

These are my hands
My knees.
I may be skin and bone,

Nevertheless, I am the same, identical woman.
The first time it happened I was ten.
It was an accident.

The second time I meant
To last it out and not come back at all.
I rocked shut

As a seashell.
They had to call and call
And pick the worms off me like sticky pearls.

Dying
Is an art, like anything else.
I do it exceptionally well.

I do it so it feels like hell.
I do it so it feels real.
I guess you could say I've a call.

It's easy enough to do it in a cell.
It's easy enough to do it and stay put.
It's the theatrical

Comeback in broad day
To the same place, the same face, the same brute
Amused shout:

'A miracle!'
That knocks me out.
There is a charge

For the eyeing of my scars, there is a charge
For the hearing of my heart—
It really goes.

And there is a charge, a very large charge
For a word or a touch
Or a bit of blood

Or a piece of my hair on my clothes.
So, so, Herr Doktor.
So, Herr Enemy.

I am your opus,
I am your valuable,
The pure gold baby

That melts to a shriek.
I turn and burn.
Do not think I underestimate your great concern.

Ash, ash—
You poke and stir.
Flesh, bone, there is nothing there—

A cake of soap,
A wedding ring,
A gold filling.

Herr God, Herr Lucifer
Beware
Beware.

Out of the ash
I rise with my red hair
And I eat men like air.

C. K. STEAD (NEW ZEALAND)

BETWEEN

Twirling an angry necklace on her fingers under the
    lamp she was saying she couldn't stand her
teachers or her mother or her life and on the other

couch her mother who she said had sulked all
afternoon was saying, "Why hasn't anyone any
    pity for *me*?" and that she was so tired
she could scream and scream and scream. Sorry for the
    both I said
    nothing, knowing if silence wouldn't help
it couldn't make anything worse. Impossible to read
    while the air was so loud with their angers.
One channel upstairs was offering a Midlands saga
    of poverty and heartbreak, the other
a California police drama with jokes and canned
    laughter. Then the row stopped. They were gone each
to her room and I could hear a tap dripping, and the cat
    snuffling after fleas, and a car cruising
down the Crescent, and what might have been stifled
    sobbing from
    behind one of those closed doors. I know how
Passion always gets a good press and why it should be so
    but have you ever thought of Reason as
the neglected child of our time? The cat has come to rest
    on my life and my ears are growing out
like vines into spaces of silence beyond the pear
    tree in blossom between the dark houses.

R. S. Thomas (Wales)

The Calling

And the word came—was it a god
spoke or a devil!—Go
to that lean parish; let them tread
on your dreams; and learn silence

is wisdom. Be alone with yourself
as they are alone in the cold room

of the wind. Listen to the earth
mumbling the monotonous song

of the soil: I am hungry, I
am hungry, in spite of the red dung
of this people. See them go
one by one through that dark door

with the crumpled ticket of your prayers
in their hands. Share their distraught
joy at the dropping of their inane
children. Test your belief

in spirit on their faces staring
at you, on beauty's surrender
to truth, on the soul's selling
of itself for a corner

by the body's fire. Learn the thinness
of the window that is
between you and life, and how
the mind cuts itself if it goes through.

ALSO HIGHLY RECOMMENDED:

Frank Bidart, "To the Dead" (in *In the Western Night*)

Rita Dove, "Parsley" (in *Selected Poems*)

Allen Ginsberg, "America" (in *Collected Poems*)

Jorie Graham, "Self-Portrait as the Gesture between Them"
    (in *The Dream of the Unified Field*)

James Merrill, "The Broken Home" (in *Selected Poems*)

Adrienne Rich, "Diving into the Wreck" (in *The Fact of a Doorframe*)

PART II

LATIN AMERICA

8

Poets of a Different Muse

Carolyn Forché

"Latin America constantly sends us poets of a different muse," Spanish poet Federico García Lorca announced before the School of Philosophy and Letters in Madrid:

> Gentle poets of the tropics, of the flatland, of the mountain: distinct rhythms and tones which add to the Spanish language a unique richness, a new language that is already somehow familiar for describing the drunken laziness of the snake, or the penguin delighting in play. But not all of these poets possess the tone of America. Many strike one as peninsular and others accentuate with their own voices the bluster of foreign poets, above all the French. But among the great ones, no. In the great ones there is the flash of a light that is full, romantic, cruel, wild, mysterious, American.

The name "America" was first given to the continents of the Western Hemisphere by German geographer Martin Waldseemüller, who honored the Florentine explorer Amerigo Vespucci by naming after him, on a 1507 map, a portion of the New World. "Latin" wasn't affixed to "America" until the mid-nineteenth century, when the French, distinguishing American speakers of Romance languages from those who spoke English, referred to the Spanish, Portuguese, and French of the "Americas," whether they lived in Canada or Chile. So the task of gathering the latter twentieth century's significant "Latin American" poetic works is complicated by conflicting geographic, historical, linguistic, and cultural identities. The European discovery and invasion of the new lands constituted a collision of humanities so cataclysmic for the Old and New Worlds that historians mark the period as the beginning of the modern age.

"Latin America" has come to refer to the republics from the Rio Grande to Cape Horn, Spanish- and Portuguese-speaking, often inclusive of the Caribbean but rarely of the French islands, and never of Canada. It is not, therefore, a place on a map corresponding to Mexico, Central, and South America. Waldseemüller's "America" is now Brazil, arguably the most racially mixed and ethnically diverse country on earth, as African as it is European. The former Iberian colonies have absorbed their nearly eradicated indigenous cultures and become mestizo, variously identifying in blood and affinity with Europe or the "Indians," whose ancestors inhabited the newly discovered "Indies," regarding the latter with a concatenation of reverence and contempt. As several of our poets, and most notably César Vallejo, are identified as "Indian" by blood and sensibility, it might be important to illuminate, however starkly and briefly, the proscenium of conquest.

Tvetan Todorov, in his moving examination of the conquest, writes:

> [I]t will be recalled that in 1500 the world population is approximately 400 million, of whom 80 million inhabit the Americas. By the middle of the sixteenth century, out of these 80 million, there remain ten. . . . It constitutes a record not only in relative terms (a destruction on the order of 90 percent or more), but also in absolute terms, since we are speaking of a population diminution estimated at 70 million human lives. None of the great massacres of the twentieth century can be compared to this hecatomb.

As to whether the Iberian colonizers were exceptionally brutal, Todorov argues: "Spaniards are not worse than other colonial powers, they just happen to be the people who occupied America at the time, and . . . no other colonizing power has had the opportunity, before or since, to cause the death of so many at once. The British and the French, in the same period, behave no differently. . . ." He further contends:

> Spaniards did not undertake a direct extermination of these millions . . . nor could they have done so. If we examine the forms taken by the diminution of the population, we realize that there are three, and that the Spaniards' responsibility is inversely proportional to the number of victims deriving from each of them: . . . by direct murder . . . by consequence of bad treatment . . . [and] by "microbe shock."

While the epic form has all but disappeared from English and American literature, it has survived and even flourished in twentieth-century Latin American poetry, in part toward recuperation of those ghost civilizations: Aztec, Maya, Inca, Araucanian, Chichimec, Olmec, Cholula, Cuzco, and in Brazil, the Tupi, Gê, Arawak, and Carib among them. Latin American poetry can be said to have begun in the epic impulse of the early soldier-poets and missionaries, but it has endured in César Vallejo, Octavio Paz, and Pablo Neruda, all of whom struggled with the possibility of a work sufficient to the continent's spatial and temporal breadth, which might awaken the slumbering Meso- and South American worlds. It is no coincidence that in each strong attempt at the epic, the ground is that of the lost civilizations. If historical modernity begins in the sixteenth century, "the search for poetic modernity," argued Octavio Paz, "was a quest in the allegorical and chivalric sense this word had in the twelfth century. Crossing several wastelands, visiting castles of mirrors, and camping among ghostly tribes."

Paz admits:

> I found no grail. But I did discover the modern tradition. Because modernity is not a poetic school but a lineage, a family dispersed over several continents and which for two centuries has survived many sudden changes and misfortunes: public indifference, isolation, and tribunals in the name of religious, political, academic and sexual orthodoxy. Being a tradition and not a doctrine, it has been able to persist and to change at the

same time. This is also why it is so diverse. Each poetic adventure is distinct, and each poet has sown a different plant in the
miraculous forest of speaking trees. Yet if the poems are different and each path distinct, what is it that unites these poets?
Not an aesthetic but a search.

It is in that spirit, given the exuberant resistance of Latin American
poets to categorization by national, racial, or ethnic identities, their fluid
aesthetic and complex social affinities, the often harsh demands of their
political circumstances, and their often radically contingent lives, that
this gathering of exemplary poets has been undertaken. From this project's inception at the behest of the late Russian-American poet Joseph
Brodsky, it was known that Latin America should be represented by Jorge
Luis Borges, Pablo Neruda, and Carlos Drummond de Andrade. To these
I have added my selections from César Vallejo and Octavio Paz, as well as
ten other poets whose work has come to prominence in the last decades of
the century.

For Latin America the century begins with the Spanish-American
War of 1898, which resulted in the dissolution of the weakened Spanish
empire. That same year, the Nicaraguan poet Rubén Darío, having
founded the literary movement *modernismo*, went to Europe as a correspondent for *La nación*, concerned with the future of Spanish America. It is
impossible to overestimate the significance of the *modernismo* break with
romanticism, nor its subsequent influence on Latin American poetry.
Darío, of mixed blood (either Afro-Peruvian, as Octavio Paz believes, or
Indian, as claims César Vallejo), was a precocious pan-American wanderer
who wrested Spanish poetics from Iberian romanticism and turned it
toward France, under the influence of the symbolists and Parnassians.

"The genius of *modernismo*," according to Stephen Tapscott, "is that it
articulated the characteristics of an identity that had been waiting to be
expressed," and that "had the effect of shifting attention away from propagandistic sentiment and naively realistic representation, and toward the
experimental European, especially French, literary models. . . . Modernism was a cosmopolitan, erudite movement of individuation and imaginative withdrawal." Its poetry was formal (Darío adapted the strict
French alexandrine line), rhythmically experimental, precise, mysterious,

and erotic; it was also open to the wild exoticism of the Latin American landscape. Darío is credited with creating an aperatura, an opening, for Latin American poets, showing them the possibilities for synthesizing European and indigenous models, balancing culture and nature, eroticism and solitude, clarity and mystery, while achieving a "quasi-narrative tension between Modernist elegance and compassionate awareness of tragedy." Through a fusion of lyric and narrative which suppresses the latter, he celebrated the Edenic while recognizing European historicity. Most important, he introduced the possibility of poetry as a form of knowledge, which would later be explored by postmodernists concerned with the philosophical status of writing itself. Just as North American poetry can be said to begin with Walt Whitman, Latin American poetry was founded by Rubén Darío.

Although César Vallejo is a contemporary of Borges and Drummond de Andrade, his untimely and self-prophesied death in 1938 places him, uniquely among his generation, as one whose work presages much of later-twentieth-century poetics, even if the brevity of his life did not permit him to realize his poetic ambitions. No other poet so fiercely assaulted the very material of his language—its grammar and syntax— producing perhaps the most forwardly experimental Latin American poetry of the century. Readers in the United States became familiar with Vallejo through translations of his later poems produced by Robert Bly and James Wright at a time when interest in Spanish surrealism and its imagery seemed to offer support to proponents of "deep image" poetry, but an apprehension of Vallejo's complexity and genius would await Clayton Eshleman's superb translation of Vallejo's major work, *Trilce,* written during an unjust three-month imprisonment.

Vallejo was born in Santiago de Chuco, near Trujillo, Peru, in 1892, the youngest of eleven children in a *cholo* (mestizo) family. He began writing poetry while still in school, and published his first poems, *Los heraldos negros,* when he was twenty. Two years later he was sentenced to jail on false charges of arson, assault, attempted homicide, robbery, and riot. Within his *cuatro paredes,* the four walls of his confinement, he broke from poetic conventions and inscribed his anguish into a language of shattered logic and syntax, rich in neologism—an inventive meditation on temporality, which is now regarded as one of the major works of Latin American

"Vanguardism." At thirty-one he left for Europe, where he lived for the remainder of his life in poverty. He visited the Soviet Union twice, joined the Communist Party in 1931, and made failed attempts at writing political novels and plays. When the Spanish Civil War began in 1936, he joined legions of others in Spain, and participated in the same Writer's Congress attended by Octavio Paz and Pablo Neruda.

If there is a single event that marked the creative lives of this generation of Latin American poets, it was the brutal defeat of Republican Spain. Vallejo supported the cause from Paris, in poor health, while lamenting his inability to take a more active role. "Spain was chewing at your soul," Pablo Neruda wrote to Vallejo, "That soul so whittled away by your own spirit, so stripped, so wounded by your own ascetic need. Spain was the daily drill into your immense virtue." Vallejo's poems of this period were resonant with an awareness of death—lucid, passionate calls for community and wholeness. Vallejo's poetry, written out of an exile's being and corporal awareness, attempts to interrupt the inexorable movement toward death and discover the possibilities of salvation, if not hope, for humankind.

Jorge Luis Borges might be considered the most British of Latin American poets, having been educated in Switzerland and England, and having immersed himself at an early age in his father's English library, reading Wilde, Wells, Poe, Chesterton, Johnson, and Stevenson, so he was most strongly able to resist *Rubéndiarísmo,* rejecting its musicality and decorative flourishes for a more austere, rigorous, intellectual, and symbolic art. He was the founder of "ultraism" in Argentina, "an enthusiastic but rather incoherent version of futurism which exalted the juxtaposition of violent metaphors as the sole poetic device." Argentinian *ultraísmo* gave way to a Borgesian concern for an authentic literature. His utopian aspiration emerges in an essay, "Palabrería para versos," which appeared in 1926:

> The world of appearances is a rush of jumbled percep-
> tions. . . . Language is an effective arrangement of the world's
> enigmatic abundance. In other words, with our nouns we

invent realities. We touch a round form, we see a glob of dawn-colored light, a tickle delights our mouth, and we falsely say these three heterogeneous things are one, known as an orange. The moon itself is a fiction. . . . All nouns are abbreviations. . . . The world of appearances is most complex and our language has realized only a very small number of the combinations which it allows. Why not create a word, one single word, for our simultaneous perception of cattle bells ringing in the afternoon and the sunset in the distance? . . . I know how utopian my ideas are and how far it is from an intellectual possibility to a real one, but I trust in the magnitude of the future and that it will be no less ample than my hope.

Born in 1899 in Buenos Aires of Spanish, English, and Portuguese-Jewish origin, Borges achieved international acclaim as a short-story writer, essayist, poet, and man of letters, professing no particular concern for genre distinctions, believing the differences between prose and poetry to be superficial. "Poetry is no less a mystery than anything else on earth," he concludes in his preface to *Elogia de la sombra*. "One or two felicitous lines can hardly stir our vanity, since they are but gifts of Chance or of the Spirit; only the mistakes belong to us. . . ." His preoccupations were with philosophical questions and his "primitive" metaphysics, which rejected all systems. He was concerned with space and time, dream and waking apprehensions, destiny, and the absurdity of existence. He postulated worlds, rejecting the disorder and contingency in which he found himself, believing that only art could transcend chaos and provide existential and formal meaning. He found his most fruitful devices in the labyrinth and mirror, parable and mystery. Borges suffered from a congenital affliction that caused his sight to deteriorate severely during the 1950s, and by 1970 he was nearly blind, so his later writing was accomplished by dictation. "Through the years," he wrote, "a man peoples a space with images of provinces, kingdoms, mountains, bays, ships, islands, fishes, rooms, tools, stars, horses, and people. Shortly before his death, he discovers that the patient labyrinth of lines traces the images of his own face."

•   •   •

Carlos Drummond de Andrade is widely regarded as the most accomplished poet of twentieth-century Brazil, having been at the forefront of Brazilian modernism, which differed from the *modernismo* in that its inspiration was Italian futurism rather than French symbolism. "Its locus was not the oneiric, otherworldly space of the *modernista* imagination with its sense of writerliness, but the verbal, self-consciously linguistic space of the poem *an sich*, as the writer aspired to the illusion of speech." Rather than valuing, as did *modernismo,* "the liminal isolation of the visionary poet," Brazilian modernism was "outspokenly nationalistic . . . democratic and demotic." Drummond de Andrade, born in 1902 in Itabira, was committed to the struggle for freedom and human dignity. Empathically concerned with the urban poor, he wrote on their behalf *crônicas,* short prose essays resembling the French and East European *feuilletons,* which commonly appeared in daily newspapers. As a poet, he wrote with sharp irony and inventiveness, in experimental and free-verse forms and was even credited with founding "concrete" poetry in Brazil. A pharmacist by training, Drummond de Andrade was director of the National and Artistic Heritage Service. He wrote fifteen books of poetry and six volumes of *crônicas.* Mark Strand included translations of Drummond de Andrade's poetry in his anthology *Another Republic,* coedited with Charles Simic, wherein the translators described his work as "ironic, compassionate meditations on the fugitive and ephemeral character of experience." Subsequently, in 1986, a volume of translations produced by Strand and Elizabeth Bishop, *Traveling in the Family,* appeared. In a conversation with George Starbuck in 1977, Bishop, who lived in Brazil for two decades, was asked about Brazilian writers. "The one I admire most of the older generation is Carlos Drummond de Andrade. I've translated him. I didn't know him at all. He's supposed to be very shy. I'm supposed to be very shy. We've met once—on the sidewalk at night. We had just come out of the same restaurant, and he kissed my hand politely when we were introduced." This shy courtliness obscured a nonetheless strong opposition to materialism, and an eventual resistance to nationalism, despite the importance of establishing a distinctly Brazilian cultural and literary identity. He eschewed literary politics, movements, and schools, preferring larger communal affiliations—whether regional, in his *Confessions from Minas* (1944) or political, in his solidarity with resistance to fascism. His work was urbane, authentic, deeply personal; its language was idiomatic and clear.

• • •

Pablo Neruda was born Neftalí Reyes in 1904 in Parral, Chile. Following his mother's death only a month after his birth, his father, a railroad engineer, moved the family to Temuco, a settlement in remote southern Chile, where the young poet grew up in an exotic wilderness of strange and as-yet-unclassified flora and fauna. This childhood paradise would forever establish a idyllic homeland for his exiled soul. He began writing poetry at ten years of age, an activity forbidden by his father; the poet persisted, choosing for himself a pseudonym: the common, working-class "Pablo" and the surname of an admired Czech novelist, Jan Neruda. Henceforth his life and work were indivisible, an articulation of the poet's "physical absorption of the world." Although Neruda was well acquainted with the avant-garde, his work was primarily intuitive rather than intellectual, and cannot be specifically located with reference to European movements. "In the house of poetry," he declared, "nothing remains except that which was written with blood to be listened to by blood."

Neruda's first experience of urban life in Santiago inflicted an excruciating loneliness that was to inspire his *Crepusculario,* as well as his best-known work, *Veinte poemas de amor y una canción desesperado* ("Twenty Love Poems and a Song of Despair"). Published in 1924, these surreal poems concerned familiar oscillations between love and solitude. Shortly thereafter he was posted as consul to Rangoon and then to Java, where—enduring five years of intensified isolation, and separated from his native language and culture—he wrote the first volumes of his *Residencia en la tierra* (Residence on Earth), a trilogy not to be completed for twenty years. The first darkly apocalyptic volumes record the disintegration of phenomena and a reversion to primordial chaos. Neruda sought to create a poetic analogue of this flux, grammatically ambiguous and imagistically restless. His temporality resembles Vallejo's in its complexity: Moments become indistinguishably suspended. The work has been read as chaotic, but it is rather an unconstructed, unintuitive, and oneiric sequence of images establishing their own associational and rhythmic order.

Between these works and the final volume, Neruda was marked by the extremity of the Spanish Civil War. After fulfilling his duties in Asia, he returned to Chile, spent time in Europe, then was sent as consul to

Barcelona in 1934, where he befriended poet Rafael Alberti and edited an avant-garde magazine, *Caballo,* in which he defended "impure poetry" against Juan Ramón Jiménez's search for a "pure poetry" of sublime essence. He also began his *Tercera* volume of *Residencia,* explicitly voicing support for the Republican cause in his first "public" poems: "I have the same wounded hand as all men,/I hold the same red cup/and the same enraged astonishment." He also makes his first public appeals: "Come and see the blood in the streets, come and see the blood in the streets, come and see the blood in the streets."

He began reading aloud, joined the Communist Party, intensified his public commitments, and was elected Senator in Chile in 1944. After denouncing President González Videla, Neruda was forced into exile, where he produced his arguably greatest work, *Canto General* (begun, as some critics have maintained, on the death of his father in 1938). This was Neruda's American epic, a work in fifteen sections, recording the flora and fauna of the new world, meditating on the lost civilization at Macchu Picchu; on conquerors and conquered; champions of the poor, workers, and peasants. He condemns the imperialism of the north and in addressing the United States, invokes Abraham Lincoln. He celebrates his origins and proclaims his faith in communism, but the strongest passages of *Canto General* are those concerning the natural world and America's lost civilizations, in which his consciousness fuses with a collective awareness of the past and the self as individuated entity dissolves, "like seed corn in the unending barn of lost events."

Without interrogating language, Neruda makes use of its rhetorical possibilities, borrowing from the high liturgy, and reading his own poems as incantation. Composing his work ritualistically, his strength is auditory rather than visual, sonorous and highly alliterative. *Canto General* marks Neruda's decisive break with artistic elitism. It was followed by poems inspired by his love for his future wife Matilda Urrutia, and poems written in response to his visits to Eastern Europe and China. The *Odas* follow, addressing wind, sea, rain, lemons, in songs of a human life no longer alienated. This is simpler work, spare and luminous but devoid of the ambiguities and allusiveness of his earlier poems. There follow the personal poems addressed to Matilda, *The Captain's Verses* in 1953, the neo-Baroque *Estravagario* in 1958, *One Hundred Love Sonnets* in 1959, and his impassioned poetic autobiography, *Memorial de Isla Negra,* published in 1964. He was awarded the Nobel Prize for Literature in 1971.

In keeping with his lifelong dedication to politics, Neruda announced his candidacy for the presidency of Chile in 1970 but withdrew to support the Socialist candidate Salvador Allende, who won the election only to be assassinated in the CIA-supported coup of 1973. Neruda, who was afflicted with cancer, died of heart failure a few weeks later. In introducing Pablo Neruda before the School of Philosophy and Letters in Madrid, Federico García Lorca announced "that you are about to hear an authentic poet, one of those who has tuned his senses to a world which is not ours, and which few people perceive. A poet closer to death than to philosophy, a poet closer to pain than to intellect, closer to blood than to ink."

Fellow Nobel laureate Octavio Paz was born in Mexico in 1914, the son of Emiliano Zapata's legal representative in New York—he grew up in a family dedicated to the revolution. In his earliest years, he divided his energies between poetry and social commitment, and in 1938 joined Vallejo and Neruda at the Writer's Congress in Republican Spain. His influences included T. S. Eliot, St. John Perse, and the European surrealists, as well as an interest in Eastern religions, and his work can be traced in direct lineage from nineteenth-century visionaries. Of the relation of poetry to society, Paz perceives an irresolvable conflict of opposites "condemned to perpetual conjunction which is immediately transformed into discord. . . . To make social life poetic, to make the poetic world social. The transformation of society into a creative community, into a living poem; and the poem into social life, into an incarnate image."

Unlike Neruda, Paz does not view poetry as an expression of emotion but rather, perhaps, as a "striving to negate succession and found a lasting realm." For Paz the word is magical and dialectical: He believes that the poet is created by language: "Words, phrases, syllables, stars which turn around a fixed center. Two bodies, many beings which meet in a word. Paper is covered with indelible letters which no one spoke, no one dictated, which have fallen there and burn, scorch and are extinguished." Paz is an imagist, regarding images as clusters of concentrated meaning, impervious to analysis: water, fire, air, mirrors, associated and interconnected in a luminous tissue of language. His early poetry proposed the creation of identity, and his later work seems intended as an experience between poet and reader.

One of his most ambitious poems, *Piedra del sol (Sunstone)* is represented through long and striking excerpts here. Structurally circular, it follows the Aztec calendar stone that stands in the Museum of Anthropology and History in Mexico City. Composed in 584 hendecasyllables (eleven-syllable lines, six of which are repeated), mirroring the Mayan system and cycle of Venus, the poem explores dualities in a densely allusive, mytho-historical reflection, against which contradictory aspects of human experience are set in motion: past selves which are in reality the same self. The central theme, according to Paz, is "recovery of the amorous instant as a recovery of true freedom," a love poem of "correspondence" between personal, historical, and cosmic life. This is poetry as communal ritual and means of transcendence, positing utopic vision and love as nearly impossible in the modern world, where the individual matters little.

Myth is viewed as a possible means of journeying beyond subjectivity. Paz shares with Borges a search for philosophical language commensurate with the flux of the world. Through Eastern religion, he developed a poetic mantra, linking tantra to meditation, and conceiving of art as a means of moving beyond selfhood and art-as-artifact. His is a world of correspondences, corporally grounded, phenomenological and concrete, in which it is possible to approach the absolute. For Paz there are two silences, that which precedes the poetic act, and the silence of meaning's plenitude in the poem. Surrealist André Breton praised him for his "surrealist spirit," his "spiritual avidity," and his conveyance of "a striking poetic image of Mexico." Without formally affiliating with Breton's circle, Paz shared its spirit, but mistrusted the dream-speed trance of automatic writing, and doubted that poetry could be artificially induced. He later claimed that he had been "seduced by [surrealism's] intransigent affirmation of certain values," but distanced himself from the cultivation of madness or the use of "chance operations" advocated by Breton's circle. He also rejected nationalism, Stalinism, and all forms of ideological commitment.

"For years I have been sustaining a small and interminable polemic, not against this or that artist but against two attitudes that seem to be identical to me: nationalism and the spirit of system." Paz advocates lucidity but shares surrealism's utopian poetics: the living of one's desire, the redemption of the passions, freedom, Eros, and intensity. For Paz, poetry is to be lived; it is a quest, an event more than an artifact, a sacred experience, an encounter—what is sought is spiritual liberty.

•   •   •

My education in the poetry of Latin America was begun in exilic space during the diaspora. I had committed to translate the poetry of the Salvadoran poet Claribel Alegría, who was then living in Mallorca, Spain, where I joined her during the summer of 1977, in despair at having failed to inhabit her poems sufficiently to bear them into English. The problem was not my inadequate command of Spanish, but rather my ignorance of the conditions out of which Alegría's poetry emerged: warfare, uprising, imprisonment, torture, and exile. While she herself was spared the worst, she witnessed from earliest childhood the brutality of repression, and her imagination was deeply marked by an extremity legible in her poetry. As a consequence I found myself unable to distinguish between concrete and figural language, hoping that an allusion to mutilated hands was a symbol of emotional pain rather than an indexical marker of physical brutality.

During that summer in Spain, Claribel Alegría patiently guided me toward intellectual comprehension of Latin American history, as well as its artistic and political life. In the mornings we worked on poetry and translation, then read to each other and suggested revisions. In the afternoons the various house guests—poets and writers from all over Latin America—gathered on the terrace overlooking the mountain Teix to discuss literature and politics as the sun disappeared into the Mediterranean sea. These meetings were poignant, and often lively, but always a sadness pervaded the house in Deya, a "golden cage" of comfortable but ineffectual exile. Within a few years the infamous Somoza dictatorship would fall in Nicaragua, and Claribel Alegría would leave this refuge behind and move back to the land of her birth. Within a year I would find myself in El Salvador, given a fellowship to write and translate poetry, on the eve of a twelve-year civil war. By 1980 I would more deeply understand a passage from the young writings of the Polish poet Czeslaw Milosz, seemingly a world away:

A man is lying under machine-gun fire on a street in an embattled city. He looks at the pavement and sees a very amusing sight: the cobblestones are standing upright like the quills of a porcupine. The bullets hitting against their edges displace and tilt them. Such moments in the consciousness of a man judge all poets and philosophers. Let us suppose, too, that a certain poet was the hero of literary cafés, and wherever he went was regarded with curiosity and awe. Yet his poems, recalled in such a moment, suddenly seem diseased and highbrow. The vision of the cobblestones is unquestionably real, and poetry based on an equally naked experience could survive triumphantly that judgement day of man's illusions.

For most of the twentieth century, patriarchal authority inherited from the Iberian Catholic monarchies dominated Latin America, which suffered under repressive authoritarian military dicatorships which protected the privilege of feudal oligarchies. During the 1980s many of these governments were democratized, and while Central America endured prolonged warfare, conflicts were, in the end, resolved through negotiated settlements and democratic elections. With the ascendance of cultural pluralism and the slow demise of oligarchic power, poets find themselves somewhat freer to address the problems of language itself, which become increasingly urgent in the administered world of free-market consumer capitalism. The anguish of the individual, so poignantly voiced in *modernismo*, may give way to a new art, reflective of the *mestizaje* Iberian, Indian, and African traditions, while continuing its negotiation between subjective expressivity and the materiality of the word.

9

JORGE LUIS BORGES

(1899–1986)

Jorge Luis Borges was born in Buenos Aires to a professional family, which recognized early his literary gifts. Between 1914 and 1921 the family lived in Europe, where Borges learned languages and began writing. In 1921 he returned to Argentina and began to write poems and essays about his native country. He translated Virginia Woolf, James Joyce, Franz Kafka, and William Faulkner into Spanish, published essays and reviews, and by his late twenties had published two volumes of poems. Despite the hereditary blindness that had already begun to claim his vision, he continued a wide-ranging literary career. It was not until 1939, after the death of his father and his own near death in an accident, that he began to write the short stories that would distinguish him for transcending boundaries of genre and blurring fact and fiction. After serving as director of the National Library at Buenos Aires, he became a professor of English and American literature at the University of Buenos Aires in 1956. He also lectured at many universities in the United States and throughout the world. His many awards and honors included France's Légion d'Honneur. He died in Geneva, Switzerland.

A PAGE TO COMMEMORATE COLONEL SUÁREZ, VICTOR AT JUNÍN

What do they matter now, the deprivations,
the alienation, the frustrations of growing old,
the dictator's shadow spreading across the land, the
    house
in the Barrio del Alto, which his brothers sold while he
    fought,
the useless days
(those one hopes to forget, those one knows are
    forgettable),
when he had, at least, his burning hour, on horseback
on the clear plains of Junín, a setting for the future?

What matters the flow of time, if he knew
that fullness, that ecstasy, that afternoon?

He served three years in the American Wars; and
    then
luck took him to Uruguay, to the banks of the Rio
    Negro.
In the dying afternoons, he would think
that somehow, for him, a rose had burst into flower,
taken flesh in the battle of Junín, the ever-extending
    moment
when the lances clashed, the order which shaped the
    battle,
the initial defeat, and in the uproar
(no less harsh for him than for the army),
his voice crying out at the attacking Peruvians,
the light, the force, the fatefulness of the charge,
the teeming labyrinths of foot soldiers,
the crossing of lances, when no shot resounded,
the Spaniard fighting with a reckless sword,
the victory, the luck, the exhaustion, a dream beginning,

and the men dying among the swamps,
and Bolívar uttering words which were marked for
    history,
and the sun, in the west by now, and, anew, the taste
of wine and water,
and death, that death without a face,
for the battle had trampled over it, effaced it . . .

His great-grandson is writing these lines,
and a silent voice comes to him out of the past,
out of the blood:

"What does my battle at Junín matter if it is only
a glorious memory, or a date learned by rote
for an examination, or a place in the atlas?
The battle is everlasting, and can do without
the pomp of the obvious armies with their trumpets;
Junín is two civilians cursing a tyrant
on a street corner,
or an unknown man somewhere, dying in prison."

(translated by Alastair Reid)

MANUSCRIPT FOUND IN A BOOK OF JOSEPH CONRAD

In the shimmering countries that exude the summer,
The day is blanched in white light. The day
Is a harsh slit across the window shutter,
Dazzle along the coast, and on the plain, fever.

But the ancient night is bottomless, like a jar
Of brimming water. The water reveals limitless wakes,
And in drifting canoes, face inclined to the stars,
Man marks the limp time with a cigar.

The smoke blurs gray across the constellations
Afar. The present sheds past, name, and plan.
The world is a few vague tepid observations.
The river is the original river. Man, the first man.

(translated by Alastair Reid)

COMPASS

All things are words of some strange tongue, in thrall
To Someone, Something, who both day and night
Proceeds in endless gibberish to write
The history of the world. In that dark scrawl

Rome is set down, and Carthage, I, you, all,
And this my being which escapes me quite,
My anguished life that's cryptic, recondite,
And garbled as the tongues of Babel's fall.

Beyond the name there lies what has no name;
Today I have felt its shadows stir the aim
Of this blue needle, light and keen, whose sweep

Homes to the utmost of the sea its love,
Suggestive of a watch in dreams, or of
Some bird, perhaps, who shifts a bit in sleep.

(translated by Richard Wilbur)

LIMITS

Of all those streets that wander to the west,
there must be one (I do not know which one)
which unawares I have walked down for a last
indifferent time, the pawn of that Someone

who fixes in advance the omnipotent laws,
tracing a secret and unyielding graph
of all the dreams, the forms, and the shadows
which thread and unthread the texture of this life.

If there is an end to everything, and an appraisal,
and a last time and nothing more and forgetfulness,
who then will point out which person, in this house,
to whom we have said, without knowing it, farewell?

Through the glass, already gray, the night
withdraws, and among the pile of volumes
throwing steep shadows on the table's gloom,
there must be one which we will never read.

There is, in the South, more than one worn gate
with its rough stone jugs and prickly pear
forbidden to my feet, as if it were
a lithograph or an old print.

For you, there is some door you are closing for ever,
and for you too, some mirror vainly waits.
The crossroads seem to you open and clear,
and yet are watched by a Janus with four heads.

There is among all of your memories one
which is irreparably lost and gone.
They will not see you going down to that fountain,
neither the white sun nor the yellow moon.

Your voice will never recover what was said once
in the Persian, the language of birds and roses,
when at your dying, before the light disperses,
you wish to utter unforgettable things.

And the ever-flowing Rhone, and the lake,
all that vast yesterday on which rests my present?
It will be as lost as Carthage was,
when the Latin scourged it out with fire and salt.

I imagine, in the dawn, I hear a worn
murmur of multitudes, faltering, fading away.
They are everything that has loved me and forgotten;
Space, Time and Borges now are leaving me.

(translated by Alastair Reid)

INFERNO I, 32

In the final years of the twelfth century, from twilight of dawn to twilight of dusk, a leopard looked upon some wooden planks, some vertical iron bars, men and women who were always different, a thick wall and, perhaps, a stone trough filled with dry leaves. The leopard did not know, could not know, that what he craved was love and cruelty and the hot pleasure of rending and the odor of a deer on the wind; and yet something within the animal choked him and something rebelled, and God spoke to him in a dream: *You live and will die in this prison, so that a man I know may look at you a certain number of times and not forget you and put your figure and your symbol in a poem which has its precise place in the scheme of the universe. You suffer captivity, but you will have furnished a word to the poem.* In the dream, God enlightened the rough beast, so that the leopard understood God's reasons and accepted his destiny; and yet, when he awoke, he felt merely an obscure resignation, a gallant ignorance, for the machinery of the world is overly complex for the simplicity of a wild beast.

Years later, Dante lay dying in Ravenna, as little justified and as much alone as any other man. In a dream, God revealed to him the secret purpose of his life and labor; in wonderment, Dante knew at last who he was and what he was and he blessed his bitter days. Tradition holds that on awakening he felt he had received and then lost something infinite, something he could not recuperate, or even glimpse, for the machinery of the world is overly complex for the simplicity of men.

(translated by Anthony Kerrigan)

THE GOLEM

If every name is (as the Greek maintains
In the *Cratylus*) the archetype of its thing,
Among the letters of *ring,* resides the ring,
And in the word *Nile* all the Nile remains.

Then, made up of vowels and consonants,
Encoding God's essence, should exist some Name
Whose exact syllables and letters frame
Within them, terribly, Omnipotence.

Adam and all the stars had known it, placed
There in the Garden. The corrosive rust
Of sin (cabalists say) has long effaced
The Name that generations have since lost.

Human innocency and human guile
Are boundless: it is known that a day came
When the Chosen People pursued the Name
Over the wakeful ghetto's midnight oil.

Unlike the way of those who, as in fog,
Beam a dim shadow in dim history,
Green and alive remains the memory
Of Judah, the Hohe Rabbi Löw of Prague.

Yearning to know that which the Deity
Knows, the Rabbi turned to permutations
Of letters in complicated variations,
And finally pronounced the Name which is the Key

The Entry Gate, the Echo, Host, and Mansion,
Over a dummy at which, with sluggish hand,
He labored hard that it might understand
Secrets of Time, Space, Being, and Extension.

The simulacrum raised its heavy, lowered
Eyelids and perceived colors and forms;
It understood not; lost in loud alarms,
I started to take groping paces forward.

And like ourselves, it gradually became
Locked in the sonorous meshes of the net
Of After, Before, Tomorrow, Meanwhile, Yet,
Right, Left, You, Me, and Different and Same.

(The cabalist from whom the creature took
Its inspiration called the weird thing Golem—
But all these matters are discussed by Scholem
In a most learned passage in his book.)

The rabbi revealed to it the universe
(*This is my foot; that's yours; this is a log*)
And after years of training, the perverse
Pupil managed to sweep the synagogue.

Perhaps there was a faulty text, or breach
In the articulation of the Name;
The magic was the highest—all the same,
The apprentice person never mastered speech.

Less a man's than a dog's, less a dog's, well,
Even than a thing's, the creature's eyes
Would always turn to follow the rabbi's
Steps through the dubious shadows of his cell.

Something eerie, gross, about the Golem,
For, at his very coming, the rabbi's cat
Would vanish. (The cat cannot be found in Scholem;
Across the years, I divine it, for all that.)

Toward God it would extend those filial palms,
Aping the devotions of its God,
Or bend itself, the stupid, grinning clod,
In hollow, Orientalized salaams.

The rabbi gazed on it with tender eyes
And terror. *How* (he asked) *could it be done
That I engender this distressing son?
Inaction is wisdom. I left off being wise.*

*To an infinite series why was it for me
To add another integer? To the vain
Hank that is spun out in Eternity
Another cause or effect, another pain?*

At the anguished hour when the light gets vague
Upon his Golem his eyes would come to rest.
Who can tell us the feelings in His breast
As God gazed on His rabbi there in Prague?

(translated by John Hollander)

CHESS

I

Set in their studious corners, the players
Move the gradual pieces. Until dawn
The chessboard keeps them in its strict confinement
With its two colors set at daggers drawn.

Within the game itself the forms give off
Their magic rules: Homeric castle, knight
Swift to attack, queen warlike, king decisive,
Slanted bishop, and attacking pawns.

Eventually, when the players have withdrawn,
When time itself has finally consumed them,
The ritual certainly will not be done.

It was in the East this war took fire.
Today the whole earth is its theater.
Like the game of love, this game goes on forever.

II

Faint-hearted king, sly bishop, ruthless queen,
Straightforward castle, and deceitful pawn—
Over the checkered black and white terrain
They seek out and begin their armed campaign.

They do not know it is the player's hand
That dominates and guides their destiny.
They do not know an adamantine fate
Controls their will and lays the battle plan.

The player too is captive of caprice
(The words are Omar's) on another ground
Where black nights alternate with whiter days.

God moves the player, he in turn the piece.
But what god beyond God begins the round
Of dust and time and sleep and agonies?

(translated by Alastair Reid)

THE OTHER TIGER

> And the craft createth a semblance.
> —Morris, *Sigurd the Volsung* (1876)

I think of a tiger. The half-light enhances
the vast and painstaking library
and seems to set the bookshelves at a distance;
strong, innocent, new-made, bloodstained,
it will move through its jungle and its morning,
and leave its track across the muddy
edge of a river, unknown, nameless
(in its world, there are no names, nor past, nor future
only the sureness of the passing moment)
and it will cross the wilderness of distance
and sniff out in the woven labyrinth
of smells the smell peculiar to morning
and the scent of deer, delectable.
Among the slivers of bamboo, I notice
its stripes, and I have an inkling of the skeleton
under the magnificence of the skin, which quivers.
In vain, the convex oceans and the deserts
spread themselves across the earth between us;
from this one house in a remote lost seaport
in South America, I dream you, follow you,
oh tiger on the fringes of the Ganges.

Afternoon creeps in my spirit and I keep thinking
that the tiger I am conjuring in my poem
is a tiger made of symbols and of shadows,
a sequence of prosodic measures,
scraps remembered from encyclopedias,
and not the deadly tiger, the luckless jewel
which in the sun or the deceptive moonlight
follows its paths, in Bengal or Sumatra,
of love, of indolence, of dying.

Against the symbolic tiger, I have planted
the real one, it whose blood runs hotly,
and today, 1959, the third of August,
a slow shadow spreads across the prairie,
but still, the act of naming it, of guessing
what is its nature and its circumstances
creates a fiction, not a living creature,
not one of those who wander on the earth.

Let us look for a third tiger. This one
will be a form in my dream like all the others,
a system and arrangement of human language,
and not the tiger of the vertebrae
which, out of reach of all mythology,
paces the earth. I know all this, but something
drives me to this ancient and vague adventure,
unreasonable, and still I keep on looking
throughout the afternoon for the other tiger,
the other tiger which is not in this poem.

(translated by Alastair Reid)

A SOLDIER OF URBINA

Beginning to fear his own unworthiness
for campaigns like the last one he fought, at sea,
this soldier, resigning himself to minor duty,
wandered unknown in Spain, his own harsh country.

To get rid of or to mitigate the cruel
weight of reality, he hid his head in dream.
The magic past of Roland and the cycles
of Ancient Britain warmed him, made him welcome.
Sprawled in the sun, he would gaze on the widening
plain, its coppery glow going on and on;
he felt himself at the end, poor and alone,

not knowing what all the music had been hiding;
Suddenly, plunging deep in a dream of his own,
he came on Sancho and Don Quixote, riding.

(translated by Alastair Reid)

EVERYTHING AND NOTHING

There was no one in him: behind his face (even the poor paintings
of the epoch show it to be unlike any other) and behind his words
(which were copious, fantastic, and agitated) there was nothing
but a bit of cold, a dream not dreamed by anyone. At first he
thought that everyone was like himself. But the dismay shown by
a comrade to whom he mentioned this vacuity revealed his error
to him and made him realize forever that an individual should
not differ from the species. At one time it occurred to him that he
might find a remedy for his difficulty in books, and so he learned
the "small Latin, and less Greek," of which a contemporary spoke.
Later, he considered he might find what he sought in carrying out
one of the elemental rites of humanity, and so he let himself be
initiated by Anne Hathaway in the long siesta hour of an after-
noon in June. In his twenties, he went to London. Instinctively,
he had already trained himself in the habit of pretending he was
someone, so it should not be discovered that he was no one. In
London, he found the profession to which he had been predes-
tined, that of actor: someone who, on a stage, plays at being
someone else, before a concourse of people who pretend to take
him for that other one. His histrionic work taught him a singular
satisfaction, perhaps the first he had ever known. And yet, once
the last line of verse had been acclaimed and the last dead man
dragged off stage, he tasted the hateful taste of unreality. He
would leave off being Ferrex or Tamburlaine and become no one
again. Thus beset, he took to imagining other heroes and other
tragic tales. And so, while his body complied with its bodily des-

tiny in London bawdyhouses and taverns, the soul inhabiting that body was Caesar unheeding the augur's warnings, and Juliet detesting the lark, and Macbeth talking on the heath with the witches who are also the Fates. No one was ever so many men as that man: like the Egyptian Proteus he was able to exhaust all the appearances of being. From time to time, he left, in some obscure corner of his work, a confession he was sure would never be deciphered: Richard states that in his one person he plays many parts, and Iago curiously says: "I am not what I am." The fundamental oneness of existing, dreaming, and acting inspired in him several famous passages.

He persisted in this directed hallucination for twenty years. But one morning he was overcome by a surfeit and horror of being all those kings who die by the sword and all those unfortunate lovers who converge, diverge, and melodiously expire. That same day he settled on the sale of his theatre. Before a week was out he had gone back to his native village, where he recuperated the trees and the river of his boyhood, without relating them at all to the trees and rivers—illustrious with mythological allusion and Latin phrase—which his Muse had celebrated. He had to be someone: he became a retired impresario who had made his fortune and who is interested in making loans, in lawsuits, in petty usury. It was in character, then, in this character, that he dictated the arid last will and testament we know, from which he deliberately excluded any note of pathos or trace of literature. Friends from London used to visit him in his retreat, and for them he would once more play the part of poet.

History adds that before or after his death he found himself facing God and said: *I, who have been so many men in vain, want to be one man, myself alone.* From out of a whirlwind the voice of God replied: *I am not, either. I dreamed the world the way you dreamed your work, my Shakespeare: one of the forms of my dreams was you, who, like me, are many and no one.*

(*translated by Anthony Kerrigan*)

POEM WRITTEN IN A COPY OF *BEOWULF*

At various times, I have asked myself what reasons
moved me to study, while my night came down,
without particular hope of satisfaction,
the language of the blunt-tongued Anglo-Saxons.

Used up by the years, my memory
loses its grip on words that I have vainly
repeated and repeated. My life in the same way
weaves and unweaves its weary history.

Then I tell myself: it must be that the soul
has some secret, sufficient way of knowing
that it is immortal, that its vast, encompassing
circle can take in all, can accomplish all.

Beyond my anxiety, beyond this writing,
the universe waits, inexhaustible, inviting.

(translated by Alastair Reid)

THE LABYRINTH

Zeus, Zeus himself could not undo these nets
Of stone encircling me. My mind forgets
The persons I have been along the way,
The hated way of monotonous walls,
Which is my fate. The galleries seem straight
But curve furtively, forming secret circles
At the terminus of years; and the parapets
Have been worn smooth by the passage of days.
Here, in the tepid alabaster dust,

Are tracks that frighten me. The hollow air
Of evening sometimes brings a bellowing,
Or the echo, desolate, of bellowing.
I know that hidden in the shadows there
Lurks another, whose task is to exhaust
The loneliness that braids and weaves this hell,
To crave my blood, and to fatten on my death.
We seek each other. Oh, if only this
Were the last day of our antithesis!

(translated by John Updike)

LIMITS (OR GOOD-BYES)

There's a line of Verlaine's that I'm not going to
     remember again.
There's a nearby street that's forbidden to my footsteps.
There's a mirror that has seen me for the last time.
There's a door I've closed until the end of the world.
Among the books in my library (I'm looking at them)
There are some I'll never open again.
This summer I'll be fifty years old:
Death invades me, constantly.

From *Inscripciones* by Julio Platero Haedo
(Montevideo, 1923)

(translated by Alan Dugan)

BORGES AND MYSELF

It's to the other man, to Borges, that things happen. I walk along
the streets of Buenos Aires, stopping now and then—perhaps out
of habit—to look at the arch of an old entranceway or a grillwork

gate; of Borges I get news through the mail and glimpse his name among a committee of professors or in a dictionary of biography. I have a taste for hourglasses, maps, eighteenth-century typography, the roots of words, the smell of coffee, and Stevenson's prose; the other man shares these likes, but in a showy way that turns into stagy mannerisms. It would be an exaggeration to say that we are on bad terms; I live, let myself live, so that Borges can weave his tales and poems, and those tales and poems are my justification. It is not hard for me to admit that he has managed to write a few worthwhile pages, but these pages cannot save me, perhaps because what is good no longer belongs to anyone—not even the other man—but rather to speech or tradition. In any case, I am fated to become lost once and for all, and only some moment of myself will survive in the other man. Little by little, I have been surrendering everything to him, even though I have evidence of his stubborn habit of falsification and exaggerating. Spinoza held that all things try to keep on being themselves; a stone wants to be a stone and the tiger a tiger. I shall remain in Borges, not in myself (if it is so that I am someone), but I recognize myself less in his books than in those of others or than in the laborious tuning of a guitar. Years ago, I tried ridding myself of him, and I went from myths of the outlying slums of the city to games with time and infinity, but those games are now part of Borges, and I will have to turn to other things. And so, my life is a running away, and I lose everything and everything is left to oblivion or to the other man.

Which of us is writing this page I don't know.

(translated by Norman Thomas di Giovanni
in collaboration with the author)

10

PABLO NERUDA

(1904–1973)

Pablo Neruda was born Neftalí Ricardo Reyes y Basoalto in Parral, Chile, the son of a railroad worker. At an early age he began to write vivid, often surreal poems, despite being forbidden to do so by his father. The name he chose honored Czech novelist Jan Neruda. He joined the Chilean diplomatic corps in 1927 and traveled widely in Asia, serving as consul in Burma, Ceylon, and Java, as well as Buenos Aires and Madrid. While in Spain he met prominent writers of the "Generation of '27," including Federico García Lorca. Influenced by the pre–civil war politics of Spain, Neruda turned form the subjective lyrics he had written earlier to a new poetry of broad political and social concern, which achieved its great expression in *Canto general*. On his return to Chile in 1944, having served as a diplomat in Mexico City throughout most of the Second World War, he was elected to the Senate as a Communist; his passionate criticism of the president forced him to flee the country and remain in exile until 1953. Among numerous other honors, Neruda was awarded the Nobel Prize in Literature in 1971.

TONIGHT I CAN WRITE . . .

Tonight I can write the saddest lines.

Write, for example, "The night is shattered
and the blue stars shiver in the distance."

The night wind revolves in the sky and sings.

Tonight I can write the saddest lines.
I loved her, and sometimes she loved me too.

Through nights like this one I held her in my arms.
I kissed her again and again under the endless sky.

She loved me, sometimes I loved her too.
How could one not have loved her great still eyes.

Tonight I can write the saddest lines.
To think that I do not have her. To feel that I have lost
    her.

To hear the immense night, still more immense without
    her.
And the verse falls to the soul like dew to the pasture.

What does it matter that my love could not keep her.
The night is shattered and she is not with me.

This is all. In the distance someone is singing. In the
    distance.
My soul is not satisfied that it has lost her.

My sight searches for her as though to go to her.
My heart looks for her, and she is not with me.

The same night whitening the same trees.
We, of that time, are no longer the same.

I no longer love her, that's certain, but how I loved her.
My voice tried to find the wind to touch her hearing.

Another's. She will be another's. Like my kisses before.
Her voice. Her bright body. Her infinite eyes.

I no longer love her, that's certain, but maybe I love her.
Love is so short, forgetting is so long.

Because through nights like this one I held her in my
     arms
my soul is not satisfied that it has lost her.

Though this be the last pain that she makes me suffer
and these the last verses that I write for her.

(translated by W. S. Merwin)

WALKING AROUND

It happens that I am tired of being a man.
It happens that I go into the tailors' shops and the
     movies
all shrivelled up, impenetrable, like a felt swan
navigating on a water of origin and ash.

The smell of barber shops makes me sob out loud.
I want nothing but the repose either of stones or of wool,
I want to see no more establishments, no more gardens,
nor merchandise, nor glasses, nor elevators.

It happens that I am tired of my feet and my nails
and my hair and my shadow.
It happens that I am tired of being a man.

Just the same it would be delicious
to scare a notary with a cut lily
or knock a nun stone dead with one blow of an ear.
It would be beautiful

to go through the streets with a green knife
shouting until I died of cold.

I do not want to go on being a root in the dark,
hesitating, stretched out, shivering with dreams,
downwards, in the wet tripe of the earth,
soaking it up and thinking, eating every day.

I do not want to be the inheritor of so many misfortunes.
I do not want to continue as a root and as a tomb,
as a solitary tunnel, as a cellar full of corpses,
stiff with cold, dying with pain.

For this reason Monday burns like oil
at the sight of me arriving with my jail-face,
and it howls in passing like a wounded wheel,
and its footsteps towards nightfall are filled with hot
        blood.

And it shoves me along to certain corners, to certain
        damp houses,
to hospitals where the bones come out of the windows,
to certain cobblers' shops smelling of vinegar,
to streets horrendous as crevices.

There are birds the color of sulphur, and horrible
        intestines
hanging from the doors of the houses which I hate,
there are forgotten sets of teeth in a coffee-pot,
there are mirrors
which should have wept with shame and horror,
there are umbrellas all over the place, and poisons, and
        navels.

I stride along with calm, with eyes, with shoes,
with fury, with forgetfulness,

I pass, I cross offices and stores full of orthopedic
        appliances,
and courtyards hung with clothes on wires,
underpants, towels and shirts which weep
slow dirty tears.

(translated by W. S. Merwin)

I EXPLAIN A FEW THINGS

You will ask: And where are the lilacs?
And the metaphysical blanket of poppies?
And the rain that often struck
your words filling them
with holes and birds?

I am going to tell you all that is happening to me.

I lived in a quarter
of Madrid, with bells,
with clocks, with trees.

From there one could see
the lean face of Spain
like an ocean of leather.

        My house was called
the house of flowers, because it was bursting
everywhere with geraniums: it was
a fine house
with dogs and children.

        Raul, do you remember?
Do you remember, Rafael?
        Federico, do you remember
under the ground,

do you remember my house with balconies where
June light smothered flowers in your mouth?

>   Brother, brother!
Everything
was great shouting, salty goods,
heaps of throbbing bread,
markets of my Arguelles quarter with its statue
like a pale inkwell among the haddock:
the olive oil reached the ladles,
a deep throbbing
of feet and hands filled the streets,
meters, liters, sharp
essence of life,
>   fish piled up,
pattern of roofs with cold sun on which
the vane grows weary,
frenzied fine ivory of the potatoes,
tomatoes stretching to the sea.

And one morning all was aflame
and one morning the fires
came out of the earth
devouring people,
and from then on fire,
gunpowder from then on,
and from then on blood.

Bandits with airplanes and with Moors,
bandits with rings and duchesses,
bandits with black-robed friars blessing
came through the air to kill the children
and through the streets the blood of the children
ran simply, like children's blood.

Jackals that the jackal would spurn,
stones that the dry thistle would bite spitting,
vipers that vipers would abhor!

Facing you I have seen the blood
of Spain rise up
to drown you in a single wave
of pride and knives!

Treacherous
generals:
look at my dead house,
look at broken Spain:
but from each dead house comes burning metal
instead of flowers,
but from each hollow of Spain
Spain comes forth,
but from each dead child comes a gun with eyes,
but from each crime are born bullets
that will one day seek out in you
where the heart lies.

You will ask: why does your poetry
not speak to us of sleep, of the leaves,
of the great volcanoes of your native land?

Come and see the blood in the streets,
come and see
the blood in the streets,
come and see the blood
in the streets!

(translated by Nathaniel Tarn)

AMOR AMERICA (1400)

I

Before the wig and the dress coat
there were rivers, arterial rivers:
there were cordilleras, jagged waves where
the condor and the snow seemed immutable:
there was dampness and dense growth, the thunder
as yet unnamed, the planetary pampas.

Man was dust, earthen vase, an eyelid
of tremulous loam, the shape of clay—
he was Carib jug, Chibcha stone,
imperial cup or Araucanian silica.
Tender and bloody was he, but on the grip
of his weapon of moist flint,
the initials of the earth were
written.
        No one could
remember them afterward: the wind
forgot them, the language of water
was buried, the keys were lost
or flooded with silence or blood.

Life was not lost, pastoral brothers.
But like a wild rose
a red drop fell into the dense growth,
and a lamp of earth was extinguished.

I am here to tell the story.
From the peace of the buffalo
to the pummeled sands
of the land's end, in the accumulated
spray of the antarctic light,
and through precipitous tunnels

of shady Venezuelan peacefulness
I searched for you, my father,
young warrior of darkness and copper,
or you, nuptial plant, indomitable hair,
mother cayman, metallic dove.
I, Incan of the loam,
touched the stone and said:

Who
awaits me? And I closed my hand
around a fistful of empty flint.
But I walked among Zapotec flowers
and the light was soft like a deer,
and the shade was a green eyelid.

My land without name, without America,
equinoctial stamen, purple lance,
your aroma climbed my roots up to the glass
raised to my lips, up to the slenderest
word as yet unborn in my mouth.

(translated by Jack Schmitt)

ODE TO THE LEMON

From blossoms
released
by the moonlight,
from an
aroma of exasperated
love,
steeped in fragrance,
yellowness
drifted from the lemon tree,
and from its planetarium
lemons descended to the earth.

Tender yield!
The coasts,
the markets glowed
with light, with
unrefined gold;
we opened
two halves
of a miracle,
congealed acid
trickled
from the hemispheres
of a star,
the most intense liqueur
of nature,
unique, vivid,
concentrated,
born of the cool, fresh
lemon,
of its fragrant house,
its acid, secret symmetry.

Knives
sliced a small
cathedral
in the lemon,
the concealed apse, opened,
revealed acid stained glass,
drops
oozed topaz,
altars,
cool architecture.

So, when you hold
the hemisphere
of a cut lemon
above your plate,

you spill
a universe of gold,
a
yellow goblet
of miracles,
a fragrant nipple
of the earth's breast,
a ray of light that was made fruit,
the minute fire of a planet.

(translated by Margaret Sayers Peden)

POET'S OBLIGATION

To whoever is not listening to the sea
this Friday morning, to whoever is cooped up
in house or office, factory or woman
or street or mine or harsh prison cell:
to him I come, and, without speaking or looking,
I arrive and open the door of his prison,
and a vibration starts up, vague and insistent,
a great fragment of thunder sets in motion
the rumble of the planet and the foam,
the raucous rivers of the ocean flood,
the star vibrates swiftly in its corona,
and the sea is beating, dying and continuing.

So, drawn on by my destiny,
I ceaselessly must listen to and keep
the sea's lamenting in my awareness,
I must feel the crash of the hard water
and gather it up in a perpetual cup
so that, wherever those in prison may be,
wherever they suffer the autumn's castigation,
I may be there with an errant wave,
I may move, passing through windows,

and hearing me, eyes will glance upward
saying 'How can I reach the sea?'
And I shall broadcast, saying nothing,
the starry echoes of the wave,
a breaking up of foam and of quicksand,
a rustling of salt withdrawing,
the grey cry of sea-birds on the coast.

So, through me, freedom and the sea
will make their answer to the shuttered heart.

(translated by Alastair Reid)

POETRY

And it was at that age . . . Poetry arrived
in search of me. I don't know, I don't know where
it came from, from winter or a river.
I don't know how or when,
no, they were not voices, they were not
words, nor silence,
but from a street I was summoned,
from the branches of night,
abruptly from the others,
among violent fires
or returning alone,
there I was without a face
and it touched me.

I did not know what to say, my mouth
had no way
with names,
my eyes were blind,
and something started in my soul,
fever or forgotten wings,
and I made my own way,

deciphering
that fire,
and I wrote the first faint line,
faint, without substance, pure
nonsense,
pure wisdom
of someone who knows nothing,
and suddenly I saw
the heavens
unfastened
and open,
planets,
palpitating plantations,
shadow perforated,
riddled
with arrows, fire and flowers,
the winding night, the universe.

And I, infinitesimal being,
drunk with the great starry
void,
likeness, image of
mystery,
felt myself a pure part
of the abyss,
I wheeled with the stars,
my heart broke loose on the wind.

(translated by Alastair Reid)

THE FLAG

My flag is blue and sprouts a fish rampant, locked in and let loose
by two bracelets. In winter, when the wind blows hard and there's
no one about in these out-of-the-way places, I like to hear the flag

crack like a whip with the fish swimming in the sky as if it were alive.

And why this fish, I'm asked. Is it mystical? Yes, I say, it is the ichthyous symbol, the prechristic, the luminocratic, the friddled, the true, the fried, the fried fish.

— And nothing else?

— Nothing else.

But in high winter, the flag thrashes up there with its fish in the air, trembling with cold, wind and sky.

(translated by Nathaniel Tarn)

11

OCTAVIO PAZ

(1914–1998)

Octavio Paz, born in 1914 in Mexico City, is considered one of Mexico's fore-most writers of the twentieth-century. His work includes essays, translations, and poems, ranging from a lyrical surrealism in his early work to more broadly inclusive poems, blending genres and exploring the cultures of Mexico and India. In the 1930s Paz lived in Spain and championed the Spanish Republic. He joined Mexico's diplomatic service in 1945 and was posted to the United States, Japan, and France, where he befriended such avant-garde writers as the surrealist André Breton. Paz resigned as ambassador to India in 1968 following a government massacre of students in Mexico City just before the opening of the Olympic Games. After 1968, considering himself a "disillusioned leftist," he became a professor of Spanish-American literature, Latin American studies, and poetry at universities abroad including Cambridge (England), Harvard, and the University of California at San Diego. He received the Nobel Prize for Literature in 1990.

NAMES, PLACES, STREETS, FACES: THE UNIVERSE IN FLAME

was it I making plans
for the summer—and for all the summers—
on Christopher Street, ten years ago,

with Phyllis, who had two dimples in her cheeks
where sparrows came to drink the light?
on the Reforma did Carmen say to me,
"the air's so crisp here, it's always October,"
or was she speaking to another I've forgotten,
or did I invent it and no one said it?
in Oaxaca was I walking through a night
black-green and enormous as a tree,
talking to myself like the crazy wind,
and reaching my room—always a room—
was it true the mirrors didn't know me?
did we watch the dawn from the Hotel Vernet
dancing with the chestnut trees—
did you say "it's late," combing your hair,
did I watch the stains on the wall and say nothing?
did the two of us climb the tower together,
did we watch evening fall on the reef?
did we eat grapes in Bidart? in Perote
did we buy gardenias?
          names, places,
streets and streets, faces, plazas,
streets, a park, stations, single
rooms, stains on the wall, someone
combing her hair, someone dressing,
someone singing at my side, rooms,
places, streets, names, rooms,

Madrid, 1937,
in the Plaza del Angel the women were sewing
and singing along with their children,
then: the sirens' wail, and the screaming,
houses brought to their knees in the dust,
towers cracked, facades spat out
and the hurricane drone of the engines:
the two took off their clothes and made love
to protect our share of all that's eternal,

to defend our ration of paradise and time,
to touch our roots, to rescue ourselves,
to rescue the inheritance stolen from us
by the thieves of life centuries ago,
the two took off their clothes and kissed
because two bodies, naked and entwined,
leap over time, they are invulnerable,
nothing can touch them, they return to the source,
there is no you, no I, no tomorrow,
no yesterday, no names, the truth of two
in a single body, a single soul,
oh total being . . .
      rooms adrift
in the foundering cities, rooms and streets,
names like wounds, the room with windows
looking out on other rooms
with the same discolored wallpaper,
where a man in shirtsleeves reads the news
or a woman irons; the sunlit room
whose only guest is the branches of a peach;
and the other room, where it's always raining
outside on the patio and the three boys
who have rusted green; rooms that are ships
that rock in a gulf of light; rooms
that are submarines: where silence dissolves
into green waves, and all that we touch
phosphoresces; and the tombs of luxury,
with their portraits nibbled, their rugs unraveling;
and the traps, the cells, the enchanted grottoes,
the birdcages and the numbered rooms,
all are transformed, all take flight,
every molding is a cloud, every door
leads to the sea, the country, the open
air, every table is set for a banquet;
impenetrable as conches, time lays siege
to them in vain, there is no more time,

there are no walls: space, space,
open your hand, gather these riches,
pluck the fruit, eat of life,
stretch out under the tree and drink!

. . . .

      better the crime,
the suicides of lovers, the incest committed
by brother and sister like two mirrors
in love with their likeness, better to eat
the poisoned bread, adultery on a bed
of ashes, ferocious love, the poisonous
vines of delirium, the sodomite who wears
a gob of spit for a rose in his lapel,
better to be stoned in the plaza than to turn
the mill that squeezes out the juice of life,
that turns eternity into empty hours,
minutes into prisons, and time into
copper coins and abstract shit;

better chastity, the invisible flower
that rocks atop the stalks of silence,
the difficult diamond of the holy saints
that filters desires, satiates time,
the marriage of quietude and motion,
solitude sings within its corolla,
every hour is a petal of crystal,
the world strips off its masks,
and at its heart, a transparent shimmer
that we call God, nameless being
who studies himself in the void, faceless
being emerged from himself, sun
of suns, plentitude of presences and names. . . .

. . . .

—and the banquet, the exile, the first crime,
the jawbone of the ass, the opaque thud
and the startled glance of the dead falling
on an ash-strewn plain, Agamemnon's
great bellow, the screams of Cassandra,
over and over, louder than the sea,
Socrates in chains (the sun rises,
to die is to wake: "Crito, a cock
for Aesculapius, I am cured of life"),
the jackal discoursing in the ruins of Nineveh,
the shade that appeared to Brutus on the eve
of the battle, Moctezuma insomniac
on his bed of thorns, the ride in the carriage
toward death—the interminable ride,
counted minute by minute by Robespierre,
his broken jaw between his hands,
Churruca on his cask like a scarlet throne,
the numbered steps of Lincoln as he left
for the theater, Trotsky's death-rattle
and his howl like a boar, Madero's gaze
that no one returned: why are they killing me?,
and the curses, the sighs, the silence
of the criminal, the saint, the poor devil,
graveyards of anecdotes and phrases scratched up
by rhetorical dogs, and the shouts of victory,
the raving, the dark sound we make
when dying and that pulsebeat of life
as it's born, and the sound of bones being crushed
in the fray and the foaming mouth of the prophet
and his scream and the scream of the hangman
and the scream of the victim . . .

                                    eyes are flames,
what they see is flames, the ear a flame

and sounds a flame, lips are coals,
the tongue is a poker, touch and the touched,
thought and the thought-of, he who thinks
is flame, all is burning, the universe
is flame. . . .

—from *Sunstone*

(translated by Eliot Weinberger)

12

CÉSAR VALLEJO

(1892–1938)

César Vallejo, the last of eleven children in a family of mestizos, was raised in the rural highlands of Peru. His early life was impoverished: He withdrew from college several times for lack of money, and finally graduated from the University of Trujillo in 1915, writing a thesis on romanticism in Spanish poetry. He supported himself for several years by teaching primary school while reading and working on his poems; his first collection appeared in 1919, the year after his mother's death. The following year he was imprisoned for 105 days for crimes he did not commit. Profoundly affected by the experience, he wrote many of the poems included in his second book, *Trilce,* published in 1922—the same year *The Waste Land* and *Ulysses* appeared. In 1923 he left Peru and settled in Paris, where his political awakening led him to become involved with socialism and eventually with the Republicans, who were to lose the Spanish Civil War. In addition to his socialist protest novel, *Tungsten,* Vallejo wrote a play, *La piedra cansada,* and many poems, most of which would be posthumously published by his widow. At age forty-six Vallejo died in Paris following a sudden fever.

THE BLACK MESSENGERS

There are some blows in life so hard . . . I don't know!
Blows that seem to come from God's hatred; as if before
     them,
the backwash of all suffering
were welling into my soul . . . I don't know!

They are few, but they are . . . They open dark furrows
in the toughest faces and the strongest backs.
Perhaps they are the colts of barbarous attilas;
or the black messengers sent us by Death.

They are the grave downfall of the soul's Christs,
of some adorable faith that destiny curses.
Those bloody blows are the crackling
of bread heating for us at the oven door.

And man . . . Poor . . . poor man! He turns his head
the way we do when a hand is clapped on our shoulder;
he turns his crazed eyes, and all living
is damned up in that glance, like a puddle of guilt.

There are some blows in life so hard . . . I don't know!

                              (translated by Rachel Benson)

TO MY BROTHER MIGUEL

     in memoriam

Brother, today I sit on the brick bench outside the house,
where you make a bottomless emptiness.
I remember we used to play at this hour of the day, and
     mama
would calm us: "There now, boys . . . "

Now I go hide
as before, from all these evening
prayers, and I hope that you will not find me.
In the parlor, the entrance hall, the corridors.
Later, you hide, and I do not find you.
I remember we made each other cry,
brother, in that game.

Miguel, you hid yourself
one night in August, nearly at daybreak,
but instead of laughing when you hid, you were sad.
And your other heart of those dead afternoons
is tired of looking and not finding you. And now
shadows fall on the soul.

Listen, brother, don't be too late
coming out. All right? Mama might worry.

(translated by John Knoepfle and James Wright)

THE ETERNAL DICE

> *For Manuel González Prada, this wild and unique
> feeling—one of these emotions which the great
> master has admired most in my work.*

God of mine, I am weeping for the life that I live;
I am sorry to have stolen your bread;
but this wretched, thinking piece of clay
is not a crust formed in your side:
you have no Marys that abandon you!

My God, if you had been man,
today you would know how to be God,
but you always lived so well,
that now you feel nothing of your own creation.
And the man who suffers you: he is God!

Today, when there are candles in my witchlike eyes,
as in the eyes of a condemned man,
God of mine, you will light all your lamps,
and we will play with the old dice . . .
Gambler, when the whole universe, perhaps,
is thrown down,
the circled eyes of Death will turn up,
like to final aces of clay.

My God, in this muffled, dark night,
you can't play anymore, because the Earth
is already a die nicked and rounded
from rolling by chance:
and it can stop only in a hollow place,
in the hollow of the enormous grave.

(translated by James Wright)

HAVE YOU ANYTHING TO SAY IN YOUR DEFENSE?

Well, on the day I was born,
God was sick.

They all know that I'm alive,
that I'm vicious; and they don't know
the December that follows from that January.
Well, on the day I was born,
God was sick.

There is an empty place
in my metaphysical shape
that no one can reach:
a cloister of silence
that spoke with the fire of its voice muffled.

On the day I was born,
God was sick.

Brother, listen to me, Listen . . .
Oh, all right. Don't worry, I won't leave
without taking my Decembers along,
without leaving my Januaries behind.
Well, on the day I was born,
God was sick.

They all know that I'm alive,
that I chew my food . . . and they don't know
why harsh winds whistle in my poems,
the narrow uneasiness of a coffin,
winds untangled from the Sphinx
who holds the desert for routine questioning.

Yes, they all know . . . Well, they don't know
that the light gets skinny
and the darkness gets bloated . . .
and they don't know that the Mystery joins things
        together . . .
that he is the hunchback
musical and sad who stands a little way off and foretells
the dazzling progression from the limits to the Limits.

On the day I was born,
God was sick,
gravely.

                              (translated by James Wright)

GOOD SENSE

—There is, mother, a place in the world called Paris.
A very big place and far off and once again big.

My mother turns up the collar of my overcoat, not
because it is beginning to snow, but so it can begin to
snow.

My father's wife is in love with me, coming and
advancing backward toward my birth and chestward
toward my death. I close her, on coming back. That is
why her eyes had given so much to me, brimming with
me, caught red-handed with me, making herself happen
through finished works, through consummated pacts.

Is my mother confessed by me, named by me. Why
doesn't she give as much to my other brothers? To
Victor, for example, the eldest, who is so old now, that
people say: He looks like his mother's younger brother!
Perhaps because I have traveled so much! Perhaps
because I have lived more!

My mother grants a charter of colorful beginning to
my stories of return. Before my returning life, remembering
that I traveled during two hearts through her womb, she
blushes and remains mortally livid, when I say, in the
treatise of the soul: That night I was happy. But more
often she becomes sad; more often she could become sad.

—My son, you look so old!

And files along the yellow color to cry, for she finds
me aged, in the swordblade, in the rivermouth of my
face. She cries from me, becomes sad from me. What
need will there be for my youth, if I am always to be her
son? Why do mothers ache finding their sons old, if the
age of the sons never reaches that of their mothers? And
why, if the sons, the more they approach death, the more
they approach their parents? My mother cries because I
am old from my time and because never will I grow old
from hers!

My farewell set off from a point in her being, more
external than the point in her being to which I return. I
am, because of the excessive time-limit of my return,
more the man before my mother than the son before my
mother. There resides the candor which today makes us
glow with three flames. I say to her then until I hush:

— There is, mother, in the world, a place called
Paris. A very big place and very far off and once again
big.

My father's wife, on hearing me, eats her lunch and
her mortal eyes descend softly down my arm.

(translated by Clayton Eshleman)

I AM GOING TO SPEAK OF HOPE

I do not suffer this pain as Vallejo. I do not ache now as an artist,
as a man or even as a simple living being. I do not suffer this pain
as Catholic, as a Mohammedan or as an atheist. Today I am sim-
ply in pain. If my name were not César Vallejo, I would still suf-
fer this very same pain. If I were not an artist, I would still suffer
it. If I were not a man or even a living being, I would still suffer
it. If I were not a Catholic, atheist or Mohammedan, I would still
suffer it. Today I am in pain from further below. Today I am sim-
ply in pain.

I ache now without any explanation. My pain
is so deep, that it never had a cause nor does it lack a cause now.
What could have been its cause? Where is that thing so impor-
tant, that it might stop being its cause? Its cause is nothing;
nothing could have stopped being its cause. For what has this
pain been born, for itself? My pain comes from the north wind
and from the south wind, like those neuter eggs certain rare birds
lay in the wind. If my bride were dead, my pain would be the
same. If they had slashed my throat all the way through, my pain
would be the same. If life were, in short, different, my pain would
be the same. Today I suffer from further above. Today I am simply
in pain.

I look at the hungry man's pain and see that his hunger is so far from my suffering, that if I were to fast unto death, at least a blade of grass would always sprout from my tomb. The same with the lover!

I believed until now that all the things of the universe were, inevitably, parents or sons. But behold that my pain today is neither parent nor son. It lacks a back to darken, as well as having too much chest to dawn and if they put it in a dark room, it would not give light and if they put it in a brightly lit room, it would cast no shadow. Today I suffer no matter what happens. Today I am simply in pain.

(translated by Clayton Eshleman)

INTENSITY AND HEIGHT

I want to write, but out comes foam,
I want to say so much and I freeze;
there is no spoken cipher which is not a sum,
there is no written pyramid, without a core.

I want to write, but I feel like a puma;
I want to laurel myself, but I stew in onions.
There is no spoken cough, which doesn't end in mist,
there is no god nor son of god, without unfolding.

Let's go, then, through this, and eat grass,
the flesh of sobbing, the fruit of groaning,
our melancholy soul preserved in jam.

Let's go! Let's go! I'm wounded;
let's go drink that already drunk,
let's go, raven, and fecundate your rook.

(translated by Clayton Eshleman)

A MAN WALKS BY WITH A LOAF OF BREAD ON HIS SHOULDER

A man walks by with a loaf of bread on his shoulder.
I'm going to write, after that, about my double?

Another sits, scratches, gets a louse out of his armpit,
cracks it. How dare one speak about psychoanalysis?

Another has entered my chest with a stick in his hand.
After that chat with the doctor about Socrates?

A cripple walks by arm in arm with a child.
After that I'm going to read André Breton?

Another shakes from cold, hacks, spits blood.
Is it possible to even mention the profound I?

Another searches in the mud for bones, rinds.
How write after that about the infinite?

A bricklayer falls from the roof, dies, and no longer
    eats lunch.
After that innovate the trope, the metaphor?

A merchant cheats a customer out of a gram.
After that talk about the fourth dimension?

A banker falsifies his balance.
With what face to cry in the theater?

An outcast sleeps with his foot behind his back.
After that, not talk about Picasso?

Someone goes to a burial sobbing.
How then enter the Academy?

Someone cleans a rifle in his kitchen.
How dare one speak about the beyond?

Someone passes by counting with his fingers.
How speak of the not-I without screaming?

(translated by Clayton Eshleman)

13

CARLOS DRUMMOND DE ANDRADE

(1902–1987)

Carlos Drummond de Andrade was born in a small mining town in Brazil, in the state of Minas Gerais. He attended boarding school in Belo Horizonte, the state capital, and was later expelled from a Jesuit school. As a young man Drummond was influenced by modernism and by a growing sense of Brazilian national identity, giving rise to a uniquely Brazilian aesthetic. Drummond founded the modernist journal *The Review* in 1925 and would later publish poems in the *Revista de Antropofagia*. In 1929, having already worked as a pharmacist, he joined the Department of Education and began to publish journalistic articles, as well as his first book of poems. In 1934 Drummond moved to Rio de Janeiro, continuing in the civil service while adding translations from the French and Spanish to his literary work. By this time he had become skeptical about a poetics of national identity; his later work would imply the political only through personal experience. Drummond became friends with his first English-language translator, Elizabeth Bishop, with whom he shared a concern for the idiom of the common Brazilian citizen. He continued to publish books of poems after he retired from the civil service in 1962.

SEVEN-SIDED POEM

When I was born, one of the crooked
angels who live in shadow said:
Carlos, go on! Be *gauche* in life.

The houses watch the men,
men who run after women.
If the afternoon had been blue,
there might have been less desire.

The trolley goes by full of legs:
white legs, black legs, yellow legs.
My God, why all the legs?
my heart asks. But my eyes
ask nothing at all.

The man behind the moustache
is serious, simple, and strong.
He hardly ever speaks.
He has a few, choice friends,
the man behind the spectacles and the moustache.

My God, why hast Thou forsaken me
if Thou knew'st I was not God,
if Thou knew'st that I was weak.

Universe, vast universe,
if I had been named Eugene
that would not be what I mean
but it would go into verse
faster.
Universe, vast universe,
my heart is vaster.

I oughtn't to tell you,
but this moon
and this brandy
play the devil with one's emotions.

(translated by Elizabeth Bishop)

IN THE MIDDLE OF THE ROAD

In the middle of the road there was a stone
there was a stone in the middle of the road
there was a stone
in the middle of the road there was a stone.

Never should I forget this event
in the life of my fatigued retinas.
Never should I forget that in the middle of the road
there was a stone
there was a stone in the middle of the road
in the middle of the road there was a stone.

(translated by Elizabeth Bishop)

YOUR SHOULDERS HOLD UP THE WORLD

A time comes when you no longer can say:
    my God.
A time of total cleaning up.
A time when you no longer can say: my love.
Because love proved useless.
And the eyes don't cry.
And the hands do only rough work.
And the heart is dry.

Women knock at your door in vain, you won't open.
You remain alone, the light turned off,
and your enormous eyes shine in the dark.
It is obvious you no longer know how to suffer.
And you want nothing from your friends.

Who cares if old age comes, what is old age?
Your shoulders are holding up the world
and it's lighter than a child's hand.
Wars, famine, family fights inside buildings
prove only that life goes on
and not everybody has freed himself yet.
Some (the delicate ones) judging the spectacle cruel
will prefer to die.
A time comes when death doesn't help.
A time comes when life is an order.
Just life, without any escapes.

(translated by Mark Strand)

RESIDUE

From everything a little remained.
From my fear. From your disgust.
From stifled cries. From the rose
a little remained.

A little remained of light
caught inside the hat.
In the eyes of the pimp
a little remained of tenderness,
very little.

A little remained of the dust
that covered your white shoes.

Of your clothes a little remained,
a few velvet rags, very
very few.

From everything a little remained.
From the bombed-out bridge,
from the two blades of grass,
from the empty pack
of cigarettes a little remained.

So from everything a little remains.
A little remains of your chin
in the chin of your daughter.

A little remained of your
blunt silence, a little
in the angry wall,
in the mute rising leaves.

A little remained from everything
in porcelain saucers,
in the broken dragon, in the white flowers,
in the creases of your brow,
in the portrait.

Since from everything a little remains,
why won't a little
of me remain? In the train
traveling north, in the ship,
in newspaper ads,
why not a little of me in London,
a little of me somewhere?
In a consonant?
In a well?

A little remains dangling
in the mouths of rivers,
just a little, and the fish
don't avoid it, which is very unusual.

From everything a little remains.
Not much: this absurd drop
dripping from the faucet,
half salt and half alcohol,
this frog leg jumping,
this watch crystal
broken into a thousand wishes,
this swan's neck,
this childhood secret . . .
From everything a little remained:
from me; from you; from Abelard.
Hair on my sleeve,
from everything a little remained;
wind in my ears,
burbing, rumbling
from an upset stomach,
and small artifacts:
bell jar, honeycomb, revolver
cartridge, aspirin tablet.
From everything a little remained.

And from everything a little remains.
Oh, open the bottles of lotion
and smother
the cruel, unbearable odor of memory.

Still, horribly, from everything a little remains,
under the rhythmic waves
under the clouds and the wind
under the bridges and under the tunnels
under the flames and under the sarcasm

under the phlegm and under the vomit
under the cry from the dungeon, the guy they
    forgot
under the spectacles and under the scarlet death
under the libraries, asylums, victorious churches
under yourself and under your feet already hard
under the ties of family, the ties of class,
from everything a little always remains.
Sometimes a button. Sometimes a rat.

(translated by Mark Strand)

AN OX LOOKS AT MAN

They are more delicate even than shrubs and they run
and run from one side to the other, always forgetting
something. Surely they lack I don't know what
basic ingredient, though they present themselves
as noble or serious, at times. Oh, terribly serious,
even tragic. Poor things, one would say that they hear
neither the song of air nor the secrets of hay;
likewise they seem not to see what is visible
and common to each of us, in space. And they are sad,
and in the wake of sadness they come to cruelty.
All their expression lives in their eyes—and loses itself
to a simple lowering of lids, to a shadow.
And since there is little of the mountain about them—
nothing in the hair or in the terribly fragile limbs
but coldness and secrecy—it is impossible for them
to settle themselves into forms that are calm, lasting,
and necessary. They have, perhaps, a kind
of melancholy grace (one minute) and with this they
    allow
themselves to forget the problems and translucent
inner emptiness that make them so poor and so lacking

when it comes to uttering silly and painful sounds:
    desire, love, jealousy
(what do we know?)—sounds that scatter and fall in the
    field
like troubled stones and burn the herbs and the water,
and after this it is hard to keep chewing away at our
    truth.

(translated by Mark Strand)

14

A Sampling of Other Latin American Poets

Nicanor Parra (Chile)

Piano Solo

Since man's life is nothing but a bit of action at a
        distance,
A bit of foam shining inside a glass;
Since trees are nothing but moving trees;
Nothing but chairs and tables in perpetual motion;
Since we ourselves are nothing but beings
(As the godhead itself is nothing but God);
Now that we do not speak solely to be heard
But so that others may speak
And the echo precede the voice that produces it;
Since we do not even have the consolation of a chaos
In the garden that yawns and fills with air,
A puzzle that we must solve before our death
So that we may nonchalantly resuscitate later on
When we have led woman to excess;
Since there is also a heaven in hell,
Permit me to propose a few things:

I wish to make noise with my feet
I want my soul to find its proper body.

                    (translated by William Carlos Williams)

João Cabral de Melo Neto (Brazil)

The Emptiness of Being a Man

I.

The emptiness of being a man is not like
any other: not like an empty coat
or empty sack (things which do not stand up
when empty, such as an empty man),
the emptiness of man is more like fullness
the swollen things which keep on swelling,
the way a sack must feel
that is being filled, or any sack at all.
The emptiness of man, this full emptiness,
is not like a sack of bricks' emptiness
or a sack of rivets', it does not have the pulse
that beats in a seed bag or bag of eggs.

2.

The emptiness of man, though it resembles
fullness, and seems all of a piece, actually
is made of nothings, bits of emptiness,
like the sponge, empty when filled,
swollen like the sponge, with air, with empty air;
it has copied its very structure from the sponge,
it has made up in clusters, of bubbles, of non-grapes.
Man's empty fullness is like a sack
filled with sponges, is filled with emptiness;

man's emptiness, or swollen emptiness,
or the emptiness that swells by being empty.

(translated by Galway Kinnell)

ROBERTO JUARROZ (ARGENTINA)

TENTH.9

Every poem is a hesitation of history.
Covering history with poems
is like displacing its layers
beyond the actions of men.

The poem also is an act,
a movement of the earth we tread,
but in the reverse direction,
toward where everything is absent.

There, where almost everything goes in the end,
but in a sad and forced procession,
invoking the bones of history,
with its Lenten, overlaid zones.

The poem leaps out of history
like a hunted animal
that overturns those layers,
and puts another layer on top: the infinite.

And then the hunted animal
discards its fossilized prey of history
and also sheathes its claws,
running at last free in the air.

(translated by Mary Crow)

ERNESTO CARDENAL (NICARAGUA)

"FOR THOSE DEAD, OUR DEAD . . ."

When you get the nomination, the award, the
    promotion,
think about the ones who died.
When you are at the reception, on the delegation,
    on the commission,
think about the ones who died.
When you have won the vote, and the crowd
    congratulates you,
think about the ones who died.
When you're cheered as you go up to the speaker's
    platform with the leaders,
think about the ones who died.
When you're picked up at the airport in the big city,
think about the ones who died.
When it's your turn to talk into the microphone,
    when the tv cameras focus on you,
think about the ones who died.
When you become the one who gives out the certificates,
    orders, permission,
think about the ones who died.
When the little old lady comes to you with her problem,
    her little piece of land,
think about the ones who died.
        See them without their shirts, being dragged,
      gushing blood, wearing hoods, blown to pieces,
submerged in tubs, getting electric shocks,
                their eyes gouged out,
      their throats cut, riddled with bullets,
dumped along the side of the road,
      in holes they dug themselves,
      in mass graves,

or just lying on the ground, enriching the soil of wild
        plants:
You represent them.
The ones who died
delegated you.

(translated by Jonathan Cohen)

JAIME SABINES (MEXICO)

IF SOMEONE TELLS YOU IT'S NOT FOR SURE

If someone tells you it's not for sure,
tell him to come here,
to put his hands over his stomach and swear,
to bear witness to the whole truth.
To see the light in the oily street,
the stopped cars,
the people passing and passing,
the four doors which face the East,
the empty bicycles,
the bricks, the affectionate quicklime,
the bookshelves tumbling behind you,
the gray hairs on your father's head,
the son your wife never had,
and the money that walks in with its mouth full of shit.
In the name of the undefeated God
in the contest of the democracies,
tell him to swear he's seen and heard.
Because he's also got to hear the crime of the cats
and keep his ears glued to the big clock they keep
        winding.

(translated by Philip Levine)

CLARIBEL ALEGRÍA (EL SALVADOR)

I AM ROOT

More than polished stone
more than morning dusk
more than the dream of the tree
and those of flower and fruit
I am root
a winding, crawling root
without luster, without a future
blind to any vision
hardening in the ground
as I work through it
testing the fallen bread
of misfortune
the opacity of wingless birds
the overshadowed dawn
and its leaden clouds
hours that pass without dark messages
an undulating, twining root
perhaps bringing up from the ground
that lightning, that stone
once on the beach moving among
weeds, along among rubbish, searching
cinerous root, mortal root
diver of my darkest regions
obscure calligraphy
inheritance of gallows, of cabala
poison root, imprisoned
by the time of a place
mirror of myself without water, thirsty
your blood tastes of the earth
your bark, summer

imprisoned you don't look
for openings, you look for death
a quiet death, disguised
as days without omens
and as time without dates
and the gray willing faces of the hours
without birds where an instant
simply dissolves
the life I've yet to live
does not inspire me
in my lips there are crevices
and my face is stone
I do not allow a storm to enter
silently, I submerge myself
in a sea which no longer moves
the murmur ends
the appearances and disappearances
all dreams in which we can only
dream of ourselves
the remains of that daggered love
and the other, hidden love
the names of Eros and Thanatos
everything vanishes
your crystal song never reaches me
nor your wet touch, nor your lips
nor the teeth of your love
I gather my fragments and slip away,
I slither, I smell the sea
in which one day my memory will be
buried and I will not know pain
demands, or fear
and I will then be no more
than a calm spin in a tomb of water.

(translated by Carolyn Forché)

ENRIQUE LIHN (CHILE)

TORTURE CHAMBER

Your alms are my salary
Your salary is the squaring of my circle, that I draw out
with my fingers to maintain their agility
Your calculator is my hand missing a finger with which
I keep myself from making calculation errors
Your alms are the capital I contribute when I go begging
Your appearance in Ahumada Mall is my debut
Your society is secret insofar as my tribe is concerned
Your personal security is my indecision
Your pocket handkerchief is my white flag
Your necktie is my Gordian knot
Your brand-name suit is my backdrop
Your right shoe is my left shoe a dozen years later
The crease of your pants is the edge I couldn't cross
even though I disguised myself as you
after tearing your clothes off
Your ascension up the staircase at the Bank of Chile
is my dream of Jacob's ladder on which a blond angel
with painted wings descends
to pay, in hand-to-hand combat, all my debts
Your checkbook is my sack of papers when I get stoned
Your signature is my illiterate's game
Your 2 + 2 = four is my 2 − 2
Your coming and going are my labyrinth in which
meditating I get lost pursued by a fly
Your office is the backstage where my name can be
condemned to death and transferred to another corpse
that will bear it in some friendly country
Your doctor's office is my torture chamber
Your torture chamber is the only hotel where I can be
received at any hour
without advance notice

Your order is my song
Your electric pen is what makes me a prolific author,
a goddam visionary, or the guy who remains silent—
depending on who I am at the moment
Your bad will is my blood
Your foot on my butt is my ascension to the heavens
that are what they are and not what God wants
Your tranquillity is my being stabbed in the back
Your liberty is my everlasting flower
Your peace is mine forever and whenever I enjoy it
     eternally
and you for life
Your real life is the end of my imagination when I get
     stoned
Your house is my lost paradise which I'm going to feel I
     own
the next time I get stoned
Your wife is in that case my squashed kitten
Your toothpick is now my fork
Your fork is my spoon
Your knife is my temptation to slit your throat
when I suck on a joint
Your police dog is the guardian of my impropriety
Your German shepherd is my beheader at the door of
     your house
as if I weren't a cursed lost sheep
Your machinegun is the lover I fuck in my dreams
Your helmet is the mold in which they emptied
the head of my son when he was born
Your military march is my wedding processional
Your garbage dump is my pantheon
as long as the corpses aren't carried off.

                              (translated by Mary Crow)

HEBERTO PADILLA (CUBA)

IN TRYING TIMES

They asked that man for his time
so that he could link it to History.
They asked him for his hands,
because for trying times
nothing is better than a good pair of hands.
They asked him for his eyes
that once had tears
so that he should see the bright side
(the bright side of life, especially)
because to see horror one startled eye is enough.
They asked him for his lips,
parched and split, to affirm,
to belch up, with each affirmation, a dream
(the great dream)
they asked him for his legs
hard and knotted
(his wandering legs)
because in trying times
is there anything better than a pair of legs
for building or digging ditches?
They asked him for the grove that fed him as a child,
with its obedient tree.
They asked him for his breast, heart, his shoulders.
They told him
that that was absolutely necessary.
they explained to him later
that all this gift would be useless
unless he turned his tongue over to them,
because in trying times
nothing is so useful in checking hatred or lies.
and finally they begged him,
please, to go take a walk.

Because in trying times
that is, without a doubt, the decisive test.

(translated by Alastair Reid and Andrew Hurley)

JOSÉ EMILIO PACHECO (MEXICO)

BOUNDARIES

All that you have lost, they told me, is yours.
and no memory remembered that, yes, it's true.
I was alive, I loved, I uttered words
the hours erased,
I felt a profound pity
for the years to come.

All you destroy, they told me, injures you.
Traces a scar forgetfulness won't cleanse;
is born again each day within you,
spreads beyond
those salty walls unable to contain you.

All you have loved, they told me, is now dead.
And I can't describe it quite,
but there's something in time
that has sailed away forever.
There are faces now I'll never
see in my mind again;
and perhaps there's a mirror, a summer, a street
that already go under the echo of one more futile shade.

All you created, they kept repeating, is false.
No god protects you,
only the wind is your shelter.
And the wind, as well you know,

is a boundless vacancy,
the sound the world makes
when a moment dies.

all you have lost, they concluded, is your own.
Your sole estate, your memory, your name.

You won't have, now, the day
you once refused.
Time
has left you on the shore
of this night
and perhaps
a fleeting light
will drown the silence.

(translated by John Frederick Nims)

HOMERO ARIDJIS (MEXICO)

EPITAPH FOR A POET

Before the mists descended on your body
long before hesitations clotted in the eyes of your mask
before the death of your first sons and the lower depths
before a confusion of sadness and destitution
and the save cry in the frankness of a man
before having murmured of desolation on the bridges
and the falsity of a cupola through the window that had
     no glass

almost when your lakes were suns
and the children were words in the air
and the days were the shadow of what was easy

when eternity was not the exact death we were looking for
nor the dust more likely than memory
nor sorrow our cruelty for being divine

then when all could have been said with impunity
and laughter like a flower of petals falling

then when you owed nothing but the death of a poem
you were your own and not mine and I had not lost you

(translated by John Frederick Nims)

PART III

EUROPE

15

THE DARKER HUMAN POSSIBILITIES

Sven Birkerts

I came to modern European poetry in my mid-twenties and was saved by it. Not saved from high ledges—nothing so dramatic—but saved from cynical depression, freed from private woes enough to be able to get on with things, indeed to start writing.

In reading European poetry, I felt that I had arrived at a new place, and that there were links and affinities between poets like Tomas Tranströmer, George Seferis, Yannis Ritsos, Vasko Popa, Zbigniew Herbert. What wonderful names! I found these poets and their work at a time when I had concluded the worst about the modern world and my place in it. And then I heard these voices, and they showed me that I was a child. Whatever I thought I knew of anxiety or despair was to these spirits *Kinderspiel;* they stared me down and shamed me. But they also gave the gift of their countering examples: stoicism, courage, the black belly laugh of true despair, and the thousand feints of irony. As I looked closer, read more, I also encountered with true awakening force the idea of history. I will say more about this shortly.

But first I should explain that I had the best possible guide to this new realm. The poet Joseph Brodsky had just recently settled in Ann Arbor, where I was then living. He had been expelled from the Soviet Union, and rescued by the late Carl Proffer, who was then running the Russian-expatriate Ardis Press. Proffer found Brodsky a teaching job at the University of Michigan, and the poet's first offering was a course on modern European poetry. Untrained, speaking an often incomprehensible demotic English, distraught over the fact of his abrupt displacement, Brodsky was nonetheless the best imaginable filter for this work, much of it strange, if not difficult. For he had himself been ballasted by it. Poets like Anna Akhmatova, Osip Mandelstam, Constantin Cavafy, Czeslaw Milosz, Eugenio Montale—these were his own figures of witness and counsel as he endured every sort of trauma at the hands of the state authorities. And in his way of teaching their work, line by line, with the fiercest interrogatory pressure, he passed along the message that helped me through my laughably minor distress.

In spite of the obvious hazards of generalizing about a subject as vast as that of postwar European poetry, the reader who spends some time with the work of the avowed major poets is sure to be struck by one thing: There is almost nothing similar in American poetry of the same period. Never mind that both American and European poetries each cover a wide spectrum. Even the spectra cannot be laid athwart one another; we see no commonly shared Venn-diagram zone. What is this central difference and how do we account for it?

Reading across the various modern European poetries, forgetting for a moment that they have been misleadingly democratized by all having been rendered into English, we encounter a range of tonalities. Elegiac, hermetic, metaphysical, mythic, ironically civilized—there are as many modes as poets. But different as they are, they share an underlying ground. The ironies of a Zbigniew Herbert are closer, finally, to the mythopoesis of a George Seferis than to the seemingly more kindred voice of Anthony Hecht. The European poets of this anthology, shaped by divergent personal imperatives, nonetheless share understandings that are not readily available to the American-born poet.

I am talking finally about History, the capitalized noun that refers not to specific events and outcomes, but to a force only perceived by what it has left in its wake. And this is surely what Walter Benjamin had in mind when he invoked, in his "Theses on the Philosophy of History," Paul Klee's painting *Angelus Novus:* "This is how one pictures the angel of history. His face is turned toward the past. Where we perceive a chain of events, he sees one single catastrophe which keeps piling wreckage upon wreckage and hurls it in front of his feet."

In any event—and I apologize for the obviousness of this—the

American looks over his shoulder and sees only a few vivid markings on what is still the relatively near foreground. The European, whatever his nationality, finds behind every trace a prior trace, lives with his geographical sense of going back and back that means a great deal, the more so because his language—its constructions, its syntax, the phonic deposits on individual words—encodes this same understanding. No good to protest that the American language is English—the yoke-rejecting impulses of democracy have long since modified the mother tongue; its ghosts have been banished. An American poet must either work in the vein of the demotic or exert great contrary force to import refinements (needless to say, the "mandarin" label is a sticky one).

History, however, is everything in European poetry, and the truth of this cannot be conveyed in a sentence or two. It pays greatly, in terms of deeper understanding—the kind we will need if we are to "get" what that poetry is about—to consider that Goethe had already written his *Werther,* triggering those myriad copycat suicides among overwrought Continental youth, by the time the American Revolution was fought. Hegel had been done expounding dialectical metaphysics for fifty years when General Custer was killed at the Little Big Horn. I say this not to assert European superiority (certainly the fact of the Warsaw Ghetto undoes the civilizing influence of a hundred Hegels) but to drive home this idea of the difference. The European writer, try as she may, cannot put words to the page without those words resounding down along the long corridors of History. The American poet is still, in this sense, trying out the echoes in an unfurnished house.

The European poet has not only the great receding vista of events in time to contemplate, but he also has, in his living memory, the trauma of our century's history. Between World War II, racism, the Holocaust, and the violent parching reign of Stalin and his successors, there is no midcentury European who did not have to confront a new truth: that civilization was bankrupt. But no, this is still too abstract. It would be more accurate—and telling—to assert that probably no writer escaped firsthand exposure to mind-numbing horror, suffering, danger, and privation, losing loved ones, and standing witness to the destruction of the idea of home. And both perspectives—the long-range and immediate—are therefore present, either as part of the subject matter or as implicit background, in everything written in the postwar period. What is the relation of atrocity to tradition? How does barbarism spring from culture? And: How does the private self negotiate meaning from these terrible contradictions?

This last question is interesting in that attempting to answer it we discover a vast range of responses—responses that bring us right up against questions of faith, morality, and the role of the poet in a world sprung loose from all deeper sense of certainty. A tour of these options as manifested in the work of certain key poets will reveal as much as anything else the soul's possible responses to the enormous pressure of irrationally adverse circumstance.

When we think of Russian poetry in our century, four names come immediately to mind—Boris Pasternak, Osip Mandelstam, Marina Tsvetaeva, and Anna Akhmatova. Each poet lived through calamities of the age, and from the impossible crushing force of history on the susceptible—generally romantic—psyche produced lyric poetry of a very high order. Of the four, the voice most broadly resonant, and also most frankly public, was that of Akhmatova (1889–1961). Indeed, it was Akhmatova who, in "Requiem," her poem cycle of witness and execration, ventured to give what might be called the reply of the Russian soul to the madness of Stalinism.

Like any poet, Akhmatova started out writing about the available materials such as love, loss of love, the exaltation and dread of making art. She then yoked urgent impulse to a classic formal reticence, producing distinctive verses, some of which might have worn the label WARNING: CONTENTS UNDER PRESSURE. But soon enough, with the coming of war and revolution, the subject matter changed dramatically. Quite early on, as in these lines from 1917, we find the poet assuming a larger and more representative moral stance. To voices that urge her to "leave Russia forever," she replies:

> But indifferently and calmly
> I blocked my ears, like a child,
> not to be tempted by dirty talk,
> not, in my mourning, to be defiled.

> *—from "When in the Throes of Suicide"*

The childlike deliberation she invokes is characteristic of the Akhmatova voice: We are dealing not with the power of indirection or reversed expectation but simple understatement. The poet risks a great deal here, takes the gamble that the reader will credit her as holding the lid on powerful feeling.

Akhmatova won her gamble. Though she was prohibited from publishing—could not put out a book for more than forty years—her reputation flourished in the underground economy of letters, which was, in those years, the only economy that mattered. During the darkest years of the Stalin terror, when her husband had been shot and her son imprisoned, Akhmatova wrote the sections of "Requiem 1935–1940," in the process dissolving any remnants of her proud poetic persona. Here she not only spoke for, but spoke as one of, the suffering masses. The poem tells a mother's story—she stands and waits for other mothers and wives in line outside the Leningrad prison where her son is being held. When a woman, recognizing her, asks "Can you describe this?" Akhmatova says, simply, "I can." And then, in line after line of dignified declarative verse, in the tonality that Joseph Brodsky called one of "controlled terror," she presented the situation, accepting its universal resonance. "That was a time when only the dead/ could smile, delivered from their wars," she writes in the Prologue. We follow then the movements of her heart, her soul, each surge of the seismograph needle signaling some exacerbation of an already unbearable situation:

> For seventeen months I have cried aloud,
> calling you back to your lair.
> I hurled myself at the hangman's foot.
> You are my son, changed into nightmare.

At moments Akhmatova can sound like Sylvia Plath (or vice versa), though in Plath the implicit historical backdrop is either nonexistent or is conjured for metaphorical usefulness ("O Panzer Man!") while for Akhmatova it is the very stuff of poetry.

After many sections (hundreds of lines that many had committed to memory) Akhmatova writes her epilogue, overtly joining her suffering—and lending her redeeming voice—to the suffering of the populace:

> And I pray not for myself alone . . .
> for all who stood outside the jail,
> in bitter cold or summer's blaze,
> with me under that blind red wall.

The reader of Akhmatova's poetry cannot help but notice how with the passing of years—and the relentless thumbscrew pressure of outside events, as propelled by the inhuman will of a single tyrant—the stuff of lyric slowly, then less slowly, turns into its opposite. Words, which first did duty for nightingales and bending willows, now line up in the same couplet and quatrain formations, only now they would show how even in the absence of hope the soul looks for ways to carry on.

The poetry of Paul Celan (1920–1970) surely adds a shadow or two to Akhmatova's dark reckoning. Where Akhmatova at least finds a kind of solidarity of suffering and allows her poetry to keen for the whole culture, Celan offers a far more private and metaphysical lyric. His suffering—the suffering of the voice of the poems—cannot be shared, unless by some spiritual entity whose very existence is cast into grave doubt by the nature of the suffering.

Celan, a Romanian-born Jew, lost both parents in the German invasion of Czernowitz (now Chernovtsy) in 1941 and was himself interned in a Nazi labor camp for eighteen months. Significantly, though he was fluent in a number of European languages, he chose to write in German, a contradiction as exalted as it is perverse.

Celan's poetry seems to rise up from a very deep linguistic well, one in which are mingled the traditions of German lyric poetry—Hölderlin shows through especially—and the compressed and often arcane expressions of Christian and Jewish mysticism. Where the language root is so deep, and where the meaning of the work is as wedded to its expressive means as Celan's, translation will be problematic. And indeed, Celan is a kind of limit case for translators. As George Steiner has written: "Celan's poems are so intransigently themselves, that they rebuke paraphrase. . . . I am not certain that any poetry we know comes closer than Celan's to the being of music, which is the conceptually and formally indissoluble embodiment of meaning within form, of form within meaning. . . ."

Still, even in its obscurity, and in what is very likely his misrepresented transposition, that music—dark and insistent—has exerted tremendous influence on poets and their determined readers. Consider the driving, almost surrealistic condensations of his "Fugue of Death":

> Black milk of daybreak we drink it at nightfall
> we drink it at noon in the morning we drink it at
>   night
> we drink it and drink it
> we are digging a grave in the sky it is ample to lie
>   there
> A man in the house he plays with serpents he writes
> he writes when the night falls to Germany your
>   golden hair
> Margarete

Celan commands a pressure, an intensity of address in the direction of the unknown strong enough to bring the reader what can be spoken from what cannot—or must not. These lines from a short, untitled lyric almost seem to be inviting the reader toward Celan's own painful vocation:

> Speak you too,
> speak as the last,
> say out your say.
>
> Speak—
> But don't split off No from Yes.
> Give your say this meaning too:
> give it the shadow.

Celan, master spirit of these murky places—where meanings are obscure and assurances even more so, and where language is no better than Eliot's "shabby deteriorating equipment"—finally could not surmount his own despair. He committed suicide by drowning in 1970.

•   •   •

There are many responses possible to oppression and not all of them are routed through the heart. The Polish poet Zbigniew Herbert (1924–1998) deploys an astringently ironic voice in his work. His characteristic modes include using the mask of an historical or a literary figure such as the fictional "Mr. Cogito," an alienated intellectual, to comment on events and situations. Herbert will also, on occasion, pose his reflections in his own voice, but even then he maintains a resolute detachment. Feelings are not to intrude on what is meant to be a poetry of philosophical and moral inquiry.

Writing under a regime in which the plain truth could not be spoken, and in which lies and rationalizations paved over the often shameful events of the past—history rewritten by the victors—Herbert made a shrewd aesthetic choice. He would not counter this propaganda with honest or heartfelt language, at least not directly. Rather, he would use an idiom itself oblique, one in tension with the plainspoken assessment of things. It therefore falls to the reader to use the sharp pick of tonal dissimulation to spring the lock of outright hypocrisy and deceit. Of course, the poet can modulate his detachment and the temperature of his irony as required.

In "The Power of Taste," Herbert begins using the very lightest touch:

> It didn't require much character at all
> our refusal disagreement and resistance
> we had a shred of the necessary courage
> but fundamentally it was a matter of taste

and later adds, still in the same register:

> So aesthetics can be helpful in life
> one should not neglect the study of beauty
>
> Before we declare our consent we must carefully
>   examine
> the shape of the architecture the rhythm of the
>   drums and pipes

But Herbert can at times also use declarative flatness to make pronouncements that the reader expects will be ironic, but that are not—that are, in fact, face-value assertions, even moral injunctions. In his famous poem "The Envoy of Mr. Cogito," he offers these austere words of guidance:

> go upright among those who are on their knees
> among those with their backs turned and those
> > toppled in the dust
>
> you were saved not in order to live
> you have little time you must give testimony

The tonality may be affectless, but the experience of reading Herbert is nonetheless often moving. We are stirred in our moral being, forced to ask the hard questions not just about what we believe but also about how we would act on behalf of those beliefs when put to the hard test.

Herbert's compass is, in a sense, considerably narrower than that of his better-known countryman, Czeslaw Milosz. He does not stand stunned, as Milosz does, before the works of time; does not evoke the detailed landscapes of childhood; nor does he turn his gaze toward the great metaphysical and religious schema. But for all that—precisely because of his intransigent self-consistency, his laserlike tonal clarity—Herbert's poems remain reliable and essential expressions of an exacting moral nature.

A great deal of European poetry in this century has pitched itself against the Symbolist tradition that had dominated the end of the last century. Poets preferred a rougher, less dreamy music and concrete domestic correlatives to the more elusive symbolic elements sought by their predecessors. Greek poet George Seferis (1900–1971) is at least a partial exception. Writing under the powerful early influence of T. S. Eliot, Seferis developed a unique idiom fusing a tragic sense of life with an ancient Greek mythic awareness. In Seferis the reader discovers an entirely new vantage on the present, one stripped of identifying bric-a-brac. There a passing moment appears to churn with archetypal joys and discords; the winds of the gods' passing can still be felt.

Seferis's is a difficult poetry—difficult in the sense of being elusive. The lines are elemental, full of sea and sky and stones. We do not so much follow the track of a poem from point to point as hand ourselves over to its alogical momentum.

In "Memory I," in many ways a representative Seferis poem, the speaker presents himself as a solitary figure with a reed flute. The time and place are indeterminate. We learn only that he is in the midst of some vast enterprise of destruction:

> The others have abolished every kind of greeting:
> they wake, shave, and start the day's work of
>   slaughter
> as one prunes or operates, methodically, without
>   passion;
> sorrow's dead like Patroclus, and no one makes a
>   mistake.
>
> I thought of playing a tune and then I felt ashamed
>   in front of the other world
> the one that watches me from beyond the night from
>   within my light
> woven of living bodies, naked hearts
> and love that belongs to the Furies
> as it belongs to man and to stone and to
>   water and to grass
> and to the animal that looks straight into the eye of
>   its approaching death
>
> So I continued along the dark path
> and turned into my garden and dug and buried the
>   reed
> and again I whispered: some morning the resurrection
>   will come,
> dawn's light will blossom red as trees glow in
>   spring,

the sea will be born again, and the wave will again
    fling forth Aphrodite.
We are the seed that dies. And I entered my empty
    house.

Here is a bracing pessimism, a sense that the harshness and finality of individual existence have been registered. Reading Seferis, we inhabit what feels like a realm of Homeric duration: Modernity is just a shimmer, and the deeper forms of consciousness are somehow transpersonal, partaking of archetype, though not necessarily in the approved Jungian manner.

We come much closer to a familiar tonality, that of the reflective cosmopolitan individual, in the poetry of Eugenio Montale (1896–1981). Montale's range is vast, fusing in ever-changing ways the psychological, philosophical, political, and spiritual awareness of the twentieth century. His gift was to find a complex, yet familiar, even confiding idiom for imbuing commonplace, indeed humble details with dramatic potentiality. In poem after poem, Montale shapes those elements toward a moment of revelation. We are guided, we feel, toward some special insight into the hidden chambers of being.

    Writing about lemon trees, for example, the poet thus lures us into a silent place in nature:

> when things
> let themselves go and seem almost
> to reveal their final secret,
> we sometimes expect
> to discover a flaw in Nature,
> the world's dead point, the link that doesn't hold,
> the thread that, disentangled, might at last lead us
> to the center of a truth

Montale is in search of the secret, the exceptional, that which flourishes in the midst of waste, that which redeems. Thus, in what is perhaps his best-known poem, "The Eel," he celebrates the very principle of renewal in the face of desolation:

eel, torchlight, lash
arrow of Love on earth,
whom only these dry gulches of ours or burned-out
Pyrenean gullies can draw back up
to Edens of generation;
the green soul seeking
life where there's nothing but stinging
drought, desolation;
spark that says
everything begins when everything seems
dead ashes, buried stump;

Needless to say, Montale is writing against the backdrop of fascism and world war. Yet even in moments of extreme doubt and despair, his poetic impulse cannot quite relinquish faith in the core rightness of creation. His "Little Testament" captures in its opening lines just how close he has come to being overwhelmed and giving in to nihilism:

This thing the night flashes
like marshlight through the skull of my mind,
this pearl necklace snails trail,
this ground glass, diamond-dust sparkle—
it is not the lamp in any church or office,
tended by some adolescent altar boy,
Communist or papist,
in black or red.
I have only this rainbow
to leave you, this testimonial,
of faith, often invaded,
of a hope that burned more slowly
than a green log on the fire.

The flickering can be construed as the lyric faith itself.

•   •   •

This glance at Montale hardly exhausts the inventory of available styles and voices—all of them at some level responses to the forceful imprint of history on the exacerbated psyche. We could as well have focused on the movement toward Eastern spiritualism in the work of Sweden's Gunnar Ekelöf, or the troubling deep-psyche image worlds of his countryman, Tomas Tranströmer; or the flat, aggressive ironies of Bertolt Brecht; or the charged folklorish incantations of Yugoslavian (now Serb) poet Vasko Popa; or the lyric surrealism of Spain's Rafael Alberti; or the intense tragi-comic brooding of Joseph Brodsky.

Still, we draw our lines, insisting on the provisionality of the selections even as we hope they will be regarded as representative. I have read through the following selections many times now, and even through the scrim of English they register their power and singularity.

I cannot quite conclude these reflections, saturated as they are with the idea of history, without noting that the last few decades have seen—alas, not everywhere—a great lifting of pressure. The Soviet state has been dismantled, living standards have been improving steadily, human rights organizations are vigilant on behalf of threatened individuals, and as the overall picture is seen to improve, much of this poetry registers differently. Stoicism, bitter irony, and other "countering modes" lose some of their point when price wars have replaced street fighting. As George Steiner suggested, what's good for humanity is not necessarily good for literature. But of course no one who has heeded the humane plea at the root of all art would think of calling back harsher times. We should be grateful when we can.

But if we have tuned in to the voice of history, then we also know that most truces are provisional, and even the fairest peace does not prevail forever. We should therefore hold the writings of these and other poets in trust. They have so much to tell us not only about the darker human possibilities, but also about the defiant light struck up in the souls of those who tried to right the balance, or at the very least simply to bear witness so that others would know.

16

ANNA AKHMATOVA

(1889–1966)

When Anna Gorenko's father learned that his daughter was about to publish a selection of her poems in a St. Petersburg magazine, he called her in and told her that although he had nothing against her writing poetry, he'd urge her "not to befoul a good name" and to use a pseudonym. The daughter agreed, and that is how "Anna Akhmatova" entered Russian literature.

The five open *a*'s of her chosen pseudonym had a hypnotic effect and put this name's carrier firmly at the top of the alphabet of Russian poetry. In a sense "Anna Akhmatova" was her first successful line, memorable in its acoustic inevitability.

Akhmatova looked positively stunning, a physical beauty. Five feet eleven, dark haired, fair skinned, with pale gray-green eyes like those of snow leopards, slim and incredibly lithe, she was for half a century sketched, painted, cast, carved, and photographed by a multitude of artists, starting with Amedeo Modigliani. The poems dedicated to her would make more volumes than do her own collected works.

As for the hidden part of the self being a perfect match for the visible, breathtaking one, there is testimony to it in her writing. Her chief characteristics are nobility and restraint. Akhmatova is the poet of strict meters, exact rhymes, and short sentences. In an era marked by so much technical experimentation in poetry, she wanted to play the game straight, without bending or inventing the rules. She felt very much at home within the confines of classical verse, thereby suggesting that her raptures and revelations were no greater than those of her predecessors who also used these meters before. Among her contemporaries she is a Jane Austen. In any case, if her sayings were dark, it wasn't due to her grammar.

Her first collections were tremendously successful with both the critics and the public. Akhmatova's success was in this respect remarkable if one takes into account its timing, especially in the case of her second and third volumes: 1914 (the outbreak of World War I) and 1917 (the October Revolution in Russia). Or perhaps it was precisely the deafening background thunder of world events that rendered the private tremolo of this young poet all the more discernible and vital.

More than any other art, poetry is a form of sentimental education, and the lines that Akhmatova readers learned by heart were to temper their hearts against the new era's onslaught of vulgarity. The note of controlled terror in her early poetry—designed to keep in check emotions of a romantic nature—proved later to be as effective when applied to mortal fears. This is why, and not only because of the epigrammatic beauty of her lines, the public committed them to memory and clung to them so unwittingly. It was an instinctive reaction—the instinct being that of self-preservation. The comprehension of the metaphysics of personal drama betters one's chances of weathering the drama of history.

By the time of the revolution she was twenty-eight years old: neither young enough to believe in it nor so old to justify it. She didn't reject the revolution; a defiant pose wasn't for her. She simply took it for what it was: a terrible national upheaval that meant a tremendous increase of grief per individual. She also knew not only that the emotions and perceptions she dealt with were fairly common but that time, true to its repetitive nature, would render them universal.

After 1922 until her death in 1966 Akhmatova couldn't publish a book of her own. *Anno Domini MCMXXI* was her fifth and last collection. In the postwar period two slim editions of her work were published, consisting of a few reprinted early lyrics plus patriotic war poems and bits of doggerel extolling the arrival of peace, written to win her son's release from the labor camps. The poems were selected by the editors of the state-run publishing house to convince the public (especially abroad) that Akhmatova was alive, well, and loyal. They totaled some fifty pieces and had nothing in common with her real output during those four decades.

For a poet of Akhmatova's stature this meant being buried alive, with a couple of slabs marking the mound. Her going under was a product of several forces, mostly that of history, whose chief element is vulgarity and whose immediate agent is the state. By *MCMXXI*, which means 1921, the new state would already be at odds with Akhmatova, whose first husband, the poet Nikolai Gumilyov, was executed by its security forces, allegedly on Lenin's direct orders. In the subsequent decade and a half the state-sponsored destruction consumed her entire circle (including her closet friends, poets Vladimir Narbut and Osip Mandelstam). It culminated in the arrests of her son, Lev Gumilyov, and her third husband, art historian Nikolai Punin, who soon died in prison. Then came World War II.

Those fifteen years preceding the war were perhaps the darkest in the whole of Russian history; undoubtedly they were so in Akhmatova's own life. If she proceeded to write, it's because prosody absorbs death, and because she felt guilty she survived. It's not that she tried to "immortalize" her dead: Most of them were already the pride of Russian literature and thus had immortalized themselves enough. She simply tried to manage the meaninglessness of existence, which suddenly gaped before her because of the destruction of the sources of meaning. Besides, addressing the dead was the only way of preventing speech from slipping into a howl.

Naturally enough, poems of this sort couldn't be published, nor could they even be written down. They could only be memorized by the author and by some seven other people, since she didn't trust her own memory. From time to time she'd meet one of the people privately and—as a means of inventory—ask him or her to recite quietly this or that selection. This precaution was far from being excessive: People would disappear forever for smaller things than a piece of paper with a few lines on it.

The power of Akhmatova's poetry lies in the fact that her biography was all too common. Her *Requiem* mourns the mourners: mothers losing sons, wives turning widows, sometimes both, as in the author's own case. No creed would help her to understand, much less forgive, let alone survive her double widowhood at the hands of the regime, the fate of her son, those forty years of being silenced and ostracized. No Anna Gorenko would have been able to take it. Anna Akhmatova did, and it's as though she knew what was in store when she took her pen name.

At certain periods of history only poetry is capable of dealing with reality by condensing it into something graspable, something that otherwise couldn't be retained by the mind. In that sense the whole nation took up the pen name of Akhmatova—which explains her popularity and which, more important, enabled her to speak for the nation as well as to tell it something it did not know.

—*J. B.*

(All translations are by Stanley Kunitz with Max Hayward.)

READING *HAMLET*

A barren patch to the right of the cemetery,
behind it a river flashing blue.
You said: "All right then, get thee to a nunnery,
or go get married to a fool . . . "

It was the sort of thing that princes always say,
but these are words that one remembers.
May they flow a hundred centuries in a row
like an ermine mantle from his shoulders.

"I WRUNG MY HANDS . . . "

I wrung my hands under my dark veil . . .
"Why are you pale, what makes you reckless?"
—Because I have made my loved one drunk
with an astringent sadness.

I'll never forget. He went out, reeling;
his mouth was twisted, desolate . . .
I ran downstairs, not touching the banisters,
and followed him as far as the gate.

And shouted, choking: "I meant it all
in fun. Don't leave me, or I'll die of pain."
He smiled at me—oh so calmly, terribly—
and said: "Why don't you get out of the rain?"

"WHEN IN THE THROES OF SUICIDE . . . "

When in the throes of suicide
our people awaited the German guests,
and the stern Byzantine spirit
abandoned our Russian Church,
I heard a voice—oh it was soothing!—
that cried: "Come here,
leave your wild and sinful country,
leave Russia forever.
I will wash the blood from your hands,
I will pluck the shame from your heart,
I will hide, with a different name,
your insults and your hurts."

But indifferently and calmly
I blocked my ears, like a child,
not to be tempted by dirty talk,
not, in my mourning, to be defiled.

"I AM NOT ONE OF THOSE WHO LEFT THE LAND . . . "

I am not one of those who left the land
to the mercy of its enemies.
Their flattery leaves me cold,
my songs are not for them to praise.

But I pity the exile's lot.
Like a felon, like a man half-dead,

dark is your path, wanderer;
wormwood infects your foreign bread.

But here, in the murk of conflagration,
where scarcely a friend is left to know,
we, the survivors, do not flinch
from anything, not from a single blow.

Surely the reckoning will be made
after the passing of this cloud.
We are the people without tears,
straighter than you . . . more proud . . .

THE MUSE

All that I am hangs by a thread tonight
as I wait for her whom no one can command.
Whatever I cherish most—youth, freedom, glory—
fades before her who bears the flute in her hand.

And look! she comes . . . she tosses back her veil,
staring me down, serene and pitiless.
"Are you the one," I ask, "whom Dante heard dictate
the lines of his *Inferno*?" She answers: "Yes."

DANTE

Even after his death he did not return
to the city that nursed him.
Going away, this man did not look back.
To him I sing this song.
Torches, night, a last embrace,
outside in her streets the mob howling.
He sent her a curse from hell

and in heaven could not forget her.
But never, in a penitent's shirt,
did he walk barefoot with lighted candle
through his beloved Florence,
perfidious, base, and irremediably home.

IN MEMORY OF M. B.

Here is my gift, not roses on your grave,
not sticks of burning incense.
You lived aloof, maintaining to the end
you magnificent disdain.
You drank wine, and told the wittiest jokes,
and suffocated inside stifling walls.
Alone you let the terrible stranger in,
and stayed with her alone.

Now you're gone, and nobody says a word
about your troubled and exalted life.
Only my voice, like a flute, will mourn
at your dumb funeral feast.
Oh, who would have dared believe that half-crazed I,
I, sick with grief for the buried past,
I, smoldering on a slow fire,
having lost everything and forgotten all,
would be fated to commemorate a man
so full of strength and will and bright inventions,
who only yesterday, it seems, chatted with me,
hiding the tremor of his mortal pain.

CLEOPATRA

I am air and fire . . .

—Shakespeare

She had already kissed Antony's dead lips,
she had already wept on her knees before Caesar . . .
and her servants have betrayed her. Darkness falls.
The trumpets of the Roman eagle scream.

And in comes the last man to be ravished by her
    beauty—
such a tall gallant!—with a shamefaced whisper:
"You must walk before him, as a slave, in the triumph."
But the slope of her swan's neck is tranquil as ever.

Tomorrow they'll put her children in chains. Nothing
remains except to tease this fellow out of mind
and put the black snake, like a parting act of pity,
on her dark breast with indifferent hand.

REQUIEM
1935–1940

No foreign sky protected me,
no stranger's wing shielded my face.
I stand as witness to the common lot,
survivor of that time, that place.

—1961

Instead of a Preface

    In the terrible years of the Yezhov terror I spent
seventeen months waiting in line outside the prison in
Leningrad. One day somebody in the crowd identified
me. Standing behind me was a woman, with lips blue
from the cold, who had, of course, never heard me called
by name before. Now she started out of the torpor

common to us all and asked me in a whisper (everyone
whispered there):

"Can you describe this?"

And I said: "I can."

Then something like a smile passed fleetingly over
what had once been her face.

—Leningrad, 1 April 1957

Dedication

Such grief might make the mountains stoop,
reverse the waters where they flow,
but cannot burst these ponderous bolts
that block us from the prison cells
crowded with mortal woe . . .
For some the wind can freshly blow,
for some the sunlight fade at ease,
but we, made partners in our dread,
hear but the grating of the keys,
and heavy-booted soldiers' tread.
As if for early mass, we rose
and each day walked the wilderness,
trudging through silent street and square,
to congregate, less live than dead.
The sun declined, the Neva blurred,
and hope sang always from afar.
Whose sentence is decreed? . . . That moan,
that sudden spurt of woman's tears,
shows one distinguished from the rest,
as if they'd knocked her to the ground
and wrenched the heart out of her breast,
then let her go, reeling, alone.
Where are they now, my nameless friends
from those two years I spent in hell?

What specters mock them now, amid
the fury of Siberian snows,
or in the blighted circle of the moon?
To them I cry, Hail and Farewell!

—March 1940

Prologue

That was a time when only the dead
could smile, delivered from their wars,
and the sign, the soul, of Leningrad
dangled outside its prison-house;
and the regiments of the condemned,
herded in the railroad-yards,
shrank from the engine's whistle-song
whose burden went, "Away, pariahs!"
The stars of death stood over us.
And Russia, guiltless, beloved, writhed
under the crunch of bloodstained boots,
under the wheels of Black Marias.

I

At dawn they came and took you away.
You were my dead: I walked behind.
In the dark room children cried,
the holy candle gasped for air.
Your lips were chill from the ikon's kiss,
sweat bloomed on your brow—those deathly flowers!
Like the wives of Peter's troopers in Red Square
I'll stand and howl under the Kremlin towers.

—1935

2

Quietly flows the quiet Don;
into my house slips the yellow moon.

It leaps the sill, with its cap askew,
and balks at a shadow, that yellow moon.

This woman is sick to her marrow-bone,
this woman is utterly alone,

with husband dead, with son away
in jail. Pray for me. Pray.

3

Not, not mine: it's somebody else's wound.
I could never have borne it. So take the thing
that happened, hide it, stick it in the ground.
Whisk the lamps away . . .
           Night.

4

They should have shown you—mocker,
delight of your friends, hearts' thief,
naughtiest girl of Pushkin's town—
this picture of your fated years,
as under the glowering wall you stand,
shabby, three hundredth in line,
clutching a parcel in your hand,
and the New Year's ice scorched by your tears.
See there the prison poplar bending!
No sound. No sound. Yet how many
innocent lives are ending . . .

5

For seventeen months I have cried aloud,
calling you back to your lair.
I hurled myself at the hangman's foot.
You are my son, changed into nightmare.
Confusion occupies the world,
and I am powerless to tell
somebody brute from something human,
or on what day the word spells, "Kill!"
Nothing is left but dusty flowers,
the tinkling thurible, and tracks
that lead to nowhere. Night of stone,
whose bright enormous star
stares me straight in the eyes,
promising death, ah soon!

6

The weeks fly out of mind,
I doubt that it occurred:
how into your prison, child,
the white nights, blazing, stared;
and still, as I draw breath,
they fix their buzzard eyes
on what the high cross shows,
this body of your death.

7
The Sentence

The word dropped like a stone
on my still living breast.
Confess: I was prepared,
am somehow ready for the test.

So much to do today:
kill memory, kill pain,
turn heart into a stone,
and yet prepare to live again.

Not quite. Hot summer's feast
brings rumors of carouse.
How long have I foreseen
this brilliant day, this empty house?

8
To Death

You will come in any case—so why not now?
How long I wait and wait. The bad times fall.
I have put out the light and opened the door
for you, because you are simple and magical.
Assume, then, any form that suits your wish,
take aim, and blast at me with poisoned shot,
or strangle me like an efficient mugger,
or else infect me—typhus be my lot—
or spring out of the fairy tale you wrote,
the one we're sick of hearing, day and night,
where the blue hatband marches up the stairs,
led by the janitor, pale with fright.
It's all the same to me. The Yenisei swirls,
the North Star shines, as it will shine forever;
and the blue lustre of my loved one's eyes
is clouded over by the final horror.

—The House on the Fontanka
19 August 1939

9

Already madness lifts its wing
to cover half my soul.
That taste of opiate wine!
Lure of the dark valley!

Now everything is clear.
I admit my defeat. The tongue
of my ravings in my ear
is the tongue of a stranger.

No use to fall down on my knees
and beg for mercy's sake.
Nothing I counted mine, out of my life,
is mine to take:

not my son's terrible eyes,
not the elaborate stone flower
of grief, not the day of the storm,
not the trial of the visiting hour,

not the dear coolness of his hands,
not the lime trees' agitated shade,
not the thin cricket-sound
of consolation's parting word.

—4 May 1940

10
Crucifixion

"Do not weep for me, Mother,
    when I am in my grave."

I

A choir of angels glorified the hour,
the vault of heaven was dissolved in fire.
"Father, why hast Thou forsaken me?
Mother, I beg you, do not weep for me . . ."

II

Mary Magdalene beat her breasts and sobbed,
His dear disciple, stone-faced, stared.
His mother stood apart. No other looked
into her secret eyes. Nobody dared.

—1940–1943

Epilogue

I

I have learned how faces fall to bone,
how under the eyelids terror lurks,
how suffering inscribes on cheeks
the hard lines of its cuneiform texts,
how glossy black or ash-fair locks
turn overnight to tarnished silver,
how smiles fade on submissive lips,
and fear quavers in a dry titter.
And I pray not for myself alone . . .
for all who stood outside the jail,
in bitter cold or summer's blaze,
with me under that blind red wall.

II

Remembrance hour returns with the turning year.
I see, hear, I touch you drawing near:

the one we tried to help to the sentry's booth,
and who no longer walks this precious earth,

and that one who would toss her pretty mane
and say, "It's just like coming home again."

I want to name the names of all that host,
but they snatched up the list, and now it's lost.

I've woven them a garment that's prepared
out of poor words, those that I overheard,

and will hold fast to every word and glance
all of my days, even in new mischance,

and if a gag should blind my tortured mouth,
through which a hundred million people shout,

then let them pray for me, as I do pray
for them, this eve of my remembrance day.

And if my country ever should assent
to casting in my name a monument,

I should be proud to have my memory graced,
but only if the monument be placed

not near the sea on which my eyes first opened—
my last link with the sea has long been broken—

nor in the Tsar's garden near the sacred stump,
where a grieved shadow hunts my body's warmth,

but here, where I endured three hundred hours
in line before the implacable iron bars.

Because even in blissful death I fear
to lose the clangor of the Black Marias,

to lose the banging of that odious gate
and the old crone howling like a wounded beast.

And from my motionless bronze-lidded sockets
may the melting snow, like teardrops, slowly trickle,

and a prison dove coo somewhere, over and over,
as the ships sail softly down the flowing Neva.

—March 1940

IN 1940

At the burial of an epoch
no psalm is heard at the tomb.
Soon nettles and thistles
will decorate the spot.
The only busy hands are those
of the gravediggers. Faster! Faster!
And it's quiet, Lord, so quiet
you can hear time passing.

Some day it will surface again
like a corpse in a spring river;
but no mother's son will claim her,
and grandsons, sick at heart,
will turn away.
            Sorrowing heads . . .
The moon swinging like a pendulum . . .

And now, over death-struck Paris,
such silence falls.

"THIS CRUEL AGE HAS DEFLECTED ME . . . "

This cruel age has deflected me,
like a river from its course.
Strayed from its familiar shores,
my changeling life has flowed
into a sister channel.
How many spectacles I've missed;
the curtain rising without me,
and falling too. How many friends
I never had the chance to meet.
Here in the only city I can claim,
where I could sleepwalk and not lose my way,
how many foreign skylines I can dream,
not to be witnessed through my tears.
And how many verses I have failed to write!
Their secret chorus stalks me
close behind. One day, perhaps,
they'll strangle me.
I know beginnings, I know endings too,
and life-in-death, and something else
I'd rather not recall just now.
And a certain woman
has usurped my place
and bears my rightful name,
leaving a nickname for my use,
with which I've done the best I could.
The grave I go to will not be my own.
But if I could step outside myself
and contemplate the person I am,
I should know at last what envy is.

THE DEATH OF SOPHOCLES

That night an eagle swooped down from the skies onto
    Sophocles' house.
And the garden suddenly rocked with a cry of cicadas.
Already the genius strode toward his immortality,
skirting the enemy camp at the walls of his native city.
Then it was that the king had a strange dream:
Great Dionysus ordered him to lift the siege,
so as not to dishonor the service for the dead
and to grant the Athenians the solace of his fame.

—1961

17

PAUL CELAN

(1920–1970)

Paul Celan was born Paul Antschel in Czernowitz, Bukovina, Romania (now Chernovtsy, Ukraine), to German-Jewish parents. He saw both his mother and father deported to a death camp in 1939, when Nazi troops invaded his homeland. Celan himself was confined for more than a year in a labor camp. After the war he lived briefly in Bucharest and Vienna before moving to Paris, where he lived until he committed suicide by drowning in 1970.

Fluent in a number of European languages, Celan nevertheless made the decision to write in German. The poems can be seen less as instances of *expression* than as investigations of the capability of language to manifest thought, emotion, and spiritual impulse.

Celan's early books, *Der Sand aus den Urnen* (The Sand from the Urn, 1948) and *Mohn und Gedächtnis* (Poppy and Remembrance, 1952)—both of which include the celebrated poem "Todesfuge" ("Fugue of Death")—use the traditional elements of lyric verse, but intensify their presentation in order to express the psychic traumas visited on Holocaust victims, even those who survived physically. *Sprachgitter* (Speech-Grille, 1959) exacerbates these elements, putting pressure on syntax, condensing and rupturing image sequences. After a turn toward themes of Jewish mysticism—and the negation of mystical faith—in *Die Niemandsrose* (The No One's Rose, 1963), Celan in his last books pushed his work further toward complexity and hermeticism.

Celan is, perhaps, more invoked than read, and more read than comprehended. Aside from the difficulty of expression itself, there is the extraordinary obstacle of the language barrier. Here is a poetry that grows best—possibly *only*—in its native linguistic soil. Everything depends on the braiding of word sounds, the echoes of traditional voices, and the rhythmic inner momentum of the German language.

Fully comprehended or not, Celan nonetheless has achieved emblematic status: He is the poet of the darkest hour, its witness and martyr.

—*S. B.*

(Translations, unless otherwise identified, are by John Felstiner.)

FUGUE OF DEATH

Black milk of daybreak we drink it at nightfall
we drink it at noon in the morning we drink it at night
we drink it and drink it
we are digging a grave in the sky it is ample to lie there
A man in the house he plays with the serpents he writes
he writes when the night falls to Germany your golden
    hair Margarete
he writes it and walks from the house the stars glitter he
    whistles his dogs up
he whistles his Jews out and orders a grave to be dug in
    the earth
he commands us strike up for the dance

Black milk of daybreak we drink you at night
we drink in the mornings at noon we drink you at
    nightfall
drink you and drink you
A man in the house he plays with the serpents he writes
he writes when the night falls to Germany your golden
    hair Margarete

Your ashen hair Shulamith we are digging a grave in the
    sky it is
ample to lie there

He shouts stab deeper in earth you there and you others
    you sing and you play
he grabs at the iron in his belt and swings it and blue are
    his eyes
stab deeper your spades you there and you others play on
    for the dancing

Black milk of daybreak we drink you at nightfall
we drink you at noon in the mornings we drink you at
    nightfall
drink you and drink you
a man in the house your golden hair Margarete
your ashen hair Shulamith he plays with the serpents

He shouts play sweeter death's music death comes as a
    master from Germany
he shouts stroke darker the strings and as smoke you
    shall climb to the sky
then you'll have a grave in the clouds it is ample to lie
    there

Black milk of daybreak we drink you at night
we drink you at noon death comes as a master from
    Germany
we drink you at nightfall and morning we drink you and
    drink you
a master from Germany death comes with eyes that are
    blue
with a bullet of lead he will hit in the mark he will hit
    you
a man in the house your golden hair Margarete

he hunts us down with his dogs in the sky he gives us a
    grave
he plays with the serpents and dreams death comes as a
    master from Germany

your golden hair Margarete
your ashen hair Shulamith.

(translated by Christopher Middleton)

YOUR HAND FULL OF HOURS

Your hand full of hours, you came to me—and I said:
Your hair is not brown.
So you lifted it lightly on to the scales of grief; it
    weighed more than I . . .

On ships they come to you and make it their cargo, then
    put it on sale in the markets of lust—
You smile at me from the depth, I weep at you from the
    scale that stays light.
I weep: Your hair is not brown, they offer brine from the
    sea and you give them curls . . .
You whisper: They're filling the world with me now, in
    your heart I'm a hollow way still!
You say: Lay the leafage of years beside you—it's time
    you came closer and kissed me!

The leafage of years is brown, your hair is not brown.

(translated by Michael Hamburger)

SHIBBOLETH

Together with my stones
grown big with weeping
behind the bars,

they dragged me out into
the middle of the market,
that place
where the flag unfurls to which
I swore no kind of allegiance.

Flute,
double flute of night:
remember the dark
twin redness
of Vienna and Madrid.

Set your flag at half-mast,
memory.
At half-mast
today and forever.

Heart:
here too reveal what you are,
here, in the midst of the market.
Call the shibboleth, call it out
into your alien homeland:
February. *No pasaran*.

Unicorn:
you know about the stones,
you know about the water;
come,
I shall lead you away
to the voices
of Estremadura.

(translated by Michael Hamburger)

ASPEN TREE

Aspen tree, your leaves glance white into the dark.
My mother's hair never turned white.

Dandelion, so green is the Ukraine.
My fair-haired mother did not come home.

Rain cloud, do you linger over the well?
My soft-voiced mother wept for everyone.

Rounded star, you coil the golden loop.
My mother's heart was cut by lead.

Oaken door, who hove you off your hinge?
My gentle mother cannot return.

CORONA

Autumn nibbles its leaf right from my hand: we're
     friends.
We shell time from the nuts and teach it to walk:
time turns back into its shell.

In the mirror is Sunday,
in dream goes sleeping,
the mouth speaks true.

My eye goes down to my lover's loins:
we gaze at each other,
we say dark things,
we love one another like poppy and memory,
we slumber like wine in the seashells,
like the sea in the moon's blood-beam.

We stand at the window embracing, they watch us from
     the street:
it's time people knew!
It's time the stone consented to bloom,
a heart beat for unrest.
It's time it came time.

It is time.

SPEAK YOU TOO

Speak you too,
speak as the last,
say out your say.

Speak—
But don't split off No from Yes.
Give your say this meaning too:
give it the shadow.

Give it shadow enough,
give it as much
as you know is spread round you from
midnight to midday and midnight.

Look around:
see how things all come alive—
By death! Alive!
Speaks true who speaks shadow.

TENEBRAE

Near are we, Lord,
near and graspable.

Grasped already, Lord,
clawed into each other, as if
each of our bodies were
your body, Lord.

Pray, Lord,
pray to us,
we are near.

Wind-skewed we went there,
went there, to bend
over pit and crater.

Went to the water-trough, Lord.

It was blood, it was
what you shed, Lord.

It shined.

It cast your image into our eyes, Lord.
Eyes and mouth stand so open and void, Lord.
We have drunk, Lord.
The blood and the image that was in the blood, Lord.

Pray, Lord.
We are near.

(THERE WAS EARTH INSIDE THEM)

There was Earth inside them, and
they dug.
They dug and dug, and so
their day went past, their night. And they did not praise
     God,
who, so they heard, wanted all this,
who, so they heard, witnessed all this.

They dug and heard nothing more;
they did not grow wise, invented no song,
devised for themselves no sort of language.
They dug.

There came then a stillness, there came also storm,
all of the oceans came.
I dig, you dig, and the worm also digs,
and the singing there says: They dig.

O one, o none, o no one, o you.
Where did it go, when it went nowhere at all?
O you dig and I dig, and I dig through to you,
and the ring on our finger awakes.

ZURICH, AT THE STORK

   for Nelly Sachs

Our talk was of Too Much, of
Too Little, of Thou
and Yet-Thou, of
clouding through brightness, of
Jewishness, of
your God.

There-
or.
On the day of an ascension, the
Minister stood over there, it came
with some gold across the water.

Our talk was of your God, I spoke
against him, I
let the heart that I had
hope:
for
his highest, death-rattled, his
wrangling word—

Your eye looked at me, looked away,
your mouth
spoke toward the eye, I heard:
We
really don't know, you know,
we
really don't know
what
counts.

PSALM

No one kneads us again out of earth and clay,
no one incants our dust.
No one.

Blessèd art thou, No One.
In thy sight would
we bloom.
In thy
spite.

A Nothing
we were, are now, and ever
shall be, blooming:
the Nothing-, the
No One's-Rose.

With
our pistil soul-bright,
our stamen heaven-waste,
our corolla red
from the purpleword we sang
over, O over
the thorn.

(THREADSUNS)

Threadsuns
over the gray-black wasteness.
A tree-
high thought
strikes the light-tone: there are
still songs to sing beyond
humankind.

(YOU WERE MY DEATH)

You were my death:
you I could hold
while everything slipped from me.

(PROFUSE ANNOUNCEMENT)

Profuse announcement
in a tomb, where
we with our
gas flags are flapping,

we stand
in the odor
of sanctity, yeah.

Burnt
fumes of Beyond
leak thick from our pores,

in every other
tooth-
cavity awakes
an undespoilable hymn.

The two bits twilight you tossed in to us,
come, gulp it down too.

(WORLD TO BE STUTTERED AFTER)

World to be stuttered after
in which I will have been
a guest, a name
sweated down from the wall
where a wound licks up high.

(THE POLES)

The Poles
are within us,
insurmountable
while waking,
we sleep across, up to the Gate
of Mercy,

I lose you to you, that
is my snow-comfort,

say, that Jerusalem *is,*

say it, as if I were this
your whiteness,
as if you were
mine,

as if without us we could be we,

I leaf you open, for ever,
you pray, you lay
us free.

18

ZBIGNIEW HERBERT

(1924–1998)

What kind of poet is Zbigniew Herbert? Is he difficult? Is he hard to follow, hard to scan, impossible to remember? Look at "Pebble," the first poem of this selection, and decide for yourself.

What kind of poem is this, and what is it about? About nature, perhaps? Perhaps. I, for one, though, think that if it is about nature, then it is about human nature. About its autonomy, about its resistance, about, if you will, its survival. In this sense it is a very Polish poem, considering that nation's recent—more exactly, modern—history. And it is a very modern poem, because Polish history, one may say, is modern history in miniature—well, more exactly—in a pebble. Because whether you are a Pole or not, what history wants is to destroy you. The only way to survive, to endure its almost geological pressure, is to acquire the features of a pebble, including the false warmth once you find yourself in somebody's hands.

No, this is not a difficult poem. It is easy to follow. It is a parable: very reticent, very stark. Starkness, in fact, is very much Herbert's signature. My impression of his poems has always been that of a geometrical figure pressed into the marshmallow of my brain. One does not so much remember his lines as find one's mind being branded by their ice-cold lucidity. One does not chant them: The cadences of one's own speech simply yield to his level, to his almost neutral timber, to the tonality of his reserve.

Though Polish, Herbert is not a romantic. In his poems he argues not by raising the temperature but by lowering it, to the point where his lines begin to burn the reader's grasping faculties, like an iron fence in winter. He is a modern poet not because he uses *verse libre* but because the reasons for which he uses it are very modern. Born in 1924, Herbert belongs to the generation of Europeans that saw the native realm reduced to rubble—and, as was his particular case, to ruble. Somewhat naively perhaps, people of that generation came to associate strict meters with the social order that brought their nations to catastrophe. They sought a new, unadorned, direct, plain form of speech. In other words, unlike its Western counterpart, Eastern European modernism appears to have been historically motivated.

Herbert's modernism is, indeed, as one perceptive critic put it, a modernism without experimental hoopla. His idiom is forged by necessity, not by the oversaturated aestheticism of his predecessors. When he was young Herbert fought in the anti-Nazi resistance; as a grown-up he had to deal with the monolith of the communist totalitarian state. While the former were murderous, the latter was both murderous and ethically corrosive. In order to survive and to temper the reader's heart, a poet's statements had to be at once self-contained and opaque: a pebble.

Yet it would be myopic to reduce this poet to the role of a resistance fighter against the two most formidable systems of political oppression our century has known. His real enemy is the vulgarity of the human heart, which always produces a simplified version of human reality. This inevitably results in social injustice at best, in utopia-turned-nightmare at worst. Herbert is a poet of tremendous ethical consequence because his verse zeroes in on the cause, not just the effects, which he treats as something incidental—which they always are. Symptoms are not the malaise.

In this sense he is a historical poet. His pen often summons history, which is after all the mother of culture, in order to enable his readers to endure and, with luck, to overcome the vulgarity of the present. His poems show that most of our beliefs, convictions, and social concepts are in bad taste, if only because they are entertained at someone else's expense. He is a supreme ironist, of course; to me, though, his irony is no more than the safety valve of his compassion, since human tragedy is repetitive.

Zbigniew Herbert is a poet for this place; above all, for this time.

—J. B.

(Translations, unless otherwise indicated, are by John and
Bogdana Carpenter.)

PEBBLE

The pebble
is a perfect creature

equal to itself
mindful of its limits

filled exactly
with a pebbly meaning

with a scent which does not remind one of anything
does not frighten anything away does not arouse desire

its ardor and coldness
are just and full of dignity

I feel a heavy remorse
when I hold it in my hand
and its noble body
is permeated by false warmth

—Pebbles cannot be tamed
to the end they will look at us
with a calm and very clear eye

(translated by Czeslaw Milosz and Peter Dale Scott)

THE ENVOY OF MR. COGITO

Go where those others went to the dark boundary
for the golden fleece of nothingness your last prize

go upright among those who are on their knees
among those with their backs turned and those toppled
    in the dust

you were saved not in order to live
you have little time you must give testimony

be courageous when the mind deceives you be
    courageous
in the final account only this is important

and let your helpless Anger be like the sea
whenever you hear the voice of the insulted and beaten

let your sister Scorn not leave you
for the informers executioners cowards—they will win
they will go to your funeral and with relief will throw a
    lump of earth
the woodborer will write your smoothed-over biography

and do not forgive truly it is not in your power
to forgive in the name of those betrayed at dawn

beware however of unnecessary pride
keep looking at your clown's face in the mirror
repeat: I was called—weren't there better ones than I

beware of dryness of heart love the morning spring
the bird with an unknown name the winter oak

light on a wall the splendor of the sky
they don't need your warm breath
they are there to say: no one will console you

be vigilant—when the light on the mountains gives the
      sign—arise and go
as long as blood turns in the breast your dark star

repeat old incantations of humanity fables and legends
because this is how you will attain the good you will not
      attain
repeat great words repeat them stubbornly
like those crossing the desert who perished in the sand

and they will reward you with what they have at hand
with the whip of laughter with murder on a garbage
      heap

go because only in this way will you be admitted to the
      company of cold skulls
to the company of your ancestors: Gilgamesh Hector
      Roland
the defenders of the kingdom without limit and the city
      of ashes

Be faithful Go

TRANSFORMATIONS OF LIVY

How did they understand Livy my grandfather my great
      grandfather
certainly they read him in high school
at the not very propitious time of the year
when a chestnut stands in the window—fervent
      candelabras of blooms—

all the thoughts of grandfather and great-grandfather
    running breathless to Mizia
who sings in the garden shows her décolleté also her
    heavenly legs up to the knees
or Gabi from the Vienna opera with ringlets like a
    cherub
Gabi with a snub nose and Mozart in her throat
or in the end to the kind-hearted Józia refuge of the
    dejected
with no beauty talent or great demands
and so they read Livy—O season of blossoms—
in the smell of chalk boredom naphthalene for cleaning
    the floor
under a portrait of the emperor
and the empire like all empires
seemed eternal

Reading the history of the City they surrendered to the
    illusion
that they are Romans or descendants of the Romans
these sons of the conquered themselves enslaved
surely the Latin master contributed to this
with his rank of Court Councillor
a collection of antique virtues under a worn-out frock
    coat
so following Livy he implanted in his pupils the
    contempt for the mob
the revolt of the people—*res tam foede*—aroused loathing
    in them
whereas all of the conquests appeared just
they showed simply the victory of what is stronger
that is why they were pained by the defeat at Lake
    Trasimeno
the superiority of Scipio filled them with pride

they learned of the death of Hannibal with genuine relief
easily too easily they let themselves be led
through the entrenchments of subordinate clauses
complex constructions governed by the gerund
rivers swollen with elocution
pitfalls of syntax
—to battle
for a cause not theirs.

Only my father and myself after him
read Livy against Livy
carefully examining what is underneath the fresco
that is why the theatrical gesture of Scevola awoke no
    echo in us
shouts of centurions triumphal marches
while we were willing to be moved by the defeat
of the Samnites Gauls or Etruscans
we counted many of the names of peoples turned to dust
    by the Romans
buried without glory who for Livy
were not worth even a wrinkle of style
those Hirpins Auleans Lucanians Osunans
also the inhabitants of Tarentum Metapontis Locri

My father knew well and I also know
that one day on a remote boundary
without any signs in heaven
in Pannonia Sarajevo or Trebizon
in a city by a cold sea
or in a valley of Panshir
a local conflagration will explode

and the empire will fall

THE TRIAL

During his great speech the prosecutor
kept piercing me with his yellow index finger
I'm afraid I didn't appear self-assured
unintentionally I put on a mask of fear and depravity
like a rat caught in a trap an informer a fratricide
the reporters were dancing a war dance
slowly I burned at a stake of magnesia

all of this took place in a small stifling room
the floor creaked plaster fell from the ceiling
I counted knots in the boards holes in the wall faces
the faces were alike almost identical
policemen the tribunal witnesses the audience
they belonged to the party of those without any pity
and even my defender smiling pleasantly
was an honorary member of the firing squad

in the first row sat an old fat woman
dressed up as my mother with a theatrical gesture she
      raised
a handkerchief to her dirty eyes but didn't cry
it must have lasted a long time I don't even know how
      long
the red blood of the sunset was rising in the gowns of
      the judges

the real trial went on in my cells
they certainly knew the verdict earlier
after a short rebellion they capitulated and started to die
one after the other
I looked in amazement at my wax fingers.

I didn't speak the last word and yet
for so many years I was composing the final speech

to God to the court of the world to the conscience
to the dead rather than the living
roused to my feet by the guards
I managed only to blink and then
the room burst out in healthy laughter
my adoptive mother laughed also
the gavel banged and this really was the end

but what happened after that—death by a noose
or perhaps a punishment generously changed to a
    dungeon
I'm afraid there is a third dark solution
beyond the limits of time the senses and reason

therefore when I wake I don't open my eyes
I clench my fingers don't lift my head
breathe lightly because truly I don't know
how many minutes of air I still have left

MR. COGITO AND THE IMAGINATION

I

Mr. Cogito never trusted
tricks of the imagination

the piano at the top of the Alps
played false concerts for him

he didn't appreciate labyrinths
the Sphinx filled him with loathing

he lived in a house with no basement
without mirrors of dialectics

jungles of tangled images
were not his home

he would rarely soar
on the wings of a metaphor
and then he fell like Icarus
into the embrace of the Great Mother

he adored tautologies
explanations
idem per idem

that a bird is a bird
slavery means slavery
a knife is a knife
death remains death

he loved
the flat horizon
a straight line
the gravity of the earth

2

Mr. Cogito will be numbered
among the species *minores*

he will accept indifferently the verdict
of future scholars of the letter

he used the imagination
for entirely different purposes

he wanted to make it
an instrument of compassion

he wanted to understand to the very end

—Pascal's night
—the nature of a diamond
—the melancholy of the prophets
—Achilles' wrath
—the madness of those who kill
—the dreams of Mary Stuart
—Neanderthal fear
—the despair of the last Aztecs
—Nietzsche's long death throes
—the joy of the painter of Lascaux
—the rise and fall of an oak
—the rise and fall of Rome

and so to bring the dead back to life
to preserve the covenant

Mr. Cogito's imagination
has the motion of a pendulum

it crosses with precision
from suffering to suffering

there is no place in it
for the artificial fires of poetry

he would like to remain faithful
to uncertain clarity

GEORG HEYM — THE ALMOST METAPHYSICAL
ADVENTURE

I

If it is true
an image precedes thought
one would believe
that the idea of Heym
originated while ice skating

—the ease of moving
over the icy surface

he was there and here
he circled among the moving center
he wasn't a planet
nor a bell
nor a farmer tied to his plough

—the relativity of movement
mirror-like interpenetration of systems

the closer left-hand shore
(the red roofs of Gatow)
was flying backwards
like a violently tugged tablecloth
while the right-hand shore
stayed (apparently) in place

the overthrow of determinism
marvelous coexistence of possibilities

—my greatness—
Heym was saying to himself
(he was now gliding backwards
with the left leg raised)

is based on the discovery
that in the contemporary world
there are no direct results
no tyranny of sequence
dictatorships of causality
all thoughts
actions
objects
phenomena
lie side by side
like the traces of skate
on a white surface

a weighty assertion
for theoretical physics
a dangerous assertion
for the theory of poetry

2

those who stood on the right shore
didn't notice the disappearance of Heym

the high school student passing him
saw everything in reverse order:

white sweater
trousers fastened below the knee
with two bone buttons

calves in orange stockings
the skates the cause of the accident

two policemen pushed a path
through the crowd of onlookers
standing over the hole in the ice

(it looked like the entrance to a dungeon
like the cold mouth of a mask)

licking their pencils
they tried to record the event
to introduce order
according to the obsolete
logic of Aristotle

with the slow-minded
indifference of authority
for the discoverer
and his thoughts
which were now
wandering helplessly
under the ice

THE RAIN

When my older brother
came back from the war
he had a little silver star on his forehead
and under the star
an abyss

a splinter of shrapnel
hit him at Verdun
or perhaps at Grünwald
(he didn't remember the details)

he talked a lot
in many languages
but most of all he liked
the language of history

until losing breath
he called to his dead comrades under the ground
Roland Jones Hannibal

he shouted
that this is the last crusade
soon Carthage will fall
and then sobbing confessed
that Napoleon doesn't like him

we watched
him become paler
his senses abandoned him
slowly he was turning into a monument

into musical shells of ears
entered a stone forest

the skin of his face
was fastened
with two blind dry
buttons of eyes

all he had left
was touch

what stories
he told with his hand
in the right he had romances
in the left soldier's memories

they took my brother
and carried him out of town

he returns now every autumn
thin and quiet

he doesn't want to enter the house
he knocks at the window for me to come out

we walk on the streets
and he tells me
unbelievable tales
touching my face
with blind fingers of weeping

THE POWER OF TASTE

For Professor Izydora Dambska

It didn't require great character at all
our refusal disagreement and resistance
we had a shred of the necessary courage
but fundamentally it was a matter of taste
                                        Yes taste
in which there are fibers of soul the cartilage
    of conscience

Who knows if we had been better and more attractively
    tempted
sent rose-skinned women thin as a wafer
or fantastic creatures from the paintings of Hieronymus
    Bosch
but what kind of hell was there at this time
a wet pit the murderers' alley the barrack
called a palace of justice
a home-brewed Mephisto in a Lenin jacket
sent Aurora's grandchildren out into the field
boys with potato faces
very ugly girls with red hands

Verily their rhetoric was made of cheap sacking
(Marcus Tullius kept turning in his grave)

chains of tautologies a couple of concepts like flails
the dialectics of slaughterers no distinctions in reasoning
syntax deprived of beauty of the subjunctive

So aesthetics can be helpful in life
one should not neglect the study of beauty

Before we declare our consent we must carefully examine
the shape of the architecture the rhythm of the drums
    and pipes
official colors the despicable ritual of funerals

      Our eyes and ears refused obedience
      the princes of our senses proudly chose exile

It did not require great character at all
we had a shred of necessary courage
but fundamentally it was a matter of taste
                    Yes taste
that commands us to get out to make a wry face draw
    out a sneer
even if for this the precious capital of the body the head
                must fall

19

EUGENIO MONTALE

(1896–1981)

Eugenio Montale was an independent and largely self-taught poet. His landmark first collection, *Ossi di seppia* (Cuttlefish Bones), published in 1925, was a quiet revolt against the pomp and high-flown rhetoric of D'Annunzio and his followers. Montale's was a humble, earthly lyricism that nonetheless suggested at every turn a complex and private individual meditating on all aspects of the world.

Montale took his first regular job in 1929, becoming director of the Gabinetto Vieusseux Library in Florence, a post he lost a decade later because of his antifascism.

In 1939 Montale published *Le Occasioni* (The Occasions), another influential collection. His work had taken a more allusive—or hermetic— turn. The shadow of history falls on the page and drives the poet inward; we read the signs of an agonized search for spiritual meaning.

In 1948 Montale moved to Milan to become a correspondent for the *Corriere della sera;* he wrote hundreds of *feuilletons* on every aspect of social, artistic, and political life. Montale published *La Bufera e altro* (The Storm and Other Things) in 1956—a work reflecting political liberation and a sense of spiritual recovery. After Montale's wife died in 1963, he wrote the beautiful cycle of memorial poems, *Xenia*.

Montale's prose is available in English in *The Butterfly of Dinard,* a collection of lyrical sketches, and *The Second Life of Art,* a book of essays. He won the Nobel Prize in 1975.

—S. B.

(DON'T ASK US FOR THE WORD)

Don't ask us for the word to frame
our shapeless spirit on all sides,
and proclaim it in letters of fire to shine
like a lone crocus in a dusty field.

Ah, the man who walks secure,
a friend to others and himself
indifferent that high summer prints
his shadow on a peeling wall!

Don't ask us for the phrase that can open worlds,
just a few gnarled syllables, dry like a branch.
This, today is all that we can tell you:
what we are *not*, what we do *not* want.

(translated by Jonathan Galassi)

THE LEMON TREES

Listen: the laureled poets
stroll only among shrubs
with learned names: lingstrum, acanthus, box.
What I like are streets that end in grassy
ditches where boys snatch
a few famished eels from drying puddles:
paths that struggle along the banks,
then dip among the tufted canes,
into the orchards, among the lemon trees.

Better, if the gay palaver of the birds
is stilled, swallowed by the blue:
more clearly now, you hear the whisper
of genial branches in that air barely astir,
the sense of that smell
inseparable from the earth,

that rains its restless sweetness in the heart.
Here, by some miracle, the war
of conflicted passions is stilled,
here even we the poor share the riches of the world—
the smell of the lemon trees.

See, in these silences when things
let themselves go and seem almost
to reveal their final secret,
we sometimes expect
to discover a flaw in Nature,
the world's dead point, the link that doesn't hold,
the thread that, disentangled, might at last lead us
to the center of a truth.
The eye rummages,
the mind pokes about, unifies, disjoins
in the fragrance that grows
as the day closes, languishing.
These are the silences where we see
in each departing human shade
some disturbed Divinity.

But the illusion dies, time returns us
to noisy cities where the sky is only
patches of blue, high up, between the cornices.
Rain wearies the ground; over the buildings
winter's tedium thickens.
Light grows niggardly, the soul bitter.
And, one day, through a gate ajar,
among the trees in a courtyard,
we see the yellows of the lemon trees;
and the heart's ice thaws,
and songs pelt
into the breast
and trumpets of gold pour forth
epiphanies of Light!

(translated by William Arrowsmith)

(Bring me sunflower)

Bring me the sunflower, I'll plant it here
in my patch of ground scorched by salt spume,
where all day long it will lift the craving
of its golden face to the mirroring blue.

Dark things are drawn to brighter,
bodies languishing in a flowing
of colors, colors in musics. To vanish,
then, is the venture of ventures.

Bring me the flower that leads us out
where blond transparencies rise
and life evaporates as essence.
Bring me the sunflower crazed with light.

(translated by William Arrowsmith)

Dora Markus

I

It was where the wooden bridge
runs to Porto Corsini over open water
and a few men, moving slowly, sink their nets
or haul them in. With a wave
of your hand you pointed toward the invisible
shore beyond, your true fatherland.
Then we followed the canal back to the city's
inner harbor, shining with soot,
in the wet flats where a sluggish springtime
was settling down, unremembering.

And here where an ancient life
is mottled with a sweet
Oriental yearning,

your words shimmered like the scales
of a dying mullet.

Your restlessness reminds me
of those migratory birds that thump against the
      lighthouse
on stormy nights:
even your sweetness is a storm
whose raging's unseen,
whose lulls are even rarer.
I don't know how, *in extremis,* you resist
in that lake of indifference that is your heart; perhaps
some amulet preserves you,
some keepsake beside your lipstick,
powder puff, or file: a white mouse,
of ivory. And so you persist.

II

Now in your Carinthia
of flowering myrtles and ponds,
leaning over the edge, you look down
at the shy carp gaping,
or under the lime trees follow the evening
star kindling among the jagged
peaks, and the water aflame with awnings
on lodging houses and piers.

The night that reaches out
over the damp inlet brings,
mingled with throbbing motors,
only the honking of geese; and an interior
of snow-white tiles tells
the blackened mirror that sees the change
in you a tale of errors calmly
accepted, etching it in
where the sponge won't reach.

Your legend, Dora!
But it's written already in the stares
of men with scraggly whiskers, dignified,
in great gilded portraits, returning
in every chord sounded
by the broken street-organ in the darkening
hour, always later.

It's written there. The evergreen
bays for the kitchen
resist, the voice doesn't change.
Ravenna's far away, a brutal
faith distills its venom. What
does it want from you? Voice,
legend, or fate can't be surrendered . . .
But it's getting late, always later.

(translated by William Arrowsmith)

(YOU KNOW: I MUST LEAVE YOU AGAIN)

You know: I must leave you again and I can't.
Like a well-targeted shot, every effort,
every cry, unsettles me, even the salt
breeze overflowing
from the quays that makes Sottoripa's
springtime so dark.

Land of iron and masts
forested in the evening dust.
A long droning comes from open space,
screeches like a fingernail on glass. I look for the lost
sign, the only pledge I had of your
grace.
        And hell is certain.

(translated by William Arrowsmith)

IN THE GREENHOUSE

The lemon-house was being over-
ridden by the moles' stampedes.
The scythe shone in a rosary
of wary waterbeads.

A spot among the quinces blazed,
a bug—cochineal.
We heard the pony rear up at
the comb—then sleep was all.

Rapt, weightless, I was drenched with you.
my hidden breathing was your form,
your face was merged into mine,
and the dark idea of God

descended on the living few
to celestial tones
and children's drums
and globes of lightning strung above

the lemons, and me, and you . . .

(translated by Jonathan Galassi)

THE EEL

The eel, coldwater
siren, who leaves the Baltic behind her
to reach these shores of ours,
our wetlands and marshes, our rivers,
who struggles upstream hugging the bottom, under the
    flood of the downward torrent,
from branch to branch, thinning,
narrowing in, stem by stem,

snaking deeper and deeper into the rock core
of slab ledge, squirming through
stone interstices of slime until
one day, light,
exploding, blazes from the chestnut leaves,
ignites a wriggle in deadwater sumps
and run-off ditches of Apennine
ravines spilling downhill toward the Romagna;
eel, torchlight, lash,
arrow of Love on earth,
whom only these dry gulches of ours or burned-out
Pyrenean gullies can draw back up
to Edens of generation;
the green soul seeking
life where there's nothing but stinging
drought, desolation;
spark that says
everything begins when everything seems
dead ashes, buried stump;
brief rainbow, twin
of that other iris shining between your lashes,
by which your virtue blazes out, unsullied, among the
    sons
of men floundering in your mud, can you
deny a sister?

(translated by William Arrowsmith)

THE PRISONER'S DREAM

Here, few signs distinguish dawns from nights.

The zigzag of starlings over the watchtowers
on battle days, my only wings,
a thread of polar air,

the head guard's eye at the peephole,
nuts cracking, fatty crackling,
in the basements, roasting
real or imagined—but the straw is gold,
the wine-red lantern is hearth light,
if sleeping I can dream I'm at your feet.

The purge goes on as before, no reason given.
They say that he who recants and enlists
can survive this slaughtering of the geese;
that he who upbraids himself, but betrays and sells
his fellow's hide grabs the ladle by the handle
instead of ending up in the paté
destined for the
pestilential Gods.

Slow-witted, sore
from my sharp pallet, I've become
the flight of the moth my sole
is turning into powder on the floor,
become the light's chameleon kimonos
hung out from the towers of dawn.
I've smelled the scent of burning on the wind
from the cakes in the ovens,
I've looked around. I've conjured rainbows
shimmering on fields of spiderwebs,
and petals on the trellis of bars,
I've stood and fallen back
into the pit where a century's a minute—
and the blows keep coming, and the footsteps,
and I still don't know if at the feast
I'll be stuffer or stuffing. The wait is long,
my dream of you isn't over.

                              (translated by Jonathan Galassi)

LITTLE TESTAMENT

This thing the night flashes
like marshlight through the skull of my mind,
this pearl necklace snails trail,
this ground glass, diamond-dust sparkle—
it is not the lamp in any church or office,
tended by some adolescent altar boy,
Communist or papist,
in black or red.
I have only this rainbow
to leave you, this testimonial
of a faith, often invaded,
of a hope that burned more slowly
than a green log on the fire.
Keep its spectrum in your pocket-mirror,
when every lamp goes out,
when hell's orchestra trembles,
and the torch-bearing Lucifer
lands on some bowsprit
in the Thames, Hudson or Seine—
rotating his hard coal wings,
half lopped by fatigue, to tell you, "Now."
It's hardly an heirloom or charm
that can tranquilize monsoons
with the transparent spider wed of contemplation—
but an autobiography can only survive in ashes,
persistence is extinction.
It is certainly a sign: whoever has seen it,
will always return to you.
Each knows his own: his pride
was not an escape, his humility
was not a meanness, his obscure
earth-bound flash
was not the fizzle of a wet match.

(translated by Robert Lowell)

20

GEORGE SEFERIS

(1900–1971)

George Seferis was born Georgios Seferiades in Smyrna, then part of the Ottoman Empire. He left his homeland in his early teens, before the 1922–23 massacre and expulsion of the Christian minority. Moving first to Athens, Seferis lived in Paris between 1918 and 1924; he studied law and literature. His studies prepared him for a diplomatic career, which he undertook in 1926, traveling to England, Albania, South Africa, and Egypt. Eventually— from 1957 to 1962—he served as Greek ambassador to London.

Poetry, then, represented a parallel path, much as it did for a time for Seferis's great influence T. S. Eliot. Seferis, too, wrote his first work inspired by French symbolism. His reading of Eliot pushed him toward an exploration of the mythic substratum, and he gradually refined his distinctive idiom. Reading Seferis, we discover how subjective urgency can be encompassed, but not entirely quenched, by the awareness of mythic timelessness. Myth is not only explanatory, it is the deepest possible connection we have with tradition—and the darkness at the heart of myth explains much about our own darkness.

Seferis's publications in English include *Collected Poems* (translated by Edmund Keeley and Philip Sherrard), *Three Secret Poems* (translated by Walter Kaiser), and a collection of essays, *On the Greek Style* (translated by Rex Warner).

Seferis was awarded the Nobel Prize in 1963. In 1969 he used his enormous prestige to speak out against the dictatorship of the "Colonels."

—S. B.

(Translations, except where noted, are by Edmund Keeley and
Philip Sherrard.)

ARGONAUTICA

And for the soul,
if it is to know itself
it is into the soul
. that it must look.
The stranger and the enemy, we have seen him in the mirror.

They were good lads, the comrades who did not grumble
because of weariness or because of thirst or because of the
          freezing.
They had the manner of trees and the manner of waves
that accept the wind and the rain,
accept the night and the sun,
and in the midst of change they do not change.
They used to sweat at the oar with downcast eyes,
breathing rhythmically together,
and their blood flushed up to a subordinate skin.
There were times when they sang, again with downcast
          eyes,
when we passed the desert island with Arabian figs,
toward the setting of the sun, beyond the cape of dogs
that howled at us.
If it is to know itself, they used to say,
it is into the soul it must look, they used to say.
And the oars beat on the golden path of the sea
in the middle of sunset.
Many the capes we passed, many the islands, the sea
which leads to the other sea, sea-gulls and seals.
There were times when unfortunate women with
          lamentations
cried out for their children gone,

and others with desperate faces looked for great
    Alexander
and glory buried in the depths of Asia.
Our anchorages were shores steeped in the perfume of
    night,
among the singing of birds, waters that left on the hands
the recollection of a great good fortune.
But there was never an end to the journeys.
Their souls became one with the oars and the rowlocks,
with the severity of the figurehead on the prow,
with the curling wake of the rudder,
with the water that flecked their faces.
One after another the comrades died
with their downcast eyes. Their oars
indicate the place where they sleep on the shores.
There is none to remember them, and the word is
    Justice.

(translated by Rex Warner)

MATHIOS PASKALIS AMONG THE ROSES

I've been smoking steadily all morning
if I stop the roses will embrace me
they'll choke me with thorns and fallen petals
they grow crookedly, each with the same rose color
they gaze, expecting to see someone go by; no one
    goes by.
Behind the smoke of the pipe I watch them
scentless on their weary stems.
In the other life a woman said to me: "You can touch
    this hand,
and this rose is yours, it's yours, you can take it
now or later, whenever you like."

I go down the steps smoking still,
and the roses follow me down excited
and in their manner there's something of that voice
at the root of a cry, there where one starts shouting
"mother" or "help"
or the small white cries of love.

It's a small garden full of roses
a few square yards descending with me
as I go down the steps, without the sky;
and her aunt would say to her: "Antigone, you forgot
      your exercises today,
at your age I never wore corsets, not in my time."
Her aunt was a pitiful creature: veins in relief,
wrinkles all around her ears, a nose ready to die;
but her words were always full of prudence.
One day I saw her touching Antigone's breast
like a small child stealing an apple.

Is it possible that I'll meet the old woman now as I go
      down?
She said to me as I left: "Who knows when we'll meet
      again?"
And then I read of her death in old newspapers
of Antigone's marriage and the marriage of Antigone's
      daughter
without the steps coming to an end or my tobacco
which leaves on my lips the taste of a haunted ship
with a mermaid crucified to the wheel while she was still
            beautiful.

INTERLUDE OF JOY

That whole morning we were full of joy,
my God, how full of joy.

First, stones leaves and flowers shone
then the sun
a huge sun all thorns and so high in the sky.
A nymph collected our cares and hung them on the trees
a forest of Judas trees.
Young loves and satyrs played there and sang
and you could see pink limbs among the black laurels
bodies of little children.
The whole morning long we were full of joy;
the abyss a closed well
tapped by the tender hoof of a young fawn.
Do you remember its laugh—how full of joy!
Then clouds rain and wet the earth.
You stopped laughing when you lay down in the hut
and opened your large eyes as you watched
the archangel practicing with a fiery sword—
"Inexplicable," you said, "inexplicable.
I don't understand people:
no matter how much they play with colors
they are all black."

DAYS OF APRIL '43

Trumpets, trams, cars backfiring, screeching brakes
chloroform his mind in the same way as one counts
so long as one holds out before being lost
in numbness, at the surgeon's mercy.

In the streets he walks carefully, not to slip
on melon-rinds thrown by indifferent Arabs
or refugee politicians and the clique;
they watch him; will he step on it?—will he not?
As one plucks a daisy.
                    He walks on
swinging an enormous bunch of useless keys;

the dry sky recalls
faded advertisements of the Greek Coastal Steamship
    Company,
windows locked on faces one loves
or a little clear water at the root of a plane tree.

He walks on, going to his work, while
a thousand starving dogs tear his pants to shreds
and strip him naked.
He walks on, staggering, pointed at,
and a dense wind whirls around him
garbage, dung, stench, and slander.

Cairo—Saria Emad-el-Din, 24 June '43

MEMORY I

And there was no more sea.

And I with only a reed in my hands.
The night was deserted, the moon waning,
earth smelled of the last rain.
I whispered: memory hurts wherever you touch it,
there's only a little sky, there's no more sea,
what they kill by day they carry away in carts and dump
    behind the ridge.

My fingers were running idly over this flute
that an old shepherd gave to me because I said good-
    evening to him.
The others have abolished every kind of greeting:
they wake, shave, and start the day's work of slaughter
as one prunes or operates, methodically, without
    passion;
sorrow's dead like Patroclus, and no one makes a
    mistake.

I thought of playing a tune and then I felt ashamed in
    front of the other world
the one that watches me from beyond the night from
    within my light
woven of living bodies, naked hearts
and love that belongs to the Furies
as it belongs to man and to stone and to water and to
    grass
and to the animal that looks straight into the eye of its
    approaching death.

So I continued along the dark path
and turned into my garden and dug and buried the reed
and again I whispered: some morning the resurrection
    will come,
dawn's light will blossom red as trees glow in spring,
the sea will be born again, and the wave will again fling
    forth Aphrodite.
We are the seed that dies. And I entered my empty
    house.

MEMORY II

Ephesus

He spoke while sitting on what seemed to be
the marble remnant of an ancient gate;
endless the plain on the right and empty,
on the left the last shadows moved down the mountain:
"The poem is everywhere. Your voice
sometimes travels beside it
like a dolphin keeping company for a while
with a golden sloop in the sunlight,
then vanishing again. The poem is everywhere,
like the wings of the wind moved by the wind

to touch for a moment the sea gull's wings.
The same as our lives yet different too,
as a woman's face changes yet remains the same
after she strips naked. He who has loved
knows this; in the light that other people see things,
the world spoils; but you remember this:
Hades and Dionysus are the same."
He spoke and then took the main road
that leads to the old harbour, devoured now
under the rushes there. The twilight
as if ready for the death of some animal,
so naked was it.

          I remember still:
he was traveling to Ionian shores,
to empty shells of theatres
where only the lizard slithers over the dry stones,
and I asked him: "Will they be full again some day?"
and he answered: "Maybe, at the hour of death."
And he ran across the orchestra howling
"Let me hear my brother!"
And the silence surrounding us was harsh,
leaving no trace at all on the glass of the blue.

EURIPIDES THE ATHENIAN

He grew old between the fires of Troy
and the quarries of Sicily.

He liked seashore caves and pictures of the sea.
He saw the veins of men
as a net the gods made to catch us in like wild beasts:
he tried to break through it.
He was a sour man, his friends were few;
when his time came he was torn to pieces by dogs.

THE LAST DAY

The day was cloudy. No one could come to a decision;
a light wind was blowing. "Not a north-easter, the
    sirocco," someone said.
A few slender cypresses nailed to the slope and the sea,
gray with shining pools, beyond.
The soldiers presented arms as it began to drizzle.
"Not a north-easter, the sirocco," was the only decision
    heard.
And yet we knew that by the following dawn
nothing would be left to us, neither the woman drinking
    sleep at our side
nor the memory that we were once men,
nothing at all by the following dawn.

"This wind reminds me of spring," said my friend
as she walked beside me gazing into the distance, "the
    spring
that came suddenly in winter by the closed-in sea.
So unexpected. So many years have gone. How are we
    going to die?"

A funeral march meandered through the thin rain.

How does a man die? Strange no one's thought about it.
And for those who thought about it, it was like a
    recollection from old chronicles
from the time of the Crusades or the battle of Salamis.
Yet death is something that happens: how does a man
    die?
Yet each of us earns his death, his own death, which
    belongs to no one else
and this game is life.
The light was sinking over the clouded day, no one
    decided anything.

The following dawn nothing would be left to us,
     everything surrendered, even our hands,
and our women slaves at the springheads and our
     children in the quarries.
My friend, walking beside me, was singing a disjointed
     song:
"In spring, in summer, slaves . . . "
One recalled old teachers who'd left us orphans.
A couple passed, talking:
"I'm sick of the dusk, let's go home,
let's go home and turn on the light."

NARRATION

That man walks along weeping
no one can say why
sometimes they think he's weeping for lost loves
like those that torture us so much
on summer beaches with the gramophones.

Other people go about their business
endless paper, children growing up, women
ageing awkwardly.
He has two eyes like poppies
like cut spring poppies
and two trickles in the corners of his eyes.

He walks along the streets, never lies down
striding small squares on the earth's back
instrument of a boundless pain
that's finally lost all significance.

Some have heard him speak
to himself as he passed by
about mirrors broken years ago

about broken forms in the mirrors
that no one can ever put together again.
Others have heard him talk about sleep
images of horror on the threshold of sleep
faces unbearable in their tenderness.

We've grown used to him, he's presentable and quiet
only that he walks along weeping continually
like willows on a riverbank you see from the train
as you wake uncomfortably some clouded dawn.

We've grown used to him; like everything else you're
        used to
he doesn't stand for anything
and I talk to you about him because I can't find
anything that you're not used to;
I pay my respects.

A Sampling of Other European Poets

Rafael Alberti (Spain)

Blue

1

Blue arrived. And its time was painted.

2

How many blues did the Mediterranean give?

3

Venus, mother of the sea of the blues.

4

The blue of the Greeks
rests, like a god, on columns.

5

The delicate, medieval blue.

6

The Virgin brought her virginal blue:
blue Mary, blue Our Lady.

7

It fell to his palette. And brought
the most secret blue from the sky.
Kneeling, he painted his blues.
Angels christened him with blue.
They appointed him: Beato Blue Angelico.

8

There were celestial palettes like wings
descended from the white of clouds.

9

The blues of Italy,
the blues of Spain,
the blues of France . . .

10

Raphael had wings.
Perugino also had wings
in order to spread his blues around.

11

When they get color from you,
indigo blue, brushes are feathers.

12

Venice of golden Titian blue.

13

Rome of Poussin blues between the pines.

14

Tintoretto blues embitter me.

15

Sulphur alcohol phosphorous Greco blue.
Toxic verdigris blue Greco.

16

On the palette of Velasquez I have
another name: I am called Guadarrama.

17

When I wander through nacreous flesh,
I am called the merry blue vein of Rubens.

18

And in the dawn of the lakes,
with a blue awakening, the echoes
of darkness repeat: Patinir.

19

There is a virginal Murillo blue,
forerunner of the brilliance of the chromes

20

Tiepolo also gave blues to his century.

21

Thinned, delicate, I am a sash—
Goya's light blue ribbon.

22

I would say to you:
         —You are beautiful,
beautiful as the glorious blue of ceilings.

23

Explosions of blue in the allegories.

24

In Manet blue echoes sing
of a far-off Spanish blue.

25

I am also called Renoir. They yell for me,
but I respond at times in lilac
with my blue voice made transparent.
I am the blue shadow,
the clear silhouette of your body.
For old eyes, the scandal.

27

The Balearics gave their blues to Painting.

28

Sometimes the sea invades the palette
of the painter and assigns him
a blue sky given only in secret.

29

The shadow is bluest when the body
that casts it has vanished.

30

Ecstatic blue, having been
pure blue in motion, is nostalgic.

31

Even if the blue is not in the picture,
it covers it like a screen of light.

32
One day blue said:
—Today I have a new name. They call me:
Blue Pablo Ruiz Blue Picasso.

(translated by Mark Strand)

INGEBORG BACHMANN (AUSTRIA)

A KIND OF LOSS

Used together: seasons, books, a piece of music.
The keys, teacups, bread basket, sheets and a bed.
A hope chest of words, of gestures, brought back, used,
     used up.
A household order maintained. Said. Done. And always
     a hand was there.

I've fallen in love with winter, with a Viennese septet,
     with summer.
With village maps, a mountain nest, a beach and a bed.
Kept a calendar cult, declared promises irrevocable,
bowed before something, was pious to nothing

(—to a folded newspaper, cold ashes, the scribbled pieces
     of paper),
fearless in religion, for our bed was the church.

From my lake view arose my inexhaustible painting.
From my balcony I greeted entire peoples, my
     neighbors,
By the chimney fire, in safety, my hair took on its
     deepest hue.
The ringing at the door was the alarm for my joy.

It's not you I've lost,
but the world.

(translated by Mark Anderson)

YVES BONNEFOY (FRANCE)

THE BOOK, FOR GROWING OLD

Stars moving from their summertime
To winter pasture; and the shepherd, arched
Over earthly happiness; and so much peace,
Like the cry of an insect, halt, irregular,
Shaped by an impoverished god. The silence
Rises from your book up to your heart.
A noiseless wind moves in the noisy world.
Time smiles in the distance, ceasing to be.
And in the grove the ripe fruit simply are.

You will grow old
And, fading into the color of the trees,
Making a slower shadow on the wall,
Becoming, as soul at least, the threatened earth,
You will take up the book again, at the still open page,
And say, These were indeed the last dark words.

(translated by Emily Grosholz)

Joseph Brodsky (Russia)

Letters from the Ming Dynasty

I

Soon it will be thirteen years since the nightingale
fluttered out of its cage and vanished. And, at nightfall,
the Emperor washes down his medicine with the blood
of another tailor, then, propped on silk pillows, turns on
     a jeweled bird
that lulls him with its level, identical song.
It's this sort of anniversary, odd-numbered, wrong,
that we celebrate these days in our "Land-under-
     Heaven."
The special mirror that smooths wrinkles even
costs more every year. Our small garden is choked with
     weeds.
The sky, too, is pierced by spires like pins in the
     shoulder blades
of someone so sick that his back is all we're allowed to
     see,
and whenever I talk about astronomy
to the Emperor's son, he begins to joke . . .
This letter to you, Beloved, from your Wild Duck
is brushed onto scented rice paper given me by the
     Empress.
Lately there is no rice but the flow of rice paper is
     endless.

II

"A thousand-li-long road starts with the first step," as
the proverb goes. Pity the road home does
not depend on that same step. It exceeds ten times
a thousand li, especially counting from zeros.
One thousand li, two thousand li—
a thousand means "Thou shalt not ever see
thy native place." And the meaninglessness, like a
    plague,
leaps from words onto numbers, onto zeros especially.

Wind blows us westward like the yellow tares
from a dried pod, there where the Wall towers.
Against it man's figure is ugly and stiff as a frightening
    hieroglyph,
as any illegible scripture at which one stares.
This pull in one direction only has made
me something elongated, like a horse's head,
and all the body should do is spent by its shadow
rustling across the wild barley's withered blade.

(translated by Derek Walcott)

REMCO CAMPERT (THE NETHERLANDS)

AVIGNON

In every hotel
We found a room waiting for us. A bed,
Four walls, hysterical over the wallpaper, to the window:
Low mud-colored roofs, schoolyard full of doves,
The light rosy from the rain: evening
In Avignon.

I read *Le Monde*.
Progressive capitalism in its last stages
Lay in my billfold. I was whole and already
Myself, dirty from traveling, desiring more dirt—
The cleanliness of motion. But a hand
Held me back

Because your chair sprawled
Beside me, and in you was dying
Some feeling, something remoter than any birth.
Your belly rounded paler than lamplight under your
    blouses
And hid under its skin, tauter than a horse's nostril,
A death.

Any tree is
Fruitful or eternal, but
Someone can die before he knows that he lives,
Blood, blue the premature bluestocking, and red
Because in vain; with a white bird between breast
                          and shoulders,
Dead before it breathes,
A death more natural than breathing.

(translated by Jeffery Paine)

MIROSLAV HOLUB (CZECHOSLOVAKIA)

THE FLY

She sat on a willow-trunk
watching
part of the battle of Crécy,
the shouts,
the gasps,

the groans,
the tramping and the tumbling.

During the fourteenth charge
of the French cavalry
she mated
with a brown-eyed male fly
from Vadincourt.

She rubbed her legs together
as she sat on a disemboweled horse
meditating
on the immortality of flies.

With relief she alighted
on the blue tongue
of the Duke of Clervaux.

When silence settled
and only the whisper of decay
softly circled the bodies

and only
a few arms and legs
still twitched jerkily under the trees,

she began to lay her eggs
on the single eye
of Johann Uhr,
the Royal Armourer.

And thus it was
that she was eaten by a swift
fleeing
from the fires of Estrées.

(translated by Ian Milner and George Theiner)

CZESLAW MILOSZ (POLAND)

ENCOUNTER

We were riding through frozen fields in a wagon at
    dawn.
A red wing rose in the darkness.

And suddenly a hare ran across the road.
One of us pointed to it with his hand.

That was long ago. Today neither of them is alive,
Not the hare, nor the man who made the gesture.

O my love, where are they, where are they going
The flash of a hand, streak of movements, rustle of
    pebbles.
I ask not out of sorrow, but in wonder.

(translated by the author and Lillian Vallee)

NELLY SACHS (GERMANY)

O THE CHIMNEYS

*And though after my skin worms destroy this body, yet
in my flesh shall I see God.*

—*Job, 19:26*

O the chimneys
On the ingeniously devised habitations of death
When Israel's body drifted as smoke
Through the air—
Was welcomed by a star, a chimney sweep,

A star that turned black
Or was it a ray of sun?

O the chimneys!
Freedomway for Jeremiah and Job's dust—
Who devised you and laid stone upon stone
The road for refugees of smoke?

O the habitations of death,
Invitingly appointed
For the host who used to be a guest—
O you fingers
Laying the threshold
Like a knife between life and death—

O you chimneys,
O you fingers
And Israel's body as smoke through the air!

(translated by Michael Roloff)

WISŁAWA SZYMBORSKA (POLAND)

UNDER A CERTAIN LITTLE STAR

I apologize to coincide for calling it necessity.
I apologize to necessity just in case I'm mistaken.
Let happiness be not angry that I take it as my own.
Let the dead not remember they scarcely smoulder in my
        memory.
I apologize to time for the muchness of the world
        overlooked per second.
I apologize to old love for regarding the new as the first.
Forgive me, far-off wars, for bringing flowers home.
Forgive me, open wounds, for pricking my finger.

I apologize to those who cry out of the depths for the
   minuet-record.

I apologize to people at railway stations for sleeping at
   five in the morning.

Pardon me, hounded hope, for laughing now and again.

Pardon me, deserts, for not rushing up with a spoonful
   of water.

And you, O falcon, the same these many years, in that
   same cage,

forever staring motionless at that self-same spot,

absolve me, even though you are but a stuffed bird.

I apologize to the cut-down trees for the table's four legs.

I apologize to the big questions for small answers.

O Truth, do not pay me too much heed.

O Solemnity, be magnanimous unto me.

Endure, mystery of existence, that I pluck out the
   threads of your train.

Accuse me not, O soul, of possessing you but seldom

I apologize to everything that I cannot be everywhere.

I apologize to everyone that I cannot be every man and
   woman.

I know that as long as I live nothing can justify me,

because I myself am an obstacle to myself.

Take it not amiss, O speech, that I borrow weighty
   words,

and later try hard to make them seem light.

(translated by Magnus J. Krynski and Robert A. Maguire)

ALSO HIGHLY RECOMMENDED:

   Gottfried Benn, "No Mourning's Possible" (in *Prose Essays Poems*)

   Bertolt Brecht, "To Posterity" (in *Selected Poems*)

   Henri Michaux, "I Am Writing to You from a Far-off Country" (in
      Selected Writings)

   Tomas Tranströmer, "Baltics" (in *Selected Poems*)

   Adam Zagajewski, "To Go to Lvov" (in *Tremor*)

PART IV

AFRICA

22

AN AFRICAN WAY WITH WORDS
Kwame Anthony Appiah

My mother read us poems from as early as I can remember. Her reading voice and her sense of the rhythm and pace of English verse are among my oldest memories. Like all children we began, of course, with nursery rhymes, but before I was nine (and went to boarding school in England) she had also taught me to love English romantic poetry and especially Wordsworth and Keats. Though my sisters and I were growing up in Ghana, surrounded by my father's Ghanaian family—grandfather across the street, aunts and uncles and cousins all over town—my mother herself was English. Looking back, it seems to me that (despite her total immersion in Kumasi, the city where we were raised) she kept in touch with the English countryside she still loved so much by constantly revisiting it in the poets with whom she had grown up. And on those journeys we were often her companions.

I learned about daffodils from Wordsworth: they don't grow in Ghana. I could imagine the shore of a winter lake because I knew from "La Belle Dame Sans Merci" how

> . . . the sedge is withered from the lake,
> And no birds sing.

I could find my way through meadows moister than our savannas, woods gentler than our forests, grasp the rhythm of seasons we did not experience, feel a nostalgia for English country churchyards, with their monuments of mossy stone, long before my first real experience of any of them. When I first spent time in England as a child, I recognized the hedgerows, copses, and fields; when I first saw the shimmering cascade of bluebells in the woods of springtime, my response had been prepared by the bluebells of English nature poetry. My mother has given me many gifts, but the sense of landscape in English poetry is one of the most precious.

But one's sense of the possibilities of poetry comes from many more places than poems read from the page. Verse forms and the sense of rhymes and half rhymes and all the metrical patterns of the language came to me from hymns in church, the cadences of the King James Bible, and, above all, from the rhythms of speech in my father's language, Twi. We learned the words of children's games naturally, chanted in our treble voices to the accompaniment of clapping and the padding of our dancing feet. And we lived in a world where ordinary people took pleasure in a conversation rich in allusion to folk tradition and family and national history, where a "way with words" was something to aim for, something to enjoy in others.

However, the richest source of everyday play with language came from the lively tradition of making and using proverbs. For in proverbs, too, there is a kind of formality, a moving away from the rhythms of ordinary "prose," everyday talk; these proverbs used words with a sense not only of what they are saying but of how they say it. It is the inevitable interdependence on the what and the how that explains why, as Robert Frost once said, "Poetry is what gets lost in translation."

One of my favorite proverbs gets lost in translation just because it is, as we say, a play on words, a potpourri of puns:

Esono esono ena esono sosono.

The words mean that there's a difference between an elephant and a worm, but, as you can see, it works because *"Esono . . . esono . . . "* (the formula for saying "There's a difference between . . . and . . . ," *esono* (elephant) and *sosono* (worm) are almost homonyms. So different, "elephant" and "worm," but sounding almost the same!

Of course Frost exaggerated: Poetry can be powerfully translated. (Keats, remember, thought his first look into Chapman's translation of

Homer was as exciting as "stout Cortez's" first sight of the Pacific Ocean.) To translate well, however, is to seek not only to echo the meanings of the words and phrases, but also to mimic the way sound and sense interact in the original language.

The challenge of proverb making, like the challenge of creating poetry, is to match form and content, intertwine them; and living with proverbs is, I am sure, a part of what prepared me for poetry.

Sometime in my late teens, one summer holiday at home in Ghana, I picked up the collected poems of Léopold Sédar Senghor, the first president of Senegal, and began to translate them from the French. My father was an African politician and diplomat of Senghor's generation, a generation whose leaders knew one another across national and linguistic divides. Senghor had sent us this elegant red volume, "the definitive version," as he wrote in his brief introduction, "of my poems." (As I write, on my desk is this copy of the *Poémes* in the 1964 Seuil edition. It is signed by the author, with this message to my mother: À *Madame Peggy Appiah, en hommage de fidèle amitié.*) I started at the beginning with "In Memoriam," the opening poem from *Chants d'ombre* (Shadow Songs), published in 1945.

> *C'est dimanche*
> *J'ai peur de la foule de mes semblables au visage de pierre.*
> (Today is Sunday./I fear the crowd of my fellows with
>   such faces of stone.)

That second rolling line, with what struck my ear as a strong, propulsive beat, is typical of Senghor's poetry. It is a long line, its rhythm emphatic, its imagery is striking; the language has a rigorous lucidity.

The poem is, in fact, a Sunday reflection on the day after All Saints', the great Catholic feast. Yet almost immediately—in the third line—we meet the "impatient Ancestors," who have followed Senghor from the Sine (a river in Senegal). These are Ancestors "who knew how to resist Death from the Sine to the Seine," from Senegal, where he was born, to Paris, the city from which the poet speaks. Senghor in these poems hovers always exactly where he always lived, at the crossroads of Africa and

Europe. And when we reach the last lines, which speak of going down to
the street,

> joining my brothers
> who have blue eyes and hard hands,

we have a final emblematic moment: the outstretched hand of friendship
to his French "brothers."

Senghor's poetry is influenced formally by the symbolist poets, who
were the dominant voices of new poetry in 1930s France. But in the circle
of young black intellectuals in Paris then—at whose center were two
extraordinary Antillean sisters, Paulette and Jane Nardal—there was also
a great deal of discussion of the Harlem Renaissance (evidence of the
salience of Harlem in Senghor's imagination is to be found in the poem
"To New York"). And then, in many of the poems one finds Senegalese
words and references, and, often, in the call and responses of verse and
chorus, an attempt to evoke the style of older oral performance.

To make sense of Senghor's work one must see it within the history of
French poetry, and, especially one must understand his home among the
symbolists. But one must also see his writing as belonging to the world of
African writing in the colonial and postcolonial worlds.

Senghor's life work began before World War II, and it is one of the start-
ing points of modern African literature in the colonial languages. Since
the War, in the period of nationalist struggle and independence, the pub-
lication of the literature of sub-Saharan Africa in those languages—
French, English, and Portuguese—has mushroomed. There are a few
other notable documents in this literature in the colonial languages before
World War II: In the Francophone world René Maran won the Prix
Goncourt in 1921 for *Batouala,* a novel set in the French colony that
became the Central African Republic—but Maran was from Martinique;
and Aimé Césaire (also from the French Antilles) and Senghor himself, as
I say, were already well known in the 1930s, through their influential the-
oretical writings and their poetry.

Still, it is with the growth of the post-Second World War novel, and especially the publication, by the Paris-based (but African-owned) publishing house Présence Africaine and many major French publishers, of a considerable volume of African poetry and prose, that contemporary Francophone African literature really explodes. A similar story can be told about the British colonies. Notwithstanding such rare early works as J. E. Casely Hayford's 1911 *Ethiopia Unbound* (as much a tract as a work of fiction), whose eclectic style perhaps accounts for its having had no literary offspring, most African writing was confined to journalism, political pamphlets, and scholarly writings on African cultures. Only with the beginnings of the Heinemann African Writers' series in 1959, under the guidance of the Nigerian novelist Chinua Achebe (whose own *Things Fall Apart,* the first book in that series, is probably still the most widely read African novel), is there a real proliferation of published fiction.

It is interesting and important that the first major Francophone African literary figure—Senghor—was a poet. For to succeed as a poet in any language (and, especially, to achieve greatness in poetry), one must, of course, not only command verbal and syntactical subtleties, but also appreciate the more elusive echoes of words and phrases, their histories within poetic and quotidian diction, and the formal traditions of verse (even where one is going to disrupt or mock them). And all this requires the sort of substantial investment in the language and its culture that is rare in people who are not native speakers. (Conrad was a great English novelist: wouldn't it have been more surprising if he had been a great poet?) That Senghor not only masters and modifies French verse forms but also ends up as a member of the Académie Française (the ancient institution charged with the responsibility of preserving the French language) is a reflection of the deep commitment of French colonial education to the assimilation of a few special colonial subjects: the creation of what they called *evolués.*

This was not an emphasis shared by the British. The practice of "indirect rule" in India was transferred to Africa, and the African colonies were governed in the first instance through political leaders. This did not require the creation of a substantial "native" class trained in the ways of the colonizer, nor did it suggest that African subjects needed to be taken out of their cultures and recreated as ersatz Englishmen. As a result, serious African poetry in English is a later development than in French.

Perhaps the first really major black African poet in English is Christopher Okigbo, whose work appears in the 1960s. (I say "perhaps" because this judgment is, I think, more controversial than Senghor's priority in the Francophone case.)

The Portuguese had a policy of assimilation similar to that of the French. There had been a tradition of anticolonial writings, both in Luanda (Angola's capital) and in Lisbon from the later nineteenth century on, but the establishment of the fascist dictatorship of Antonio Salazar in Lisbon in 1928 led to a vigorous crackdown on colonial dissent. Contemporary Angolan literature—and especially its poetry—really derives from the writings of such revolutionary authors as Agostinho Neto, the first president of independent Angola.

There are older African literate traditions: in pharaonic Egypt, of course, but also in Ethiopia, and in areas of Africa where Islam brought writing before the European empires. (Much of North Africa belongs straightforwardly to the world of Arab literature; but there is also a Swahili tradition in East Africa, and a Hausa one in northern Nigeria, both of which begin in Arabic script.) Still, until the modern period, sub-Saharan African literature is fundamentally the oral productions of more than a thousand precolonial languages. There is little point in arguing the definitional question whether the oral histories, myths, praise-poems, love-songs, and proverbs of Africa are "really" literature. But even if, by some criterion or other, such works are not truly "literary," they are important to modern African literature because they provide so much of the background to contemporary works created on the page.

More than this, it is a central fact about oral forms that they invite many of the same modes of critical appreciation and evaluation that we standardly apply to the literatures of Europe and North America with which we are familiar. Thus: we may study their genres; we may explore their plots; we may appreciate—even in translation—their metaphors and their symbolism; and above all, we may learn through them of other ways of interpreting, appreciating, and evaluating the social and natural worlds, and thus increase our appreciation of the range of human and cultural experience.

Nevertheless, it is important to be aware of some basic differences between written and oral literatures, differences that were first studied by

European and American literary scholars in the context of such canonical texts as the Anglo-Saxon *Beowulf* and Homer's *Odyssey*. I want to focus on a central feature of orature (as such oral literature is now called) that differentiates it from much literature crafted in writing.

Until we reduce it to writing, orature is fundamentally a form of performance. Myths, histories, poems are sung or spoken to audiences—often with their participation, often with musical accompaniment—and the quality of the total performance is central to the audience's appreciation. We are used to thinking of plays (which also exist, in a certain sense, only in performance) as nevertheless defined by the text—the script—that is performed. We speak of good and bad performances of *Lear* or *La Misanthrope,* but we also speak of them as a great tragedy and comedy respectively, independently of any particular performance. Thinking of a play this way, as defined by a script, is natural enough for us, but it is not the natural way to think of performances in an oral tradition. For one thing, the script usually has a single author, often one we know by name. But what the oral performer is interpreting, though it is always based on materials handed down to him or her, is often not thought of as having been produced by a particular named individual. This is in part because what was handed down was almost always not the very words that the performer is saying or singing but only certain structures: the plot, certain phrases and formulas, perhaps some songs that intersperse the performance. (We have a familiar model to hand, of course, for such a situation, in the fairy tales we tell to children. Most people do not think of Cinderella as a story with a particular author: we think of it, rather, as a plot, which is retold to each generation of children with additions and embellishments that differ from performance to performance.)

The centrality of verbal performance in older African cultures, and the persistence of these modes of performance into the present, helps account for the fact that poetry is a favorite form of many contemporary African readers and writers (both in the colonial languages and in scores of other tongues). And the poems here represent the extraordinary range of languages and linguistic situations out of which poetry has grown in modern Africa.

Like much traditional oral poetry, a great deal of modern African poetry is directly engaged with problems of social and political life. (There is, of course, a great deal of political poetry in Europe and in North America: consider, for example, the celebrations of the French Revolution in Romantic poetry or the poetry of the Black Arts movement in the United States.) In the poetry of Africa in the colonial languages, a very substantial preponderance of work attends to questions that are political in the broadest sense; issues of kinship and kingship, marriage and war, nation and empire, power and possession. There is less of the celebration of romantic love that runs through Western poetry from Sappho on; or of the small moments of the everyday that are among the greatest subjects of modern poetry; and there is little of the cult of nature that we associate with English poetry since Romanticism. The rhythmic language of many oral performances, with its poetic drift away from the ordinary syntax of everyday speech, was already in wide use throughout Africa in praise-poems (which address rulers and others of high stature) and in funeral dirges (which mourn, but also locate the social position of the deceased). In a whole host of forms the poetic vernacular addressed questions of social life and history, hymning the ancestors, the heroes, the gods. It is natural enough, in places where oral poetry formed a fundamental part of the background, that modern writers should have chosen to attend to questions that mattered to them in a poetic form. Without the Western conventions that separate the proper subjects of poesy from those of prose (a distinction that arises most easily in written traditions), it is more than natural—it is, perhaps, inevitable—that writers addressed the questions that engaged them most intensely with the intensity of feeling that the formal features of poetry makes possible.

I do not want to overstate this point, since, as you will see, there are poems here that are not, in even the broadest sense, political. But that politics was at the center of the preoccupations of the five poets whose work is most extensively reproduced here is evident in the fact that two were Presidents, one a political prisoner in Nigeria, and the other two were active in struggles against racism in South Africa and neocolonialism in Kenya. In this political focus they are not unusual: the class of Africans educated in the Western manner in this century had to face profound political questions, because their situation was the product of an encounter with European military and economic power, and in this encounter their own societies had been vanquished. They had to think deeply about their situation and what their conquest meant for the fate of their cultures and traditions and for the future of the peoples they seemed destined to lead.

It is one of the great ironies of history that the concept most central to that reflection—the very idea of Africa—was itself a product of the encounter with European empires. Western-educated intellectuals articulated a resistance to colonialism not in the name of the specific precolonial societies whose heirs they were, but, almost always, in the name of Africa. The many colonial students gathered in London, Paris, and Lisbon in the years after the Second World War were brought together in their common search for political independence from a single metropolitan state. They were brought together too by the fact that their colonial rulers—those who helped as well as those who hindered—saw them all as Africans, first of all, because "race" was central to Europe's vision of them. But they were able to articulate a common vision of postcolonial Africa through a discourse inherited from prewar Pan-Africanism—a discourse that was the product, largely, of black citizens of the New World. Since what bound those African-American and Afro-Caribbean Pan-Africanists together was the African ancestry they shared, a racial understanding of their solidarity was, perhaps, an inevitable development. The tradition on which the Francophone intellectuals of the postwar era drew, whether articulated by Aimé Césaire, from the New World, or Léopold Senghor from the Old, shared the European and American view of race. Like Pan-Africanism, Negritude began with the assumption of the racial solidarity of the Negro.

The irony here is compounded if we reflect that Europe, as an idea, plays almost no role in the poetry of Europe, despite the fact that, since the Enlightenment, the intellectual and cultural life of the continent has been one of great interchange and mutual knowledge. By contrast, amid Africa's enormous cultural diversity—hundreds of mutually unintelligible languages and a great diversity of religious traditions and ideas of politics and of family life, only lately brought together through a shared relationship to the modern economy and to global politics—the poets, like other intellectuals, have taken Africa as a shared point of reference.

Appreciating these ironies, we can begin to notice that the Africa these poets assume is almost always, in fact, a way of referring to something much more local and particular than the continent as a whole. To put it simply, Africa in Senghor's poetry is almost always Senegal.

Who, then, apart from Senghor are the other major poets represented here? Agostinho Neto was a leader of the Angolan independence movement and, like Senghor, he was the first president of his country after its independence. But the struggle for Angolan independence was a long and bloody war, while Senegalese independence was the result of a gradual accommodation. There is, as a result, more conspicuously political energy in these poems than in Senghor's, though it is reflected in a sympathy with the oppressed rather than in a hostility to Portuguese (or to European) culture. Neto has been lucky in his translators: There is something especially powerful in W. S. Merwin's translations of "African Poem" and "Kinaxixi" in their unaffected lyricism.

In the Francophone and Lusophone (Portuguese-speaking) cultures of assimilation, the political leaders were poets. But in the English-speaking world, while they were intellectuals—Ghana's Kwame Nkrumah was a philosopher, Jomo Kenyatta in Kenya an anthropologist, Nnamdi Azikiwe in Nigeria a journalist—they were not, by and large, poets. Poetry was nourished in the universities, in journals like *Black Orpheus* (which first published the Merwin translations of Neto). Since Nigeria is by far the largest of the Anglophone states and has the largest number of universities, it is perhaps not surprising that it is the home of some of the finest Anglophone poetry: particularly noteworthy are Christopher Okigbo, with his substantial achievement, and Wole Soyinka, who became the first African to win the Nobel Prize for Literature. Soyinka's Nobel Prize reflects, perhaps foremost, the just assessment of his dramatic works as among the great literary achievements of our time, but that he has felt the urge to work in poetry is, I believe, a reflection, as much as anything else, of the call of oral poetry in the Yoruba cultural world from which he has drawn his sustenance.

Senghor, Neto, Okigbo, and Soyinka represent high points in poetry in the main colonial languages. Breyten Breytenbach's situation is hard to fit simply into the narrative of native and colonizer, because of the peculiar situation of Afrikaner culture in Southern Africa. Though Afrikaans is as central to the identity of many "Colored" South Africans as it is to the white Boers, from the point of view of most black South Africans, Afrikaans is just a colonial language and one that comes with a particularly brutal history of oppression. Afrikaner consciousness, in the period since World War II, has been shaped on the one hand as a culture of political domination, one that created the apartheid state, but on the other as a culture of resentment and insecurity. It is, in short, a culture typical of postcolonial elites.

From the sixties on, Afrikaners were increasingly aware of the pariah status of the racist state they had created. In this context it is a quite extraordinary act for an Afrikaner poet who is antiracist to seek to mobilize the Afrikaans language for modernist poetry. Typically the celebration of Afrikaans in South Africa has been a central project of the apartheid state, and that celebration has been culturally reactionary in the extreme. Breytenbach's unsentimental rigor, the bracing quality of his poetic idiom, reflects the almost quixotic character of his project of creating a space for a poetry in Afrikaans that is in revolt against apartheid.

The final poet, represented here by a significant number of lines, is Okot p'Bitek. P'Bitek's *Song of Lawino* has always struck me as capturing wonderfully something about the conflicts and confluences of our own life in Ghana, something representative of our lives on the cusp of the transition from colonial to postcolonial. P'Bitek, who grew up in Uganda, was conscious, as we were, of European cultures and of their impact on our own, but he also saw these interactions as moments not just of crisis but also of cultural opportunity, and he had, like us too, an attachment to the traditions we inherited that managed to combine the sentimental with the ironic.

In a sense Okot p'Bitek represents, in the panoply of modern African poetry, the persistence into contemporary poetry of an older—in this case Acholi—tradition. In *Song of Lawino,* he speaks in the voice of Lawino, an Acholi woman whose husband has been distanced from her by his (partial) assimilation of European culture. (P'Bitek also published a *Song of Ocol,* a cycle of poems in the voice of the husband. He was himself responsible for both the Acholi and the English versions of both poems.)

Much of the dramatic irony of these poems depends on the supposition that we know more than the speaker about the meaning of the European cultural practices that she describes from her own perspective. So the poems are at a crossing point between Acoli and English in ways that already distance them from older Acoli poetry. But we know that they work as Acoli poetry, because they have had a long and popular life in Acoli . . . including in p'Bitek's legendarily magical performances of them.

I have tried to construct a sampler of African poets worth attending to. In seeking excellence it is hard to be representative, especially in a world as multifarious as Africa. It is, after all, a continent of more than fifty nations, thirty million square kilometers, more than a thousand languages, and, to put it mildly, some considerable ecological, cultural, and ideological diversity. Paulin Hountondji, a leading Beninese intellectual, has written that it is a "simple, obvious truth that Africa is above all a continent and the concept of Africa an empirical, geographical concept and not a metaphysical one." If the experience of colonialism, the imposition of a few European languages, and a century of dialogue among African intellectuals across countries have produced some commonalities, it remains true that all the modern African poets worth reading have struggled in their own way with the call of older forms and alien models, of mother tongues and colonial dialects. These African masters begin with materials given by their tradition—genres, languages, notions of plot, historical references, other literary works that can be subtly echoed or alluded to—and add to it their own individual contribution, making from this rich cultural brew something of their own.

I learned in my childhood that once you have taken a poem in, it lives with you. Like a good old friend it will sit with you for long periods in silence, present but not pressing, surfacing suddenly to remind you that it still has things to say. Poems you have learned, that you have recited out

loud to yourself or to others, have an uncanny way of coming back when
you least expect them. Like Wordsworth's daffodils they "flash upon that
inward eye which is the bliss of solitude"—and you dance with them.

I have lived—and danced—with some of these poems all my adult
life. Others I have come to know more recently; they are new friends. I do
not know which of my friends—old and new—will become yours. All I
can do is introduce you to them and invite you to see which of them stays
with you, flashing upon *your* inward eye, filling *your* heart with pleasure.

LÉOPOLD SÉDAR SENGHOR

(1906–   )

Léopold Sédar Senghor was born in a multiethnic region of Senegal called Sine-Saloum, to Basile Digoye Senghor, a rich trader and landowner, and his wife, Gnilane Bakhoum. Koumba Ndofène Diouf, last king of the region, "called my father 'Uncle,' and they exchanged riddles," Senghor was to write later.

At the age of seven Senghor was dispatched to a Catholic mission school. Thereafter he was educated in French, going on to secondary school in Dakar, capital of the newly created Federation of French West Africa. A brilliant student, he won a scholarship to study in Paris, enrolling in the Lycée Louis-le-Grand, opposite the Sorbonne, where his classmates included another future president, Georges Pompidou. In 1935 he took the highly competitive French national exam, the *agrégation,* and, by passing, became the first African to qualify to teach in the French school and university system.

In the early thirties in Paris, Senghor met many of the blacks from the French Caribbean who formed the circle of the extraordinary Nardal sisters, Paulette and Jane. He was also introduced to African-American poetry and the literature of the Harlem Renaissance. It was within this milieu that Senghor and Aimé Césaire, from Martinique, articulated the ideas of Negritude, the most important modern literary movement in Africa and its diaspora. And it was under these influences that he developed into a major French—and at the same time a major African—poet.

Born a colonial subject, Senghor was by now a French citizen. He was drafted into the French army (in a regiment of colonial infantry) and taken prisoner by the Germans. After the war he became increasingly involved in politics. In 1949 he was elected to the European Assembly in Strasbourg. He continued to be deeply committed to literary life, publishing poems and editing in 1948 the *Anthology of the New Black and Malagasy Poetry in the French Language*. Despite its clumsy title, this book (with its controversial introduction by Jean-Paul Sartre) remains one of the models of African and Afro-Caribbean literary achievement.

But Senghor's political interests increasingly absorbed him, and his involvement in the movement for independence left him, in 1960, the first president of the new nation of Senegal. When he stepped down, on New Year's Day 1981, it was after two decades as the respected Catholic leader of a largely Moslem country.

His poems by themselves would justify Senghor a place in the history of our times. But they were written by the cofounder of the Negritude movement; by the first black member of the Académie Française, the highest cultural honor in a country that honors culture highly; by a man who was for twenty years the democratically elected president of Senegal, and who retired and handed over power constitutionally at the end of 1980. Each of these three considerable achievements would also warrant him more than a footnote in any history of our century, and it should astonish us that these accomplishments are the work of a single man and a splendid poet.

(All translations are by Melvin Dixon.)

IN MEMORIAM

Today is Sunday.
I fear the crowd of my fellows with such faces of stone.
From my glass tower filled with headaches and
    impatient Ancestors,
I contemplate the roofs and hilltops in the mist.
In the stillness—somber, naked chimneys.

Below them my dead are asleep and my dreams turn to
    ashes.
All my dreams, blood running freely down the streets
And mixing with blood from the butcher shops.
From this observatory like the outskirts of town
I contemplate my dreams lost along the streets,
Crouched at the foot of the hills like the guides of my
    race
On the rivers of the Gambia and the Saloum
And now on the Seine at the foot of these hills.
Let me remember my dead!
Yesterday was All Saints' Day, the solemn anniversary of
    the Sun,
And I had no dead to honor in any cemetery.
O Forefathers! You who have always refused to die,
Who knew how to resist Death from the Sine to the
    Seine,
And now in the fragile veins of my indomitable blood,
Guard my dreams as you did your thin-legged migrant
    sons!
O Ancestors! Defend the roofs of Paris in this dominical
    fog,
The roofs that protect my dead.
Let me leave this tower so dangerously secure
And descend to the streets, joining my brothers
Who have blue eyes and hard hands.

PORTE DORÉE

I have chosen to live near the rebuilt walls of my
    memory,
And from the top of the high ramparts
I remember Joal-of-the-Shades,
The face of the land of my blood.
I have settled down between City and country,

Where the City opens on the first breath of rivers and
      woods.
I miss the rooftops, nestled in private shrubs,
Draining away the water.
The smallest taxi makes my heart roll and dip
As if on the swells of the Atlantic.
Just one cigarette makes me stagger
Like a sailor on shore leave returning to ship.
And I say as awkwardly as the long-ago schoolboy from
      the bush:
"Good morning, Miss . . . How do you do?"

ALL DAY LONG . . .

All day long on the long and narrow rails
This iron will upon the listless sands
Through the drought in Cayor and Baol where baobab
      trees
Twist their arms in anguish
All day long and all along the line
Past the same small stations, the chattering black girls
Bursting from birdcages and school
All day long tossed about on the hard, bumpy benches
Of this iron train puffing and dusty
Here I am trying to forget Europe in the heartland of the
      Sine.

TOTEM

I must hide him down in my deepest veins
The Ancestor whose stormy skin
Streaks with lightning and thunder
He is the guardian animal I must hide
Lest I burst the dam of scandal.

He is my loyal blood demanding loyalty,
Protecting my naked pride against myself
And the arrogance of fortunate races . . .

CAMP 1940

To the Guélowâr

Guélowâr!
We have listened to you, we have heard you
With the ears of our heart.
Your voice has burst radiantly through our prison night
Like the roar of the Lord of the bush, and what a thrill
Raced up the spines of our bent backs!
We are small birds fallen from the nest,
Drooping bodies without hope,
Beasts with clipped claws, soldiers without weapons,
Naked men.
And here we are numb and clumsy as blind men without
      hands.
The purest among us have died: they couldn't swallow
The bread of shame. And here we are trapped in the nets,
Victims of the cruelty of civilized men,
Exterminated like wild boars. Glory to the tanks,
Glory to the airplanes!
We have searched for support but it crumbled like sand
From the dunes; sought leaders and they were absent;
Friends, and they no longer recognized us.
And we no longer recognized France.
We have cried out our despair into the night. No one
      answered.
The princes of the Church remained silent, and
      statesmen
Claimed the magnanimity of hyenas:
"It's a question of black men! It's about mankind! No!
Not when it concerns Europe."

Guélowâr!
Your voice tells us of honor, hope, and battle
And its wings rustle in our chest
Your voice tells us Republic, that we will build the City
In the blue daylight,
In the equality of fraternal people.
And we answer, "Present, O *Guélowâr!*"

Amiens Camp, September 1940

TO NEW YORK
(for jazz orchestra and trumpet solo)

New York! At first I was bewildered by your beauty,
Those huge, long-legged, golden girls.
So shy, at first, before your blue metallic eyes and icy
        smile,
So shy. And full of despair at the end of skyscraper
        streets
Raising my owl eyes at the eclipse of the sun.
Your light is sulphurous against the pale towers
Whose heads strike lightning into the sky,
Skyscrapers defying storms with their steel shoulders
And weathered skin of stone.
But two weeks on the naked sidewalks of Manhattan—
At the end of the third week the fever
Overtakes you with a jaguar's leap
Two weeks without well water or pasture all birds of the
        air
Fall suddenly dead under the high, sooty terraces.
No laugh from a growing child, his hand in my cool
        hand.
No mother's breast, but nylon legs. Legs and breasts
Without smell or sweat. No tender word, no lips,
Only artificial hearts paid for in cold cash

And not one book offering wisdom.
The painter's palette yields only coral crystals.
Sleepless nights, O nights of Manhattan!
Stirring with delusions while car horns blare the empty
    hours
And murky streams carry away hygienic loving
Like rivers overflowing with the corpses of babies.
See your rivers stirring with musk alligators
And sea cows with mirage eyes. No need to invent the
    Sirens.
Just open your eyes to the April rainbow
And your ears, especially your ears, to God
Who in one burst of saxophone laughter
Created heaven and earth in six days,
And on the seventh slept a deep Negro sleep.

SUDDENLY STARTLED

Suddenly startled at the fresh sound, the stabbing
    dagger.
I hover around the hurricane lamp, possessed like a
    moth,
Burning the wings of my soul on the siren song of your
    letters.
Here I am torn and charred, caught between the fear of
    death
And the terror of living. And no book can ease this
    anguish.
The spirit is more of a desert than the Sahara.

Here are the bitter ashes of my heart like a withered
    flower.
Only you, your presence, can save my hope.
You, my present tense, my indicative, my imperfect,

You, my perfect, not your letters, but your sunny lips
Of eternal summer.

And I await you with the expectation of reviving the
   dead.

I AM ALONE

I am alone in the plains
And in the night
With trees curled up from the cold
And holding tight, elbow to body, one to the other.

I am alone in the plains
And in the night
With the hopeless pathetic movement of trees
That have lost their leaves to other islands.

I am alone in the plains
And in the night.
I am the solitude of telegraph poles
Along deserted
Roads.

24

OKOT P'BITEK

(1931–1982)

Okot p'Bitek was born in Gulu, in the Acholi region of Uganda. He was educated there and later at King's College, Budo, and at the Teachers College in Mbarara. He began his career as a teacher at Sir Samuel Baker's School, in Gulu, before going on to acquire a diploma in education at Bristol University, in England; a law degree at Aberystwyth University, in Wales; and, finally, a B.Lit. in social anthropology at Oxford University.

Okot taught at Makerere University in Kampala, Uganda, at a time when it was perhaps the liveliest intellectual center in Anglophone Africa, and also lectured at the University of Ife, in Nigeria. His scholarly work included a critique of the way in which Africa's traditional religions were represented in Western scholarship and his own contribution to the field of the study of African religion, a book on the *Religion of the Central Luo*. He also collected and published Acholi proverbs, folk songs, and folk tales, as well as several volumes of essays on African culture and values.

Not only was Okot a prominent poet, critic, scholar, and folklorist, he was also the Director of the National Theatre of Uganda. But he is best known, in Uganda and elsewhere, for his work as a poet, both in English and Acholi; and especially for his *Song of Lawino* (1966) and *Song of Ocol* (1970). Okot p'Bitek died at fifty-one, while still actively engaged as a poet, critic, and folklorist.

The English-language versions of Okot's major poetic works represent a highly successful attempt to build on Acholi verse traditions, and both of these poems exist in Acholi versions, which have had a very successful life in performance for Acholi audiences. Okot's own performances, of these poems in both English and Acholi have an almost legendary status in the annals of contemporary African poetry, and anyone who reads them can see that they would work well as dramatic monologues. Still, the poems are not just translations of a preexisting Acholi form. The extended narrative of the wife's complaint about her Westernized husband in *Song of Lawino* depends on establishing an ironic gap between the speaker's knowledge—which is that of a "traditional" Acholi village woman—and that of the audience, which is presumed to know something of the "modern" world of the literate husband. The result is that the poem explicitly requires a distance between Acholi cultural tradition and the world of its audience.

Nevertheless, it is clear that the poem is far from being simply "on the side of modernity." While the audience needs to be familiar with the world of modern literacy, it is not assumed to identify with it wholly. Indeed *Song of Lawino* (like its companion poem *Song of Ocol*) is clearly hostile to the materialism of the new educated middle class: It rejects their shallow assumption of superiority to their unlettered brethren, and it criticizes their failure to appreciate the Acholi cultural traditions that Okot p'Bitek did so much to record, sustain, and develop.

The Woman with Whom I Share My Husband

Ocol rejects the old type.
He is in love with a modern woman,
He is in love with a beautiful girl
Who speaks English.

But only recently
We would sit close together, touching each other!
Only recently I would play
On my bow-harp
Singing praises to my beloved.
Only recently he promised

That he trusted me completely.
I used to admire him speaking in English.

Ocol is no longer in love with the old type;
He is in love with a modern girl.
The name of the beautiful one
Is Clementine.

Brother, when you see Clementine!
The beautiful one aspires
To look like a white woman;

Her lips are red-hot
Like glowing charcoal,
She resembles the wild cat
That has dipped its mouth in blood,
Her mouth is like raw yaws
It looks like an open ulcer,
Like the mouth of a field!
Tina dusts powder on her face
And it looks so pale;
She resembles the wizard
Getting ready for the midnight dance.

She dusts the ash-dirt all over her face
And when little sweat
Begins to appear on her body
She looks like the guinea fowl!

The smell of carbolic soap
Makes me sick,
And the smell of powder
Provokes the ghosts in my head;
It is then necessary to fetch a goat
From my mother's brother,
The sacrifice over
The ghost-dance drum must sound

The ghost be laid
And my peace restored.

I do not like dusting myself with powder:
The thing is good on pink skin
Because it is already pale,
But when a black woman has used it
She looks as if she has dysentery;
Tina looks sickly
And she is slow moving,
She is a piteous sight.

Some medicine has eaten up Tina's face;
The skin on her face is gone
And it is all raw and red,
The face of the beautiful one
Is tender like the skin of a newly born baby!

And she believes
That this is beautiful
Because it resembles the face of a white woman!
Her body resembles
The ugly coat of the hyena;
Her neck and arms
Have real human skins!
She looks as if she has been struck
By lightning;
Or burnt like the *kongoni*
In a fire hunt.

And her lips look like bleeding,
Her hair is long
Her head is huge like that of the owl,
She looks like a witch,
Like someone who has lost her head
And should be taken

To the clan shrine!
Her neck is rope-like,
Thin, long and skinny
And her face sickly pale.

Forgive me, brother,
Do not think I am insulting
The woman with whom I share my husband!
Do not think my tongue
Is being sharpened by jealousy.
It is the sight of Tina
That provokes sympathy from my heart.

I do not deny
I am a little jealous.
It is no good lying,
We all suffer from a little jealousy.
It catches you unawares
Like the ghosts that bring fevers;
It surprises people
Like earth tremors:

But when you see the beautiful woman
With whom I share my husband
You feel a little pity for her!

Her breasts are completely shrivelled up,
They are all folded dry skins,
They have made nests of cotton wool
And she folds the bits of cow-hide
In the nests
And calls them breasts!

O! my clansmen
How aged modern women
Pretend to be young girls!

They mould the tips of the cotton nests
So that they are sharp
And with these they prick
The chests of their men!
And the men believe
They are holding the waists
Of young girls that have just shot up!
The modern type sleep with their nests
Tied firmly on their chests.

How many kids
Has this woman suckled?
The empty bags on her chest
Are completely flattened, dried.
Perhaps she has aborted many!
Perhaps she has thrown her twins
In the pit latrine!

Is it the vengeance ghosts
Of the many smashed eggs
That have captured her head?
How young is this age-mate of my mother?

The woman with whom I share my husband
Walks as if her shadow
Has been captured,
You can never hear
Her footsteps;

She looks as if
She has been ill for a long time!
Actually she is starving
She does not eat,
She says she fears getting fat,
That the doctor has prevented her
From eating,

She says a beautiful woman
Must be slim like a white woman;

And when she walks
You hear her bones rattling,
Her waist resembles that of the hornet.
The beautiful one is dead dry
Like a stump,
She is meatless
Like a shell
On a dry river bed.

But my husband despises me,
He laughs at me,
He says he is too good
To be my husband.

Ocol says he is not
The age-mate of my grandfather
To live with someone like me
Who has not been to school.

He speaks with arrogance,
Ocol is bold;
He says these things in broad daylight.
He says there is no difference
Between me and my grandmother
Who covers herself with animal skins.

I am not unfair to my husband,
I do not complain
Because he wants another woman
Whether she is young or aged!
Who has ever prevented men
From wanting women?

Who has discovered the medicine for thirst?
The medicines for hunger
And anger and enmity
Who has discovered them?
In the dry season the sun shines
And rain falls in the wet season.
Women hunt for men
And men want women!

When I have another woman
With whom I share my husband,
I am glad
A woman who is jealous
Of another, with whom she shares a man,
Is jealous because she is slow,
Lazy and shy,
Because she is cold, weak, clumsy!

The competition for a man's love
Is fought at the cooking place
When he returns from the field
Or from the hunt,

You win him with a hot bath
And sour porridge.
The wife who brings her meal first
Whose food is good to eat,
Whose dish is hot
Whose face is bright
And whose heart is clean
And whose eyes are dark
Like the shadows:

The wife who jokes freely
Who eats in the open
Not in the bedroom,

One who is not dull
Like stale beer,
Such is the woman who becomes
The head-dress keeper.

I do not block my husband's path
From his new wife.
If he likes, let him build for her
An iron-roofed house on the hill!
I do not complain,
My grass-thatched house is enough for me.

I am not angry
With the woman with whom
I share my husband,
I do not fear to compete with her.

All I ask
Is that my husband should stop the insults,
My husband should refrain
From heaping abuses on my head.
He should stop being half-crazy,
And saying terrible things about my mother
Listen Ocol, my old friend,
The ways of your ancestors
Are good,
Their customs are solid
And not hollow
They are not thin, not easily breakable
They cannot be blown away
By the winds
Because their roots reach deep into the soil.

I do not understand
The ways of foreigners
But I do not despise their customs.

Why should you despise yours?
Listen, my husband,
You are the son of a Chief.
The pumpkin in the old homestead
Must not be uprooted!

—from *Song of Lawino*

25

Antonio Agostinho Neto

(1922–1979)

Antonio Agostinho Neto was born in the village of Kaxicane in Icolo-i-Bengo, nearly forty miles from Luanda, the capital of what was then the Portuguese colony of Angola. His father, Agostinho Pedro Neto, was a Methodist minister, in a country where Protestantism was associated with resistance to an officially Catholic colonial administration. The family soon moved to Luanda, where Pedro Neto had been offered a large urban church, as a result of which the young Agostinho was able to get the best education available for an African in the colony. There were only two public high schools in the country at the time, one of them in Luanda and the other in Lubango, and Neto was one of the few Africans of his generation to complete his secondary education.

After finishing high school in 1944, Neto went to the Salvador Coreia Lyceum in Luanda, where he distinguished himself academically. He went on to work in the health ministry, beginning a career as a civil servant. At the same time he became involved in setting up and developing a range of literary organizations, whose ostensibly cultural aims provided a cover for social and political discussion. The colonial administration of General Salazar banned all political organizations that might have proved hostile to the Portuguese regime, and as a result, for much of the period from World War II into the beginning of the military struggle for independence, literature was one of the main sites of anticolonial expression in the Lusophone world.

In 1947, with the help of an American Methodist missionary organization in New York, Neto received the funding to make his way to Portugal, to begin his studies as a medical student, first in Coimbra, and then at Lisbon University.

Lisbon at midcentury had a large number of students from the Portuguese colonies, especially in Africa, who met together at the Casa dos Estudantes do Império (a government-sponsored social center for students from the Portuguese colonies). There Neto came to know Amilcar Cabral, who was to be the leader of the anticolonial struggle in Portuguese Guinea, and Eduardo Mondlane, who was to found FRELIMO, the movement that led the struggle for the independence of Mozambique.

The young Lusophone intellectuals who met at the Casa dos Estudantes do Império were influenced both by the Negritude movement, led by the Senegalese Léopold Senghor and the Martiniquan Aimé Césaire, and also by their reading of the writers of the American Harlem Renaissance. But Neto's literary taste was also much influenced by Portuguese poets, including Fernando Pessõa, by the French poets Louis Aragon, Paul Éluard, and Jacques Prévert, and by his reading of modern fiction from Maxim Gorky to Jorge Amado to John Dos Passos.

Neto was a member of a group of Angolans in Lisbon who published in 1951 and 1952 the short-lived journal *Mensagem*, whose culturally nationalist slogan was "Let's discover Angola." Despite the obvious affinities of the *Mensagem* group with the spirit of Negritude, by the middle fifties Neto had come to believe that Negritude was too far removed from the lives of ordinary Africans and that it failed to recognize adequately the differences between the conditions in the different African colonies.

Throughout the late forties and early fifties, Neto was involved in political organizations affiliated with the Portuguese Communist Party, even while he was becoming known internationally as a major Lusophone poet. In 1951 he was imprisoned for the first time in Lisbon, for three months, because of this political work. In 1955 he was arrested and imprisoned again, and it was only after an international campaign led by intellectuals like Sartre and Aragon in France, Nicolas Guillén in Cuba, and Diego Rivera in Mexico, that he was released, in June 1957.

For the rest of his life Neto was involved in the struggle for Angolan independence. He worked from bases in Zaire, the People's Republic of

the Congo, and, finally, as president of the MPLA, the party that led
Angola to independence, from within Angola beginning in 1968. In
November 1975 the MPLA declared the independence of Angola, and
Neto became the new republic's first president. Four years later, in
September 1979, knowing that he was fatally ill, Neto flew to Moscow for
medical treatment. He died on September 10, 1979, in Moscow.

Because the first president of the Republic of Angola was both a
much-loved leader and a distinguished poet, Neto's poetry is regarded in
Angola as one of his legacies, and many Angolans can recite lines from his
work. While his poetry, like all his life's work, is grounded in the struggle
for independence and the development of a new nation, it also reflects a
love for the people and the landscape of his native land. It is crafted by a
poet who drew on a deep knowledge of modern poetry in Portuguese,
French, and English.

KINAXIXI

I was glad to sit down
on a bench in Kinaxixi
at six o'clock of a hot evening
and just sit there . . .

Someone would come
maybe
to sit beside me

And I would see the black faces
of the people going uptown
in no hurry
expressing absence in the
jumbled Kimbundu they conversed in.

I would see the tired footsteps
of the servants whose fathers also were servants
looking for love here, glory there, wanting

something more than drunkenness in every
alcohol.

Neither happiness nor hate.

After the sun had set
lights would be turned on and I
would wander off
thinking that our life after all is simple
too simple
for anyone who is tired and still has to walk.

(translated by W. S. Merwin)

AFRICAN POEM

There on the horizon
the fire
and the dark silhouettes of the imbondeiro trees
with their arms raised
in the air the green smell of burnt palm trees

On the road
the line of Bailundo porters
groaning under their loads of crueira*

in the room
the sweet sweet-eyed mulatress
retouching her face with rouge and rice-powder
the woman under her many clothes moving her hips
on the bed
the sleepless man thinking
of buying knives and forks to eat with at a table

On the sky the reflections
of the fire

*Crueira = maize flower.

and the silhouette of the blacks at the drums
with their arms raised
in the air the warm tune of marimbas

On the road the porters
in the room the mulatress
on the bed the sleepless man

The burning coals consuming
consuming with fire
the warm country of the horizons.

(translated by W. S. Merwin)

Saturday in the Sand-Slums

The sand-slums are humble townships
for humble folk

Comes Saturday
then everything is topsy-turvy with life itself
transformed into despair
into hope and into mystical anxiety

Anxiety encountered
in the meaning of things
and of human beings

in the full moon
burning instead of lamps
of street lighting:
how well poverty and moonlight
are paired

Anxiety
felt in uproar
and in the smell of alcoholic drinks
wafted through the air
with cries of grief and happiness
jumbled in bizarre orchestration
Anxiety
in the uniformed man
trapping another man
whom he subdues and lards with kicks
and when he has seen blood flow
puffs out his chest with satisfaction
at having maltreated a man

    Others will shy at passing
    where the truncheon has downed the man
    will turn on their heels
    will jump over walls
    will tread on prickles
    in unshod feet will cut themselves
    on the shards of bottles
    smashed by innocent children
    and every wife
    will sigh with relief
    when her husband comes safely home.

Anxiety
in the soldiers having fun
as they lurk in the shade of the cashew trees
in wait for the unwary passers-by

    At intervals
    moans of grief
    assail the ears
    wound timid hearts
    and steps move away

in a nerve-racking scurry
and after the laughter of some
unbridled louts
only uncanny silence tears of hatred
and flesh lacerated
by belt buckles

Anxiety
in those who wander
in search of easy pleasure
Anxiety in the man
skulking in a dark corner
violating a child

His wealth will silence her father
and the child
only belatedly
will cry out against fate

Anxiety heard
in a bar-room brawl

Partners arguing
shamelessly
over an old debt of a couple of quid
against the whispers
of numerous bystanders

Anxiety
in women
who have left their menfolk
to go and hear
their neighbor with angry shouts
railing against her husband's poverty

There are heard
hysterical sobs
the din of falling chairs
panting breath
the sorrowful clatter
of enamelled plates
and the crowd pours into the house
the squabblers push them out
and later comes the reconciliation
with soft giggles of pleasure

Anxiety
in the cinema loudspeakers
with gaping mouths
blaring swing
by the ticket offices
while a circus roundabout
trails in the whirligig of fancy
twinkling bulbs of reds greens blues
and as well
in exchange for twopence-halfpenny
lovers and children

Anxiety
in the homesick drumbeats
of Tchokwe contract workers
providing there in the encampment
a ground bass for all the din

    Lunda without frontiers
    to enclose the stirring
    of mutinous thirst

Anxiety
in the lowly child
who flees in fear from the policeman
on duty

Anxiety
in the sound of a guitar
accompanying a voice
which sings distant sambas
delightfully lazy
    burdening the air
    with the urge to burst into tears
    With the voice
    goes the cry of longing
    the multitude have for days unlived
    days of liberty
    and the night
    drinks their cares of life

Anxiety
in the drunkards falling in the streets
at dead of night

Anxiety
in the mothers with their shouts
in search of missing children

in the women who stagger by drunk

in the man
who consults the healer
to keep his job

in the woman
who begs philters from the fetishist
to keep her husband

in the mother
who asks the soothsayer
if her little girl will survive
pneumonia

in the hut
of old cracked tins

in the women beseeching
compassion
from Our Ladies

in the families at prayer
    while they worship
    drunkards urinate in the street
    huddling close to the wall
    then moving away
    to sneer at the prayers
    they have glimpsed
    through the window blinds

Anxiety in the masque
danced by the acetylene light
or the Petromax paraffin lamp
in a blue-painted hall
full of dust
and the reek of sweating bodies
and the swaying of haunches
and the contact of sexes

Anxiety
in those who laugh and in those who cry
in those who have insight
and in those who have breath but no understanding

Anxiety
in the dance halls
spewing out folk
where within moments
the lover bickers with his girlfriend

insults are hurled into the open
filling the locale with arguments
which spill out into the street
bringing the police flocking with their whistles

Anxiety
in the skeleton of stick and mud
bent threateningly
as it bears the weight of the zinc roof

and in the backyards
sown with excrement and foul smells
in the grease-stained sticks of furniture
in the sheets full of holes
and in the beds without mattresses

Anxiety
in those who discover passive crowds
awaiting their hour

In men
burns the desire to make the supreme effort
so that Man
shall be reborn in every man
and hope
shall turn no longer
into the lamentation of the crowd

Life itself
makes more purpose bloom
in the anxious looks of those who go by

Saturday jumbled night
in the townships
with mystical anxiety

and implacably
marches on unfurling heroic banners
in the enslaved souls.

(translated by Michael Wolfers)

THE GRIEVED LANDS

The grieved lands of Africa
in the tearful woes of ancient and modern slave
in the degrading sweat of impure dance
of other seas
grieved

The grieved lands of Africa
in the infamous sensation of the stunning perfume of the
flower
crushed in the forest
by the wickedness of iron and fire
the grieved lands

The grieved lands of Africa
in the dream soon undone in jinglings of gaolers' keys
and in the stifled laughter and victorious voice of
    laments
and in the unconscious brilliance of hidden sensations
of the grieved lands of Africa

      Alive
      in themselves and with us alive

They bubble up in dreams
decked with dances by baobabs over balances
by the antelope
in the perpetual alliance of everything that lives

They shout out the sound of life
shout it
even the corpses thrown up by the Atlantic
in putrid offering of incoherence and death
and in the clearness of rivers

They live
the grieved lands of Africa
in the harmonious sound of consciences
contained in the honest blood of men
in the strong desire of men
in the sincerity of men
in the pure and simple rightness of the stars' existence

They live
the grieved lands of Africa
because we are living
and are imperishable particles
of the grieved lands of Africa.

(translated by Michael Wolfers)

26

BREYTEN BREYTENBACH

(1939–)

Breyten Breytenbach was born in the small town of Bonnievale in the eastern Cape region of South Africa, into a conventional Afrikaner family. He studied painting at the University of Cape Town, but left South Africa in 1959 before finishing his degree. Then only twenty, he worked at various jobs in Europe, from the Mediterranean to Scandinavia, before finally settling in Paris, where he took up a career as a painter. In the 1960s he established a reputation substantial enough to warrant inclusion in exhibitions in France, Holland, and elsewhere.

In 1964 Breytenbach married a Vietnamese woman, Hoang Lien Ngo, thus entering into a relationship that would have been illegal (because "transracial") in his homeland. Breytenbach's failure to conform in his personal life to the racialist demands of his country (and his family) went along with explicit and public opposition to apartheid and with antiapartheid activism in Europe. His views were in stark contrast to those of his brothers, Jan—eventually a brigadier general in the South African army, whom Breytenbach described as "a trained (and enthusiastic) killer" and "a dirty tricks expert for Military Intelligence"—and Cloete, who was, again according to Breytenbach himself, a "fellow traveller" of the security police.

In 1964 Breytenbach was persuaded to publish some of the poems and short stories he had been writing for his own amusement. Two works—*Catastrophes,* a collection of short stories, and *The Iron Cow Must Sweat,* a volume of poetry—appeared to enormous critical acclaim in his native country. When he sought to travel home to receive a literary prize for these books, however, the South African authorities denied his wife a visa. Because of his reputation, both as painter and poet, this event provided ammunition for opponents of apartheid, and Breytenbach was drawn into the international apartheid movement as a South African celebrity in exile. There is therefore something of an irony in the fact that, despite his public opposition to a South African government that saw itself as the guardian of Afrikaner culture, his literary work was consistently well received in the Afrikaans literary establishment.

Over the next ten years or so, Breytenbach published six more volumes of poetry, as well as a novel and the nonfiction *A Season in Paradise,* an account of a trip he made with his wife to South Africa in 1972, when the authorities finally relented and allowed her a ninety-day visa.

In 1975 Breytenbach returned to South Africa, in disguise, under the name of Christian Galaska, to work underground for an offshoot of the African National Congress called Okhela. As it happens, Breytenbach's arrival back home was known to the South African security police, since it had been revealed by an informer within his circle in Europe, and after trailing him for a few days, the police arrested him. His family arranged for him to be legally represented by lawyers who were not used to dealing with such cases, and they persuaded him to agree to make a sort of confession in return for a reduction in the charges and a shortened sentence. In the end he was sentenced to nine years (having been given to understand that he would get five) of which he served seven, two of them in solitary confinement in Pretoria Central Prison. While in solitary confinement he wrote the beginnings of *Mouroir: Mirrornotes of a Novel* (which appeared first in French translation in 1983). The better-known *True Confessions of an Albino Terrorist,* which gives a (somewhat fragmentary) account of his trial and imprisonment, was published in 1984.

Breytenbach's writing draws on a fascinating range of sources. One is Zen Buddhism, which accounts, as the South African writer André Brink has written, for "the dazzling marriage of the real, the ordered, the rigorously disciplined world of the senses on the one hand, and the mystical and imaginary on the other." Another source is Rimbaud (Breytenbach's *A Season in Paradise* echoes and reverses the title of Rimbaud's *Saison en enfer*) and the formal devices of French symbolist poetry. Finally, his poetry falls into an Afrikaans tradition as well as having resonances occasionally with the work of the Negritude poets, including Aimé Césaire.

In a note on the politics of Afrikaans as a language at the end of *True Confessions,* Breytenbach writes: "To me it is of little importance whether the language dies of shame or is preserved and strengthened by its revolutionary impact. Of course it will be a loss if it were to die. . . . But I most certainly do not agree with the need to wage a struggle for the survival or the imposition of Afrikaans." As South Africa moves beyond the era of apartheid, the meaning of Afrikaans and its traditions continues to be debated—and in that debate one hope for its future as a language that need not "die of shame" must surely be the poetry of Breyten Breytenbach.

THREAT OF THE SICK

(for B. Breytenbach)

Ladies and Gentlemen, allow me to introduce you to Breyten
     Breytenbach,
the lean man in the green sweater; he is devout
and braces and hammers his oblong head
to fabricate a poem for you   for example:
I am scared to close my eyes
I don't want to live in the dark *and* see what goes on
the hospitals of Paris are crammed with pasty people
standing at the windows making threatening gestures
like the angels in the furnace
it's raining the streets flayed and slippery

my eyes are starched
on a wet day like this they/you will bury me
when the sods are raw black flesh
the leaves and jaded flowers snapped and stained with
    wetness

before the light can gnaw at them,   the sky sweats
    white blood
but I will refuse to coop up my eyes

pluck my bony wings
the mouth is too secretive not to feel pain
wear boots to my funeral so I can hear the mud
kissing your feet
like black blossoms the starlings tilt their smooth
    leaking heads
the green trees are monks, muttering

plant me on a hill near a pool under snapdragons
let the furtive bitter ducks crap on my grave
in the rain
cats are possessed by the souls of crazed yet cunning
    women
fears fears fears with drenched colourless heads
and I will refuse to comfort (soothe) my black tongue

Look he is harmless, have mercy on him

(translated by Denis Hirson)

DUNG-BEETLE

Anyone here ever seen a white beetle?

Neither have I

But it's a terrible creature
Like a missionary in Africa
with helmet and dark glasses

White beetles live in bright rooms: camouflage
Scampering lumps of sunlight on the wall

Up,
Beware the white beetle with its sting/its poison flask

Keep your eye peeled, do be sure
to look carefully under your bed at night.

(translated by André Brink)

BREYTEN PRAYS FOR HIMSELF

There is no need for Pain Lord
We could live well without it
A flower has no teeth

It is true we are only fulfilled in death
But let our flesh stay fresh as cabbage
Make us firm as pink fish
Let us tempt each other, our eyes deep butterflies

Have mercy on our mouths our bowels our brains
Let us always taste the sweetness of the evening sky
Swim in warm seas, sleep with the sun
Ride peacefully on bicycles through bright Sundays

And gradually we will decompose like old ships or trees
But keep Pain far from Me o Lord
That others may bear it
Be taken into custody, Shattered
> Stoned
> Suspended
> Lashed
> Used
> Tortured
> Crucified
> Cross-examined

Placed under house arrest
Given hard labor
Banished to obscure islands till the end of their days
Wasting in damp pits down to slimy green imploring
    bones
Worms in the stomachs heads full of nails
But not *Me*
But we never give Pain or complain

(translated by Denis Hirson)

WRITE OFF

why should the arabs come to my window
at night when only the clocks are alive
droning their miserable tunes
full of need and nostalgia

I must also go to bed and wait
for the rats of my feet to stifle
and grow still under the blankets. I also
like stroking an Africa of green

clay in the chart of my brain.
Go spew out your gruesome bat-like emotions
somewhere else: the chambers of
my head are all occupied

(translated by Denis Hirson)

CONSTIPATION

"No one has ever written or painted, sculpted,
modelled, built, invented except to get out of
hell."

Artaud referring to Van Gogh

For all true poetry is cruel

                                    it's not some sparrow
says Antonin Artaud somewhere
in an essay on the failure of Coleridge
or elsewhere in breaking down the success of Van Gogh
failure and decline relative
relative to the tongue of Artaud
                    for he had no soul
                    but a large mouth without teeth
                    that could fit a harness to the tongue

Not that Coleridge doesn't belong to the school of
        damned poets
            he says
the outcasts capable of ejecting at a given moment
a waxy fart of hideous pain
through the tunnel and turnstile of blood
        and there I agree
for what is a poem
other than a black wind?

Perhaps that is what Artaud wanted to say
that the anus of his own flesh was shod with teeth
from which sparrows could escape
                            but the crows stayed to nest
to devour
the tunnels and turnstiles and waiting rooms of blood

Coleridge travelled the oceans flat in search of the white
                            of an albatross
and that ideal is dead
Van Gogh's fears fly like black birds of prey
                        over the waves with eyes of corn
and he dies with a bullet in the belly

Artaud opens his jaws wide
the black and flabby crow tussles his nest
and dies without being able to lay a tooth

Excrement doesn't fly
                    and doesn't excrete

                              (translated by A. J. Coetzee)

THE BLACK CITY

above all guard yourself against bitterness, black child,
this, and that you are not allowed to dream;
take care not to choke in red eyes—fished in slop-pail,
not to let your body grow thick and rank from the gall
that will push on and on through your phosphorous
        veins
(between the cradle and the coffin there's only a screw);
rather cut and comb your papaw tree constantly
and remember the clouds perform for you too
and rats eat rubbish

I want to remember a black city, black child,
where you too swell in the sombre light;
seagulls dance like red balloons above the beach,
you too can laugh and live it up,
can fondle the water and build towns of sand
run up and down among hundreds of jokes

above all watch out for the slimy black papaw
of bitterness, black child
he that eats of it dies on bayonets
and in libraries,
dies alone in the mouth

look, over the sea the sun will be born
and the sun has a right hand and a left hand
and he'll be brown,
as war, and brown as the tickle throats of cocks

(translated by Leon de Kock and Sonia van Schalwyk)

EAVESDROPPER

for Stephen L.

you ask me how it is living in exile, friend—
what can I say?
that I'm too young for bitter protest
and too old for wisdom or acceptance
of my Destiny?
that I'm only one of many,
the maladjusted,
the hosts of expatriates, deserters,
citizens of the guts of darkness
one of the "Frenchmen with a speech defect"
or even that here I feel at home?

yes, but that I now also know the rooms of loneliness,
the desecration of dreams, the remains of memories,
a violin's thin wailing
where eyes look far and always further,
ears listen quietly inward
—that I too like a beggar
pray for the alms of "news from home,"
for the mercy of "do you remember,"
for the compassion of "one of these days"

but I do not remember,
songs have faded,
faces say nothing,
dreams have been dreamt

and as if you're searching for love in a woman's seaweed
    hair
you forget yourself in a shuffling nameless mass
of early ageing revolutionaries
of poets without language and blind painters,
of letters without tidings like seas without tides
of those who choke of the childishness of longing,
of those who call up spirits from the incense,
conjure up landscapes on their tongues,
throwing up the knowledge of self
—must I too give a deeper meaning?
that all of us are only exiles from Death
soon to be allowed to "go home"?

no, for now I begin, groping with hands rotted off
to understand those who were here before us
and all I ask of you
in the mane of what you want to know
be good to those who come after us

(translated by Ernst van Heerden)

PADMAPANI

Padmapani
No your body is no prison
your understanding has petals
sweeter than moonlight
your hair is a secret
black wave
a banner against the light
two butterflies have settled
on the twigs above your nose
if only to upset my pen
and each ear is a beach
against the wash of tides

your eyes are two shelters in the desert
two tents with brilliant peacocks
and my eyelashes lament on your shoulders
your back is a glistening lance in water
and soon after dusk your small dunes
rose from my palms
your heart moves with the quick
soundlessness of chewing peanuts
your hands are tom thumb
and all his brownish friends
where your thighs meet your belly
struts a small proud plume
o hail to the jewel in the lotus
how sweet it must be
to dive upwards
into that nothingness
no your body is no prison
Padmapani

(translated by André Brink)

27

WOLE SOYINKA

(1934–)

Is it any wonder, really, that modern African poetry is so often political? Few histories are more politicized than that of twentieth-century Africa. Unfortunate, then, that American critics often find poetry that is political somehow "off" or complain of its odor of propaganda. And yet if stirrings of heartstrings can serve poetry's purposes, it is probable that the heartrending tragedies of African colonial and postcolonial politics might also do the same trick.

Part of the politics in Africa is language: the official languages are not native ones, and, as conquered people will tell you, a language imposed is a language transformed. So it is for Wole Soyinka, who has written his way into Nigeria's history via an English that takes into account African rhythms, patterns, priorities, tonalities, cadences. Born in 1934 to Yoruba parents in western Nigeria, Wole Soyinka talked his way into school at the ripe age of two. He has never stopped talking since or, rather, taking command of the language, as a poet, playwright, critic, novelist, essayist, autobiographer, and translator, all. In 1986, he became the first African to win the Nobel Prize in Literature.

Formally educated at the Universities of Ibadan (Nigeria) and Leeds (England) in the 1950s, Soyinka's earliest and in a sense deepest education was growing up amid cultural clashes in Nigeria. The Yoruba people, so rich in tradition and art, gave Soyinka a deep sense of his Africanness. His father, Essay, fostered his intellectual growth: known throughout the village of Ake as a man who could work an argument from morning to midnight, Essay encouraged his son in the art of the well-turned argument, much to his mother's dismay. Once, when caught speaking in church, young Wole demanded, amid a congregation full of worshipers, could the sexton be absolutely sure that it was Wole who had spoken? Upon hearing of his son's heresy, the normally strict Essay pondered for a moment—and then agreed that perhaps the sexton had met his match. Wole was yet three years old. He was on his way to a life full of pointed questions.

Though Soyinka didn't join a political party till the 1970s—some twenty-five years after he began writing—Nigerian, and African, politics fueled, in ways both implicit and explicit, much of his writing. He resigned his post at the University of Ife in 1963 to protest the government's crackdown on free expression. Arrested in 1967 and held nearly incommunicado for twenty-six months, his jail experience formed his second volume of poetry, *A Shuttle in the Crypt*. Once released from prison, he spent the next six years in exile, returning to Nigeria in 1975. The following year he published *Ogun Abibiman,* his epic poem interpreted as a direct call to action against South Africa's white government. As Soyinka's pen steeped itself in personal and public crises—colonialism's crimes, his country's civil wars and bloody turnovers, his two years in solitary confinement, liberation both political and personal—it deftly blended African (particularly Yoruban) traditions, language, and vision with a locally produced English which sharply defines what it is to be African in the twentieth century.

For Soyinka, like too many of his fellow Africans, his road led him into "voluntary" exile. Only quite recently has it become safe for Soyinka to return to his homeland, and he now alternates between living in Nigeria and teaching in the United States. In America his reputation as a poet has been overshadowed by his work in other genres, notably the theater. The inclusion of his poetry here, along with a passage of poetic prose and verse lines from a play, is testimony to a singularly vital intelligence working in a renaissance variety of forms.

—*Anne Detrick*

IKEJA, FRIDAY, FOUR O'CLOCK

They were but gourds for earth to drink therefrom
the laden trucks, mirage of breath and form

Unbidden offering on the lie of altars
A crop of wrath when hands retract and reason falters

No feast but the eternal retch of human surfeit
No drink but dregs of reckoning of loss and profit

Let nought be wasted, gather up for recurrent session
Loves of led, lusting in the sun's recession

POST MORTEM

there are more functions to a freezing plant
than stocking beer, cold biers of mortuaries
submit their dues, harnessed—glory be!

in the cold hand of death . . .
his mouth was cotton filled, his man-pike
shrunk to sub-soil grub

his head was hollowed and his brain
on scales—was this a trick to prove
fore-knowledge after death?
his flesh confesses what has stilled
his tongue; masked fingers think from him
to learn, how not to die

let us love all things of grey: grey slab
grey scalpel, one grey seep and form,
grey images

TELEPHONE CONVERSATION

The price seemed reasonable, location
Indifferent. The landlady swore she lived
Off premises. Nothing remained
But self-confession. "Madam," I warned,
"I hate a wasted journey—I am African."
Silence. Silenced transmission of
Pressurized good-breeding. Voice, when it came,
Lipstick-coated, long gold-rolled
Cigarette-holder pipped. Caught I was, foully.
"HOW DARK?" . . . I had not misheard . . . "ARE
    YOU LIGHT
OR VERY DARK?" Button B. Button A. Stench
Of rancid breath of public hide-and-speak.
Red booth. Red pillar-box. Red double-tiered
Omnibus squelching tar. It *was* real! Shamed
By ill-mannered silence, surrender
Pushed dumbfoundment to beg simplification.
Considerate she was, varying the emphasis—
"ARE YOU DARK? OR VERY LIGHT?" Revelation came.
"You mean—like plain or milk chocolate?"
Her assent was clinical, crushing in its light
Impersonality. Rapidly, wave-length adjusted,
I chose, "West African sepia"—and as afterthought,
"Down in my passport." Silence for spectroscopic
Flight of fancy, till truthfulness changed her accent
Hard on the mouthpiece. "WHAT'S THAT?" conceding
"DON'T KNOW WHAT THAT IS." "Like brunette?"
"THAT'S DARK, ISN'T IT?" "Not altogether.
Facially, I am brunette, but madam, you should see
The rest of me. Palm of my hand, soles of my feet
Are a peroxide blond. Friction, caused—
Foolishly, madam—by sitting down, has turned
My bottom raven black—One moment, madam!"—
    sensing

Her receiver rearing on the thunderclap
About my ears—"Madam," I pleaded, wouldn't you
    rather
See for yourself?"

ISARA, THE ANCESTRAL VILLAGE

. . . bored voices, vacant stares, stirring to life only
when the *mallam*'s sporadic whip beat a slow tattoo on
their docile heads. Nothing really stirred, not the sheep
with huge pregnancies hugging the shadows of red mud
walls. The solitary hawker made the rounds of the few
tenanted passages, her hawking cries more dirged than
full-throated, no rousing accent to entice the indifferent.
Built into the hillside of red laterite, Isara at such
periods was neither hostile nor welcoming; it was simply
indifferent, the stone shrapnels of its walls and rust of
corrugated roofs belying the lushness of the valley below,
which wove a moist sash round the town on nearly every
side. Why, Akinyode sometimes wondered, had his
ancestors chosen to build on such inclement soil? Was it
a need for safety in those earlier, uncertain times? Yet the
town looked exposed to any determined incursion. The
wooded valleys were perfect hiding places for an enemy;
he could lay indefinite siege to these birdcages tucked
precariously against the naked sides and ridges of a
natural cantilevered hill.

One did not notice these features when the town
came to life in season. Then Isara metamorphosed into a
giddy butterfly. . . .

—from *Isara*

CIVILIAN AND SOLDIER

My apparition rose from the fall of lead,
Declared, "I'm a civilian." It only served
To aggravate your fright. For how could I
Have risen, a being of this world, in that hour
Of impartial death! And I thought also: nor is
Your quarrel of this world.
                    You stood still
For both eternities, and oh I heard the lesson
Of your training sessions cautioning—
Scorch earth behind you, do not leave
A dubious neutral to the rear. Reiteration
Of my civilian quandary, burrowing earth
From the lead festival of your more eager friends
Worked the worse on your confusion, and when
You brought the gun to bear on me, and death
Twitched me gently in the eye, your plight
And all of you came clear to me.
                    I hope some day
Intent upon my trade of living, to be checked
in stride by your apparition in a trench,
Signalling, I am a soldier. No hesitation then
But I shall shoot you clean and fair
With meat and bread, a gourd of wine
A bunch of breasts from either arm, and that
Lone question—do you friend, even now, know
What it is all about?

A MAN'S FIRST DUTIES

Baroka: [*more and more desperate.*]
    Does he not beget strength on wombs?
    Are his children not tall and stout-limbed?
Sidi: Once upon a time.
Baroka: Once upon a time?
    What do you mean, girl?
Sidi: Just once upon a time.
    Perhaps his children have of late
    Been plagued with shyness and refuse
    To come into the world. Or else
    He is so tired with the day's affairs
    That at night, he turns his buttocks
    To his wives. But there have been
    No new reeds cut by his servants,
    No new cots woven.
    And his household gods are starved
    For want of child-naming festivities
    Since the last two rains went by.
Baroka: Perhaps he is a frugal man.
    Mindful of years to come,
    Planning for a final burst of life, he
    Husbands his strength.
Sidi [*giggling. She is actually stopped, half-way,*
    by giggling at the cleverness of her remark.]
    To husband his wives surely ought to be
    A man's first duties—at all times.

—from *The Lion and the Jewel*

ABIKU

> *Wanderer child. It is the same child who dies and*
> *returns again and again to plague the mother.*
> —*Yoruba belief*

In vain your bangles cast
Charmed circles at my feet
I am Abiku, calling for the first
And repeated time.

Must I weep for goats and cowries
For palm oil and the sprinkled ash?
Yams do not sprout amulets
To earth Abiku's limbs.

So when the snail is burnt in his shell,
Whet the heated fragment, brand me
Deeply on the breast—you must know him
When Abiku calls again.

I am the squirrel teeth, cracked
The riddle of the palm; remember
This, and dig me deeper still into
The god's swollen foot.

Once and the repeated time, ageless
Though I puke, and when you pour
Libations, each finger points me near
The way I came, where

The ground is wet with mourning
White dew suckles flesh-birds
Evening befriends the spider, trapping
Flies in wine-froth;

Night, and Abiku sucks the oil
From lamps. Mothers! I'll be the
Suppliant snake coiled on the doorstep
Yours the killing cry.

The ripest fruit was saddest;
Where I crept, the warmth was cloying.
In silence of webs, Abiku moans, shaping
Mounds from the yolk.

FROM "FUNERAL IN SOWETO"

We wish only to bury our dead. Shorn
Of all but name, our indelible origin,
For indeed our pride once boasted empires,
Kings and nation builders. Seers. Too soon
The brace of conquest circumscribed our being
Yet found us rooted in that unyielding
Will to life bequeathed from birth; we
Sought no transferred deed of earthly holding.
Slaves do not possess their kind. Nor do
The truly free.

We wished to bury our dead,
We rendered unto Caesar what was Caesar's.
The right to congregate approved;
Hold procession, eulogize, lament
Procured for a standard fee. All death tariff
Settled in advance, receipted, logged.
A day to cross the barriers of our skins,
Death was accorded purchase rights, a brief license
Subject to withdrawal—we signed acceptance
On the dotted line—"orderly conduct" et cetera.
We now proceed to render earth's to earth.

We wish to mourn our dead. No oil tycoons
We, Mandela, no merchant princes, scions
Of titled lineage. No peerage aspirants
Nor tribal chieftains. Only the shirtless
Ghetto rats that briefly left
The cul-de-sac of hunger, stripes,
Contempt. The same that rose on hind legs
That brief hour in Sharpeville, reddening
The sleepy conscience of the world. We,
The sludge of gold and diamond mines,
Half-chewed morsels of canine sentinels
In Nervous chain stores, snow-white parks.
Part-crushed tracks of blinded Saracens,
The butt of hippo trucks, water cannon mush.

We, the bulldozed, twisted shapes of
Shanty lots that mimic black humanity.
Our dead bore no kinship to the race
Of lordly dead, sought no companion dead
To a world they never craved.
We set to mourn dead, bugling
No Last Post, no boom of guns in vain salute.

But others donned a deeper indigo than the bereaved.
Unscheduled undertakers spat their lethal dirge
And fifty-eight were sudden bright-attired,
Flung to earth in fake paroxysms of grief.
And then we knew them, counted, laid them out,
Companion voyages to the dead we mourned.

And now, we wish to bury our dead. . . .

28

A Sampling of Other African Poets

Dennis Brutus (South Africa)

Nightsong: City

Sleep well, my love, sleep well:
the harbour lights glaze over restless docks,
police cars cockroach through the tunnel streets

from the shanties creaking iron-sheets
violence like a bug-infested rag is tossed
and fear is immanent as sound in the wind-swung bell;

the long day's anger pants from sand and rocks;
but for this breathing night at least,
my land, my love, sleep well.

Antonio Jacinto (Angola)

Letter from a Contract Worker

I wanted to write you a letter
my love.

a letter that would tell
of this desire
to see you
of this fear
of losing you
of this more than benevolence that I feel
of this indefinable ill that pursues me
of this yearning to which I live in total surrender . . .

I wanted to write you a letter
my love.
a letter of intimate secrets,
a letter of memories of you.
of you
of your lips red as henna
of your hair black as mud
of your eyes sweet as honey
of your breasts hard as wild orange
of your lynx gait
and of your caresses
such that I can find no better here . . .
I wanted to write you a letter
my love.
that would recall the days in our haunts
our nights lost in the long grass
that would recall the shade falling on us from the plum
trees
the moon filtering through the endless palm trees
that would recall the madness
of our passion
and the bitterness
of our separation

I wanted to write you a letter
my love.

that you would not read without sighing
that you would hide from papa Bombo
that you would withhold from mama Kieza
that you would reread without the coldness
of forgetting
a letter to which in all Kilombo
no other would stand comparison . . .

I wanted to write you a letter
my love
a letter that would be brought to you by the passing
   wind
a letter that the cashews and coffee trees
the hyenas and buffaloes
the alligators and grayling
could understand
so that if the wind should lose it on the way
the beasts and plants
with pity for our sharp suffering
from song to song
lament to lament
gabble to gabble
would bring you pure and hot
the burning words
the sorrowful words of the letter
I wanted to write to you my love . . .

I wanted to write you a letter . . .

But oh my love, I cannot understand
why it is, why it is, why it is, my dear
that you cannot read
and I—Oh the hopelessness!—cannot write!

(translated by Michael Wolfers)

LENRIE PETERS (GAMBIA)

ISATOU DIED

Isatou died
When she was only five
And full of pride
Just before she knew
How small a loss
It brought to such a few.
Her mother wept
Half grateful
To be so early bereft
And did not see the smile
As tender as the root
Of the emerging plant
Which sealed her eyes
The neighbors wailed
As they were paid to do
And thought how big a spread
Might be her wedding too.
The father looked at her
Through marble eyes and said:
"Who spilled the perfume
Mixed with morning dew?"

BERNARD DADIÉ (IVORY COAST)

I GIVE YOU THANKS MY GOD

I give you thanks my God for having created me black,
For having made of me
The total of all sorrows,
and set upon my head
the World.

I wear the livery of the Centaur
And I carry the World since the first morning.

White is a color improvised for an occasion
Black, the color of all days
And I carry the World since the first night.

I am happy
with the shape of my head
fashioned to carry the World,
satisfied with the shape of my nose,
Which should breathe all the air of the World,
happy
with the form of my legs
prepared to run through all the stages of the World.

I give you thanks my God, for having created me black,
for having made of me
the total of all sorrows.
Thirty-six swords have pierced my heart.
Thirty-six brands have burned my body,
And my blood on all the calvaries has reddened the
        snow,
And my blood from all the cast has reddened nature.
And yet I am
Happy to carry the World,
Content with my short arms,
with my long legs,
with the thickness of my lips.

I give you thanks my God, for having created me black,
White is a color for an occasion,
Black the color of all days
And I carry the World since the morning of time.
And my laughter in the night brought forth day over
        the World.
I give you thanks my God for having created me black.

ABENA BUSIA (GHANA)

LIBERATION

We are all mothers.
and we have that fire within us,
of powerful women
whose spirits are so angry
we can laugh beauty into life
and still make you taste
the salt tears of our knowledge—
For we are not tortured
anymore:
we have seen beyond your lies and disguises,
and *we* have mastered the language of words,
we have mastered speech
And know
we have also seen ourselves
We have stripped ourselves raw
and naked piece by piece until our flesh lies flayed
with blood on our *own* hands
What terrible thing can you do to us
which we have not done to ourselves?
What can you tell us
which we didn't deceive ourselves with
a long time ago?
You cannot know how long we cried
until we laughed
over the broken pieces of our dreams.
Ignorance
shattered us into such fragments
we had to unearth ourselves piece by piece,
to recover with our own hands such unexpected relics
even we wondered
how we could hold such treasure.
Yes, we have conceived

to forge our mutilated hopes
into the substance of visions
beyond your imaginings
to declare the pain if our deliverance
So do not even ask,
do not ask what it is we are labouring with *this* time.
Dreamers remember their dreams
when we are disturbed—
And you shall not escape
what we *will* make
of the broken pieces of our lives.

GABRIEL OKARA (NIGERIA)

ONE NIGHT AT VICTORIA BEACH

The wind comes rushing from the sea,
the waves curling like mambas strike
the sands and recoiling hiss in rage
washing the Aladuras' feet pressing hard
on the sand and with eyes fixed hard
on what only hearts can see, they shouting
pray, the Aladuras pray; and coming
from booths behind, compelling highlife
forces ears; and car lights startle pairs
arm in arm passing washer-words back
and forth like haggling sellers and buyers—

Still they pray, the Aladuras pray
with hands pressed against their hearts
and their white robes pressed against
their bodies by the wind; and drinking
palmwine and beer, the people boast
at bars at the beach. Still they pray.

They pray, the Aladuras pray
to what only hearts can see while dead
fishermen long dead with bones rolling
nibbled clean by nibbling fishes, following
four dead cowries shining like stars
into deep sea where fishes sit in judgment;
and living fishermen in dark huts
sit round dim lights with Babalawo
throwing their souls in four cowries
on sand, trying to see tomorrow.

Still they pray, the Aladuras pray
to what only hearts can see behind
the curling waves and the sea, the start
and the subduing unanimity of the sky
and their white bones beneath the sand.

And standing dead on dead sands,
I felt my knees touch living sand—
but the rushing wind killed the budding words.

MICERE GITHAE MUGO (KENYA)

WHERE ARE THOSE SONGS?

Where are those songs
my mother and yours
always sang
fitting rhythms
to the whole
vast span of life?

What was it again
they sang
      harvesting maize, threshing millet, storing the grain

What did they sing
bathing us, rocking us to sleep . . .
and the one they sang
stirring the pot
(swallowed in parts by choking smoke)?

What was it
the woods echoed
as in long file
my mother and yours and all the women on our ridge
beat out the rhythms
trudging gaily
as they carried
piles of wood
· through those forests
miles from home
What song was it?

And the row of bending women
hoeing our fields
to what beat
did they
break the stubborn ground
as they weeded
our *shambas*?

What did they sing
at the ceremonies
    child-birth
    child-naming
    second birth
    initiation . . . ?
how did they trill the *ngemi*
What was
the warriors' song?
how did the wedding song go?

sing me
the funeral song
What do you remember?

Sing
    I have forgotten
    my mother's song
    my children
    will never know
This I remember:
Mother always said
    sing child sing
    make a song
    and sing
    beat out your own rhythms
    and rhythms of your life
    but make the song soulful
    and make life
    sing
Sing daughter sing
around you are
unaccountable tunes
some sung
others unsung
sing them
to your rhythms
observe
listen
absorb
soak yourself
bathe
in the stream of life
    and then sing
    sing
    simple songs
    for the people

for all to hear
and learn
and sing
with you

KOFI AWOONOR (GHANA)

SONG OF WAR

I shall sleep in white calico;
War has come upon the sons of men
And I shall sleep in calico;
Let the boys go forward,
Kpli and his people should go forward:
Let the white man's guns boom.
We are marching forward;
We all shall sleep in calico.

When we start, the ground shall shake;
The war is within our very huts;
Cowards should fall back
And live at home with the women;
They who go near our wives
While we are away at battle
Shall lose their calabashes when we come.

Where has it been heard before
That a snake has bitten a child
In front of its own mother
The war is upon us
It is within our very huts
And the sons of men shall fight it
Let the white man's guns boom
And its smoke cover us
We are fighting them to die

We shall die on the battlefield
We shall like death at no other place.
Our guns shall die with us
And our sharp knives perish with us
We shall die on the battlefield

MAZISI KUNENE (ZULU–SOUTH AFRICA)

ELEGY FOR MY FRIEND E. GALO

You died without my knowing
When I was out collecting firewood
To roast the meat,
That we may dance over the earth,
Even with white fat oxen;
And dance, not caring for the shape of their horns.
You died without my knowing,
When I thought I would tell you stories
Saying 'once upon a time on the earth'—
Meaning we who are one with the years
Meaning the beating of the hearts
Beating against the muscles of their desires.
I bought them expensively with gold.
You died without my knowing
You covered me with shame
As I followed you,
Admonishing those who carried you
Not to imitate you
And say death is a common thing.
If it were true I would not be here,
I would not have known that locusts
Greedily reap the fields
Leaving the discordant symphony of naked stars.
It is these that wept over the centuries.

CHRISTOPHER OKIGBO (NIGERIA)

ON THE NEW YEAR

Now it is over, the midnight funeral that parts
The old year from the new;
And now beneath each pew
The warden dives to find forgotten missals
Scraps of resolutions and medals;
And over lost souls in the graves
Amid the tangled leaves
The Wagtail is singing:
Cheep cheep cheep the new year is coming;
Christ will come again, the churchbell is tinging
Christ will come again after the argument in heaven
Christ . . . Nicodemus . . . Magdalen . . .
Dung dong ding . . .

And the age rolls on like a wind glassed flood,
And the pilgrimage to the cross is the void . . .

And into the time time slips with a lazy pace
And time into time
And need we wait while time and the hour
Roll, waiting for power?

II

To wait is to linger
With the hope that the flood will flow dry;
To hope is to point an expectant finger
At fate, fate that has long left us to lie
Marooned on the sands
Left with dry glands
To suckle as die.

Wait indeed, wait with grief laden
Hearts that throb like a diesel engine.
Throbbing with hopes:
Those hopes of men those hopes that are nowhere,
Those nebulous hopes, sand castles in the air—

Wait and hope?
The way is weary and long and time is
Fast on our heels;
Or forces life to a headlong conclusion
Nor yet like crafty Heracles
Devolve on someone else
The bulk of the globe?

III

Where then are the roots, where the solution
To life's equation?

The roots are nowhere
There are no roots here
Probe if you may
From now until doomsday.

We have to think of ourselves as forever
Soaring and sinking like dead leaves blown by a gust
Floating choicelessly to the place where
Old desires and new born hopes like bubbles burst
Into nothing—blown to the place of fear
To the cross in the void;
Or else forever playing this zero-sum game
With fate as mate, and forever
Slaying and mating as one by one
Our tombstones rise in the void.

PART V

ASIA

29

INDIA

WHAT IS INDIAN LITERATURE?

Anita Desai

If the words "Russian literature" instantly evoke a picture of a dacha in the snowy birch woods, the barbed wire of Siberian camps, white nights, and brooding darkness; and "American literature" conveys a picture of the rolling Mississippi, log cabins in cotton fields, and high-rise commotion in neon-lit cities, then what do the words "Indian literature" convey?

Antiquity, first of all—traditions that go so far back in time as to enter a primeval world that is arboreal rather than pastoral, a formal wilderness in which sages meditate and courtesans dance. Old set-in-stone orthodoxies—of family, caste, and religion. Patterns as timeless as the constellations in the sky.

This timeless archetype is now overlaid by the quite contemporary strife, violence, and chaotic motion that are a result of the true pluralities and the volatility of a country on the move, asserting the varied identities of its many-segmented society.

The word often used by Indians to describe the present scene is "fissi-parous"—and yet, if one explores Indian literature, one would come away with a sense of its underlying unity and immutability. All Indian writers would describe a landscape with the stock features of a mango grove, a river-bank, cattle raising dust along a country path, a village well, and a crescent moon. All Indian writers—and painters and filmmakers—depict mothers as self-sacrificing and hardworking, fathers as stern and authoritarian, money-lenders as cruel and vicious, peasants as ignorant and starving victims.

This may be a sweeping generalization—but to dip into Indian literature—or into Indian film or television—is to discover that there are really very few exceptions, and to realize that exceptions are not what is wanted of art (any more than of a family, or society). What *is* wanted is ever-new variations of old themes, not anything unfamiliar or unexpected, but what is known to give satisfaction through the centuries, to be instantly recognized, and therefore provide this satisfaction once again. The great epics, the *Ramayana* and the *Mahabharata,* will never cease to yield that—they can be counted on for that.

This is not to accuse the art scene of stagnation and stultification but to point out that the Indian writers use character as they do the features of the landscape—to represent wider truths. Typically, they do not regard a character, or a tree, or a hill, as unique and particular. They see them as symbols of the larger concepts that are considered the only fit subjects for art: A river represents all rivers, a tree all trees, a lover all lovers, and the beloved always the beloved.

This is the literature to which I was born—more important, the way of thinking to which I was born. So I took for granted the stability, the intrinsic steadfastness, of the Indian literary scene I came upon when I started to write. The scene was dominated by the idols who had stood the test of time—Kalidas, Tagore, Bharati—and, in the language I chose to use, by the triumvirate of Raja Rao, R. K. Narayan, and Mulk Raj Anand. All I could expect to do was to bring along my own little pebble to place at their feet. T. S. Eliot had described this circumstance thus: "[T]he existing monuments form an ideal order among themselves, which is modified by the introduction of the new work of art among them."

Even those of us who read and wrote the colonial tongue, English, a mere upstart with only three hundred years in India, felt the same aura of tradition. We received it twofold—from Indian classical literature and from the Victorian literature of the West. Both had a towering presence, casting us, the younger writers, into the shadows in which we dwelt.

If I were asked to characterize the literary scene when I was young, then it would be by that image: shadows. We were muted, chastened, terribly conscious of our own insignificance. No Indian publisher wanted to publish new writers, and no publisher in the West was interested in writing from such a remote, unknown area. We had readers nowhere—Indians preferred the classics and, if in search of the contemporary, looked to the West.

An entirely unexpected event occurred in 1980: Salman Rushdie wrote *Midnight's Children.* Not only did his book break upon the Western scene with its novelty of voice and vision but he was presenting present-day, postindependence India in the language spoken on Indian streets, recognizable to all. This, we said, was our India. Here, we saw, was the circular style of narrative, that serpent's tail of an epic that Raja Rao had described in *Kanthapura:* "Our paths are interminable . . . we have neither punctuation nor the treacherous 'ats' and 'ons' to bother us—we tell one interminable tale. Episode follows episode, and when our thoughts stop, our breaths stop, and we move on to another thought. This was and still is the ordinary style of our story-telling."

Now retold by Rushdie's hero, Saleem Sinai: "There were so many tales to tell, too many, such an excess of intertwined lives events, miracles plans rumours, so dense a commingling of the improbable and the mundane! I have been a swallower of lives, and to know me, just one of me, you'll have to swallow the whole lot as well."

In the West readers saw in it the "magical realism" of Latin America and Eastern Europe. But in India we knew better—this was the ancient style of storytelling that had traveled so far westward that, the world being the shape it is, it had come around to the East again. Rushdie was of the here and now, writing in the language of today; it had hardly mattered if it was English or Hindi or Urdu, it was dense, rich, and vital.

Younger writers rose to the challenge with a kind of delight reflected in the work of such writers as Amitav Ghosh, Allan Searly, Upmanyu Chatterji, and Mukul Keshvani. It was as if their tongues had found release. In response Indian publishers—an almost nonexistent species in my youth, dusty and spidery creatures content endlessly to churn out reprints of old textbooks—bestirred themselves to publish these writers who were suddenly in the limelight, both in India and the West. It is true that it was the novel that seemed the chosen form for this new wave of expression: Poetry has remained the art of the minority. If it too adapts the new freedom of tongue, it may become central to Indian life, as it was in the past. At the moment it is the lyrics of the songs sung in the Indian films that revel in such centrality.

Certainly, however, a new energy seems to course through that sluggish old serpent asleep on a ledge in the shadowy cave. It raises its head, it flicks its tongue, blinks at the glare of publicity, puzzled by the huge audience, the new celebrity status of authors: What is this? Is it good? Is it bad? Then it yawns and retreats, coil upon coil upon coil on the ledge in the shadows of the cave. Let another thousand years pass. . . .

A. K. RAMANUJAN (1929–1993)

Attipat Krishnaswami Ramanujan was born into a Tamil-speaking family living in Mysore, where his father taught astronomy and mathematics at the university. Originally a student of science, Ramanujan turned to English at the University of Mysore. Shakespeare was his first and abiding love, and the subject of his first courses when he became a teacher successively at Kerala and Dharwar. In 1957 he entered the Rockefeller-sponsored program in linguistics at the Deccan College, and in 1958 came to the United States to pursue a Ph.D. program in that subject at Indiana University. He received that degree in 1963, with a dissertation on generative grammar in the Kannada language. He was invited to join the Department of Linguistics at the University of Chicago, which remained his academic home for the rest of his life. His teaching of the Tamil languages, among other things, led him back to the literature of one of his native languages.

He was in fact trilingual: Tamil was spoken at home, Kannada throughout the rest of his environment, and English was the language of his education from an early age. The first volume of his poetry originally written in English, *The Striders,* appeared in 1966. It was the precise scholarship and pithy craft of his first volume of translations from the classical Tamil anthologies, *The Interior Landscape* (1967), that however announced a scholar of such breadth and sensitivity, as well as a poet of such skill, that understanding of the literatures of India would be forever changed. The first poem in that volume, "What She Said," is illustrative:

> Bigger than Earth, certainly
> higher than the sky,
> more unfathomable than the waters
> is this love for this man
>   of the mountain slopes
>   where bees make rich honey
>   from the flowers of the *kurinci*
>   that has such black stalks.

The precision of movement from the metaphysical to the domestic, stunning in a poet of the very early centuries of this era, would also be

Ramanujan's trademark for the next two books of translations (*Speaking of Shiva*, from Kannada; and *Hymns for the Drowning,* from Tamil) and three of his own poetry: *Relations* (1971), *Selected Poems* (1976), and *Second Sight* (1986). A posthumous volume, *The Black Hen,* has also appeared, in *Collected Poems* (1994).

Living and writing between two cultures, deeply learned in both, Ramanujan recognized with wry humor the difficulties implicit in his situation. His themes of the relationship of the self to one's body and to history, to his traditional Hindu upbringing and to his modern American environment, resonate because, although his poems are often highly particular and even personal, they are veins that run deep in human experience.

Ramanujan was the author of many essays in anthropology, linguistics, criticism, literature, and folklore; the translator of fiction (for example, Anantha Murthy's Kannada novel *Samskara*); the collector, editor, and often translator of *The Folktales of India;* and coauthor or coeditor of four other books.

When he died, on July 13, 1993, he had been honored by the Government of India's Padma Sri Award; he was also a grantee of the MacArthur Foundation, a member of the American Academy of Arts and Sciences, a lecturer whose charm, humor, wit, and sensitivity made him much in demand at universities throughout the United States and beyond, and a man beloved by all who knew him.

—*Edward C. Dimock*

SELF-PORTRAIT

I resemble everyone
but myself, and sometimes see
in shop-windows,
despite the well-known laws
of optics,
the portrait of a stranger,
date unknown,
often signed in a corner
by my father.

A HINDU TO HIS BODY

Dear pursuing presence,
dear body: you brought me
curled in womb and memory.

Gave me fingers to clutch
at grace, at malice; and ruffle
someone else's hair; to fold a man's
shadow back on his world;
to hold in the dark of the eye
through a winter and a fear
the poise, the shape of a breast;
a pear's silence, in the calyx
and the noise of a childish fist.

You brought me: do not leave me
behind. When you leave all else,
my garrulous face, my unkissed
alien mind, when you muffle
and put away my pulse

to rise in the sap of trees
let me go with you and feel the weight
of honey-hives in my branching
and the burlap weave of weaver-birds
in my hair.

DEATH AND THE GOOD CITIZEN

I know, you told me,
your nightsoil and all
your city's, goes still
warm every morning
in a government
lorry, drippy (you said)
but punctual, by special
arrangement to the municipal
gardens to make the grass
grow tall for the cows
in the village, the rhino
in the zoo: and the oranges
plump and glow, till
they are a preternatural
orange.

Good animal yet perfect
citizen, you, you are
biodegradable, you do
return to nature: you will
your body to the nearest
hospital, changing death into small
change and spare parts;
dismantling, not de-
composing like the rest
of us. Eyes in an eye bank
to blink some day for a stranger's

brain, wait like mummy wheat
in the singular company
of single eyes, pickled,
absolute.

Hearts,
        with your kind of temper,
may even take, make connection
with alien veins, and continue
your struggle to be naturalized:
beat, and learn to miss a beat
in a foreign body.
                    But
you know my tribe, incarnate
unbelievers in bodies,
they'll speak proverbs, contest
my will, against such degradation.
Hidebound, even worms cannot
have me: they'll cremate
me in Sanskrit and sandalwood,
have me sterilized
to a scatter of ash.

        Or abroad,
they'll lay me out in a funeral
parlor, embalm me in pesticide,
bury me in a steel trap, lock
me out of nature
till I'm oxidized by left-
over air, withered by my own
vapors into grin and bone.
My tissue will never graft,
will never know newsprint,
never grow in a culture,
or be mold and compost
for jasmine, eggplant

and the unearthly perfection
of municipal oranges.

FOUNDLINGS IN THE YUKON

In the Yukon the other day
miners found the skeleton
of a lemming
curled around some seeds
in a burrow:
sealed off by a landslide
in Pleistocene times.

Six grains were whole,
unbroken: picked and planted
ten thousand
years after their time,
they took root
within forty-eight hours
and sprouted
a candelabra of eight small leaves.

A modern Alaskan lupine,
I'm told, waits three years to come
to flower, but these
upstarts drank up sun
and unfurled early
with the crocuses of March
as if long deep
burial had made them hasty

for birth and season, for names,
genes, for passing on:
like the kick
and shift of an intra-uterine

memory, like
this morning's dream of being
born in an eagle's
nest with speckled eggs and the screech

of nestlings, like a pent-up
centenarian's sudden burst
of lust, or maybe
just elegies in Duino unbound
from the dark,
these new aborigines biding
their time
for the miner's night-light

to bring them their dawn,
these infants compact with age,
older than the oldest
things alive, having skipped
a million falls
and the registry of tree-rings,
suddenly younger
by an accident of flowering

than all their timely descendants.

SALAMANDERS

Again, here it comes, the nothing,
the zero where numbers die or begin,
the sunless day, the moonless month,
where sounds do not become words
nor words the rivals of silence.

How describe this nothing
we, of all things, flee in panic

yet wish for, work towards,
build ships and shape whole cities with?

Salamanders I'd heard live
in fire and drink the flame
as we the air: but when I met
them in the sludge of September

woods after rain, they were ember-
red but cold, born new and blind,
naked earthlings, poor yet satin
to the eye, velvet to the touch.

We, denizens of this nowhere nothing,
flame within black flame, where red
marries green and annuls it in the act,
yellow shade in yellow shadow, empty hub
of the turning wheel, mother and father

of the forever unborn, obeying edicts
written in smoke by war for countries
that never were—we, we burn
and eat fire no less than salamanders

but live in the wet, crawl in the slush,
five-toed lizards eating dragonflies,
waiting no less than the three-toed for a turn
of the body's season to copulate and people
the woods with babies satin to the eye

and velvet to the touch, surprising
only Hollywood Aliens who know us only
through legends or medieval woodcuts,
who suddenly meet us one day, blind,
actual, underfoot in the woods.

PLEASURE

A naked Jaina monk
ravaged by spring
fever, the vigor

of long celibacy
lusting now as never before
for the reek and sight

of mango bud, now tight, now

loosening into petal,
stamen, and butterfly,
his several mouths

thirsting for breast,
buttock, smells of finger,
long hair, short hair,

the wet of places never dry,

skin roused even by
whips, self touching self,
all philosophy slimed

by its own saliva,
cool Ganges turning
sensual on him

smeared by his own private

untouchable Jaina
body with honey
thick and slow as pitch,

and stood continent
at last on an anthill
of red fire ants, crying

his old formulaic cry;

at every twinge,
"Pleasure, Pleasure,
Great Pleasure!"—

no longer a formula
in the million mouths
of pleasure-in-pain

as the ants climb, tattooing

him, limb by limb,
and covet his body,
once naked, once even intangible.

30

THE MIDDLE EAST AND CENTRAL ASIA

GHAZALS, QASIDAS, RUBAIS, AND A LITERARY GIANT

Agha Shahid Ali

Literary forms find a way to move across borders, not with the predictability of conquerors but with the inevitability of lovers. They are willing to be caressed into other languages.

And so it is perhaps not wrong to see some Islamic-world poets as emerging from a background that is both Middle Eastern and Central Asian. In saying this, I am not giving in to the pervasive "Western" penchant for reducing the Islamic world to a homogenous entity—which it is not. I find myself paradoxically both resisting and endorsing the desire to see so many countries as a unit.

From Turkey to Pakistan—can that entire area for some purposes be seen as one, considering its immense diversity? And can a literary figure be considered as its representative? After all, Pablo Neruda, César Vallejo, and Octavio Paz seem to belong to all the Americas (well, the Latin part). While recognizing the immense heterogeneity of the Muslim world, I think one can argue that for that contiguous area—Turkey, Lebanon, Palestine, Syria, Iran, Afghanistan, Pakistan, and extending even to northern India and Bangladesh—there is more than a shadow of semblance of literary unity. Certain poetic forms and themes have pervaded that area because of a generous cosmopolitanism that has evolved there over the centuries. Just as sonnets are written in various European languages—perhaps in all of them—similarly *ghazals, qasidas, rubais,* and *masnavis* have been written in every living language of that area. Dramatic similarities in form and content make the literary cultures of Arabic,

Persian, Turkish, and Urdu (and their varied cousins) distant relatives in one family. Whether this results from the spread of Islam or whether it would have occurred anyway can be debated forever.

In this century, particularly in its latter part, what further unites the poets of those languages (even when one of them branches off into his own dynamic version of free verse) is the sense of shared history. Colonialism, despotic governments, capitalism—as well as the program of various First World powers to depict that region as one big Oriental abstraction—all contribute to certain shared responses.

Pakistan certainly makes for an interesting case. Its culture is both Hindu and Muslim (despite the protestations of purists to see it as only Muslim). In fact, the national language of Pakistan, Urdu, has its roots (as does Hindi) in Sanskrit. In everyday terms, Urdu and Hindi are almost one. It literary matters, however, Urdu has tended—particularly in poetry—to receive its forms and images and sensibilities from the practices of Arabic and Persian, especially Persian (Farsi).

When one takes poets such as Nazim Hikmet of Turkey, Adonis of Syria, Mahmoud Darwish of Palestine, and Faiz Ahmed Faiz of (technically) Pakistan but really of South Asia, one sees them as belonging to similar sensibilities and similar persuasions—all of them Muslim, all of them left wing, all of them deeply hostile to colonialism, all of them loved and damned in their countries for their impassioned pleas for freedom and justice.

Faiz Ahmed Faiz emerges as the most compelling presence of what I have, for my purposes, treated as a unified literary region. No matter how hard one tries, one cannot think of Adonis, Darwish, and Hikmet as South Asian. And one cannot think of—let's say—Tagore as Middle Eastern. But then we have the giant figure of Faiz, straddling simultaneously the "Muslim" Middle East and "Hindu" India.

Faiz takes much from the Persian tradition via the great Urdu poets of the nineteenth century, particularly Ghalib. But leaving that tradition behind, immersing himself in local realities, he also sees and finds himself in Punjabi and Hindi. His celebration of the hybrid cultures of South Asia in part explains his popularity in "Hindu" India. His passion, in his verse, for the rights of the Palestinians—and the years he spent in exile in Beirut—make him a Middle Eastern poet also. His translations of Nazim Hikmet further contribute to his Middle Eastern identity. He is thus the only poet who is celebrated in Bangladesh, India, Pakistan, Iran, Turkey, Palestine, Egypt—and beyond.

Acknowledged enthusiastically—both for his impassioned politics on behalf of the peoples of those countries (he had the courage to damn Pakistan for its genocide in Bangladesh, then East Pakistan) and for his poetry—he belonged to all of them. No government has been able to appropriate him, though he is quoted by the leaders of both India and Pakistan. He is lionized, particularly in Hindi/Urdu-speaking regions, by the literary elite and by the masses—a dream of so many poets. A nonsubcontinental audience may begin to understand his stature as a poet and public figure by imagining a combination of Pablo Neruda, Nazim Hikmet, Octavio Paz, and Mahmoud Darwish.

Born in Sialkot in the Punjab in 1911 (long before it was partitioned between India and Pakistan), Faiz earned two master's degrees, one in Arabic literature, the other in English. During World War II he served in the (British) Indian army, attaining the rank of lieutenant colonel. After independence in 1947, which accompanied the partition of the subcontinent, Faiz chose to live in Pakistan and became editor of the *Pakistan Times,* a daily English-language newspaper. In 1951, along with several left-wing army officers, he was arrested on the charge of planning a Soviet-sponsored coup. He spent four years in prison, mostly in solitary confinement, under sentence of death, but was released in 1955. He returned to work on the *Pakistan Times*.

In 1958 he was removed from that post when a new military government took over. Interestingly, President Ayub Khan, despite having Faiz jailed briefly, mentioned him first when UNESCO was approaching various governments to nominate their countries' representative writers for the purpose of translating them into other languages. After translations of his work appeared in Russian, he was awarded the Lenin Peace Prize in 1962 (there's a wonderful photograph of Faiz and Neruda in Moscow at that time, with Neruda's arm around Faiz's shoulder). When Zulfikar Ali Bhutto (Benazir Bhutto's father, who was later hanged by Zia ul-Haq's government) became prime minister, Faiz was appointed chair of the

National Council on the Arts, a position he lost when Bhutto was over-thrown. After that—till the Israeli invasion of 1982—Faiz lived in exile in Beirut and edited *Lotus,* the journal of the Afro-Asian Writers' Association. He died in Lahore in November 1984, an event that was reported, often in banner headlines, in India, Pakistan, the former Soviet Union, and throughout the Middle East.

Given Faiz's political commitments, particularly his Marxist under-standing of history, audiences may hastily assume that he was a poet of slogans. Faiz's genius, however, lay in his ability to balance his politics with his (in some ways stringently classical) aesthetics without compro-mising either. He once advised a poet to avoid didactic and rhetorical ges-tures. He also said that "the future of all poetry . . . depends above all on the talent of its future practitioners. Pedantically speaking, there is noth-ing good or bad in any poetic form, but that the poet makes it so." A mas-ter of the *ghazal,* a form that can be traced back to seventh-century Arabia, he transformed its every stock image and, magically, brought absolutely new associations into being. For example, the Beloved—an archetypal figure in Urdu and Persian poetry—can mean friend, God, lover. Besides tapping into these meanings, Faiz extended them to include the revolution. Waiting for the Revolution can be as agonizing and intoxicating as waiting for one's lover.

In Faiz's poetry suffering is seldom, perhaps never, private (in the con-fessional sense). Though deeply personal, it is almost never isolated from a sense of history and injustice. In a very famous poem, "Don't Ask Me for That Love Again," Faiz breaks from Urdu's traditional way of looking at the Beloved. Not only does he refuse to despair but, in a radical departure from convention, asks the Beloved—even while acknowledging her immense importance—to accept that his social commitment is more important than their love. This was a revolutionary poem, envied by many Urdu poets who wished they had first broken from the tradition in which everything was either the Beloved or nothing. Faiz did not discard the tra-dition: The poem clearly establishes the importance of the Beloved and her ravishing beauty. But it does some plain speaking (and not in any plain style—minimalism and Urdu simply don't go together), granting love its due but almost no more.

In "Don't Ask Me for That Love Again," Faiz draws a line of demarcation between the political and the romantic. But often a mingling of the two pervades his poetry. Sometimes the two are entangled in such a way that there is no point in trying to separate them: the political meaning informs the romantic, and the romantic the political. Nevertheless, Faiz, a man jailed for his beliefs, certainly does have poems, many in fact, that can be read as exclusively political. The fact that Faiz's poems are symbolic rather than direct is, in itself, a political statement. Indeed, Urdu has a long-enough tradition of concealing politics in symbols. In nineteenth-century Urdu poetry, the stock figure of the Executioner often represented the British (a way of dodging the censors as well as the gallows: In the summer of 1857, the British had hanged almost thirty thousand people from the trees of Delhi to terrorize the population and punish it for what is often called the Mutiny). In Pakistan, under the censorship of various military dictatorships, it was once again impossible to name things exactly.

Faiz Ahmed Faiz (1911–1984)

When Autumn Came

This is the way that autumn came to the trees:
it stripped them down to the skin,
left their ebony bodies naked.
It shook out their hearts, the yellow leaves,
scattered them over the ground.
Anyone could trample them out of shape
undisturbed by a single moan of protest.

The birds that herald dreams
were exiled from their song,
each voice torn from its throat.
They dropped into the dust
even before the hunter strung his bow.

Oh, God of May, have mercy.
Bless these withered bodies
with the passion of your resurrection;
make their dead veins flow with blood again.

Give some tree the gift of green again.
Let one bird sing.

(translated by Naomi Lazard)

The Day Death Comes

How will it be, the day death comes?
Perhaps like the gift at the beginning of night,
the first kiss on the lips given unasked,
the kiss that opens the way to brilliant worlds
while, in the distance, an April of nameless flowers
    agitates the moon's heart.

Perhaps in this way: when the morning,
green with unopened buds, begins to shimmer
in the bedroom of the beloved,
and the tinkle of stars as they rush to depart
can be heard on the silent windows.

What will it be like, the day death comes?
Perhaps like a vein screaming
with the premonition of pain
under the edge of a knife, while a shadow,
the assassin holding the knife,
spreads out with a wingspan
> from one end of the world to the other.

No matter when death comes, or how,
even though in the guise of the disdainful beloved
> who is always cold,
there will be the same words of farewell to the heart:
"Thank God it is finished, the night of the broken-
    hearted.
Praise be to the meeting of lips,
the honeyed lips I have known."

(translated by Naomi Lazard)

DON'T ASK ME FOR THAT LOVE AGAIN

That which then was ours, my love,
don't ask me for that love again.
The world was then gold, burnished with light—
and only because of you. That's what I had believed.
How could one weep for sorrows other than yours?
How could one have any sorrow but the one you gave?
So what were these protests, these rumors of injustice?

A glimpse of your face was evidence of springtime.
The sky, wherever I looked, was nothing but your eyes.
If you'd fall into my arms, Fate would be helpless.

All this I'd thought, all this I'd believed.
But there were other sorrows, comforts other than love.
The rich had cast their spell on history:
dark centuries had been embroidered on brocades and
    silks
Bitter threads began to unravel before me
as I went into alleys and in open markets
saw bodies plastered with ash, bathed in blood.
I saw them sold and bought, again and again.
This too deserves attention. I can't help but look back
when I return from those alleys—what should one do?
There are other sorrows in this world,
comforts other than love.
Don't ask me, my love, for that love again.

(translated by Agha Shahid Ali)

WE WHO WERE EXECUTED

*(After reading the letters of Julius and Ethel
    Rosenberg)*

I longed for your lips, dreamed of their roses:
I was hanged from the dry branch of the scaffold.
I wanted to touch your hands, their silver light:
I was murdered in the half-light of dim lanes.

And there where you were crucified,
so far away from my words,
you still were beautiful:
color kept clinging to your lips—
rapture was still vivid in your hair—
light remained silvering in your hands.

When the night of cruelty merged with the roads you
    had taken,
I came as far as my feet could bring me,
on my lips the phrase of a song,
my heart lit up only by sorrow.
This sorrow was my testimony to your beauty—
Look! I remained a witness till the end,
I who was killed in the darkest lanes.

It's true—that not to reach you was fate—
but who'll deny that to love you
was entirely in my hands?
So why complain if these matters of desire
brought me inevitably to the execution grounds?

Why complain? Holding up our sorrows as banners,
new lovers will emerge
from the lanes where we were killed
and embark, in caravans, on those highways of desire.
It's because of them that we shortened the distances of sorrow,
It's because of them that we went out to make the world
    our own,
we who were murdered in the darkest lanes.

(translated by Agha Shahid Ali)

BEFORE YOU CAME

Before you came,
things were as they should be:
the sky was the dead-end of sight,
the road was just a road, wine merely wine.

Now everything is like my heart,
a color at the edge of blood:
the gray of your absence, the color of poison, of thorns,

the gold when we meet, the season ablaze,
the yellow of autumn, the red of flowers, of flames,
and the black when you cover the earth
with the coal of dead fires.

And the sky, the road, the glass of wine?
The sky is a shirt wet with tears,
the road a vein about to break,
and the glass of wine a mirror in which
the sky, the road, the world keep changing.

Don't leave now that you're here—
Stay. So the world may become like itself again:
so the sky may be the sky,
the road a road,
and the glass of wine not a mirror, just a glass of wine.

(translated by Agha Shahid Ali)

You TELL US WHAT TO DO

When we launched life
on the river of grief,
how vital were our arms, how ruby our blood.
With a few strokes, it seemed,
we would cross all pain,
we would soon disembark.
That didn't happen.
In the stillness of each wave we found invisible currents.
The boatmen, too, were unskilled,
their oars untested.
Investigate the matter as you will,
blame whomever, as much as you want,
but the river hasn't changed,
the raft is still the same.

Now *you* suggest what's to be done,
you tell us how to come ashore.

When we saw the wounds of our country
appear on our skins,
we believed each word of the healers.
Besides, we remembered so many cures,
it seemed at any moment
all troubles would end, each wound heal completely.
That didn't happen: our ailments
were so many, so deep within us
that all diagnoses proved false, each remedy useless.
Now do whatever, follow each clue,
accuse whomever, as much as you will,
our bodies are still the same,
our wounds still open.
Now tell us what we should do,
you tell us how to heal these wounds.

(translated by Agha Shahid Ali)

31

SOUTHEAST ASIA AND THE PACIFIC

A THOUSAND YEARS WITHOUT ANY SEASON

Burton Raffel

Aku mau hidup seribu tahun lagi. I suspect that even without knowing Indonesian one can feel at least some of the blunt force of this, the final line in Chairil Anwar's best-known poem, "Aku," "Me." Now add the fact that there are no long vowels in Indonesian and thus no weak syllables. Rather like Puerto Rican Spanish, Indonesian comes at one in a steady sequence of even-spaced bursts. It is a strongly "fortis" language—meaning that the muscles at the side of the mouth are taut, not relaxed ("lenis") as in English. It helps, too, to know that *p*, *t*, and *k* are not aspirated (that is, they have no accompanying puff of air), and that there is a sharply felt rhythmic pause after *hidup,* thus breaking the line into the distinct parts.

> *Aku* = I
> *man* = to want, wish, desire
> *hidup* = life, to live
> *seribu* = a thousand
> *tahun* = year(s)
> *lagi* = more

And then, when one knows what Anwar is saying—"I want to live another thousand years"—the line acquires a singularly powerful impact. I knew an American woman who had spent eight years in Indonesia and grown to know and love its poetry. Seriously ill, she underwent major surgery, and as she began to emerge, fuzzily, from the anesthesia, she heard a voice saying, over and over, *"Aku man hidup seribu tahun lagi."*

It took a while before she realized that it was not only a female voice but her own.

By far the largest physical and cultural area in all of Southeast Asia and the Pacific is the three-thousand-mile-long archipelago of Indonesia. Its rapidly growing population, now the fourth largest in the world and fairly soon to become the third largest (only China and India will then contain more people), has already gone well over the two hundred million mark. Malaysia, though much, much smaller, closely shares the language and many—perhaps most—of the physical and cultural characteristics of Indonesia. In lesser or greater degrees, so too do the other nations of the region. All are inhabited by brown-skinned peoples who for centuries have been basically sailors and farmers, and sometimes merchants and traders. All have led essentially easygoing if careful lives, dwelling in smallish, closed, but neither sealed nor basically suspicious communities. Deeply and traditionally religious, the inhabitants of Southeast Asia and the Pacific have a long record of combat and petty wars but no history of evangelism. It is no accident that *adat,* the word for "custom" or "tradition" in Malay/Indonesian, is also a word for "law." Thailand is not Vietnam, as Malaysia is not Cambodia, and Singapore, long the great metropolis of the region, is not Hong Kong (though its population is largely Chinese). But though the nations and peoples of Southeast Asia and the Pacific have no history of imperial rule over others, all have distinct, often bitterly living memories of Western colonialism—English, French, and Dutch.

Still, Marjorie Sinclair can more or less speak for the whole region when she observes, introducing her anthology of traditional Polynesian poetry, "The[se] poems . . . were composed by a race of seafarers and island dwellers who crossed thousands of miles of ocean in frail vessels, guiding themselves by the stars and the feel of wave and wind. The poems reflect the ways in which they saw their universe of sea and sky and the scattered fragments of land they found and settled." So, too, Carol Rubenstein speaks for the whole region, after a fashion, when in describing the Dayak tribes of Borneo she tells us that "their songs offer the fullest expression of the thoughts, feelings, and environment of the

Dayaks. Taken by themselves, the songs alone entirely encapsulate and tell the story of Dayak life." Linguists necessarily put all these matters less romantically. "A great deal of the comparative research on Austronesian languages has been inspired by curiosity as to the origins and migration of the far-flung Austronesian-speaking peoples," one linguist typically wrote. These are people for whom songs and singing are profoundly important: Poetry is given impressive weight. These are also people who have done a great deal of wandering. Their recently recorded singing, like the poems that follow, is deeply rooted in their history and experience.

Nor can we forget that this entire region is tropical, steamily hot, perpetually, lushly green; most of it is amazingly fertile and unthreatened by violent storms. There is no snow, no frost, and not only no winter but virtually no seasons at all—not as most of the Indo-European-speaking world knows and has experienced seasons. Some aspects of that tropical world (though not yet the climate) are changing, to be sure. Oil wells have been going down, and skyscraping buildings have been going up. Malaysia now boasts the tallest human-made structure anywhere on the planet. Tiny Brunei has the largest per capita income in the world. In Singapore one can safely drink tap water. Computers, television sets, and even air conditioners are an ever-increasing presence; factories, tractors, cars, and planes have become commonplace.

But just like the burning sun and the moist, heavy air, a sense of scattered and once-upon-a-time deeply transient existence hangs over the region. Vietnam, physically (and culturally) closest to the massive, long-settled bulk of China, not surprisingly presents us with a more and determined nationhood than does either Malaysia or Indonesia. At the end of "Green Nostalgia: Soliloquy of a Tiger in the Zoo," Nguyen The Luc, one of the first and most important modern poets of Vietnam, has the caged jungle animal declare, "O majestic lands/Where our holy race ruled,/Where I knew freedom,/Where I will never come again!" The longing is indomitable—"I cannot forget. I hate this . . . place"—but one must have a powerful awareness of home to miss it thus desperately. There is remarkably little nostalgia, and an infinitely greater degree of defiance, in Indonesia's *Ur*-poet, Chairil Anwar: "The hell with all those tears!/I'm a wild beast/Driven out of the herd."

Legal structures, like those of commerce, trade, and government, draw on the same basic roots from which poetry springs. Traditional

Malay society, for example, framed much of its discourse around the careful use of proverbial sayings—all of them linguistically tightly wound and compressed, the Malay/Indonesian tongue being (as Hugh Clifford and Frank Swettenham once said) "essentially a diplomatic language and one admirably adapted for concealing the feelings and cloaking the real thoughts. Not even in French is it possible to be so polite, or so rude, or to say such rude things with every appearance of exaggerated courtesy, as in the case of Malay." Traditional Malay/Indonesian poetry features exactly such indirection.

> *Dari man, hendak kemana?*
>> (Where have you come from, where are you
>> going?)
> *Tinggi rumput dari padi.*
>> (Grass grows faster than grain.)
> *Tahun mana, bulan yang mana?*
>> (What ever year, what ever month?)

This is a *pantum*, and if poets of the last fifty years no longer write *pantum*, they still write in the same languages their ancestors and predecessors used, and write under the same sky. And since these are not connections quickly or easily broken, in poetry—or anything else—we will not be disappointed if we expect the *pantum*'s taut compression, its quicksilver emotionality, its flashing, subtly managed glimpses of power joined with delicacy to go on manifesting themselves in perpetually new and different ways—as indeed, in today's Indonesian poetry, they are doing. I cannot imagine a poet in Tokyo or Beijing, in New Delhi or, for that matter, New York or London or Paris writing with exactly the wry, slashing pungency of Sapardi Djoko Damonno in "Siapapak engkau [Who are you]":

> I am Adam
> who ate the apple;
> Adam suddenly aware of himself,
> startled and ashamed,
> I am Adam who realized
> good and evil, passing

from one sin to another;
Adam continuously suspicious
of himself,
hiding his face.
I am Adam floundering
in the net of space and time,
with no help from reality:
paradise lost
because of my mistrust
of the Presence.
I am Adam
who heard God say
farewell, Adam.

Though Indonesia is predominantly Islamic, this poem creates a unique blend of Hebraic, Christian, and Koranic inner universes.

How many other countries or cultures could have produced such a stark poetic blending? We are all unique and so too are all cultures. But—as George Orwell might have said—some are more unique than others.

A Force in Indonesian Poetry

Denise Levertov

Chairil Anwar lived only twenty-seven years and left only about seventy-five poems. Yet he has been a major force in Indonesian poetry. Turn to almost anywhere in this selection, and you know at once that this was a pure poet. Anwar was not one of those who chooses to be a poet and earnestly and with more or less ambition cultivates a talent—a way of life that accounts for about 95 percent of contemporary poetry—but one who could not help himself, who did not choose but (even though he wrote little and not easily) was chosen: a poet as García Lorca was one, or Hart Crane.

This by itself might not have made his work influential in the development of other young poets. But Anwar's brief years of literary activity not only coincided with the social and political ferment preceding and immediately following the end of Japanese rule in Indonesia, they were also coterminous with a period of flux and development in the Indonesian language. In his stripping away of flounces, his brilliant use of what he found in foreign poets, his searching candor and technical courage, Anwar was "purifying the language of the tribe."

Anwar was born in Sumatra in 1922, moved to Java as a boy, and for financial reasons was unable to continue his formal education beyond the second year of high school. He fought as a guerrilla against the Dutch, consorted with sailors and prostitutes, and died in 1949 from the combined attack of typhus and tuberculosis upon a system already weakened by syphilis. Certain Dutch writers—Multatuli ("an eccentric breaker-of-images" and "the one exciting writer in the doldrums of the Dutch nineteenth century," says James Holmes) and Henrik Marsman, whose poetry of the early twenties perhaps gave Anwar his first example of the possibilities of organic form; and after the war the contemporary English and American poets whose books he found in the libraries of the British and United States information services in Djakarta—these seem to have been nourishing influences, as was the folk poetry of the archipelago. But even in translation one can feel that Anwar was continually absorbing anything and everything into his *own* life, his *own* poetry. "I'll dig down," he had written to a friend during the war, "and root out every word until I've gone deep enough to find the germinal word, the germinal image."

Burton Raffel, whose work as a translator is notably intelligent and artistic, makes us feel the fascination of Anwar's poetic presence. Raffel points out that he has adhered to Anwar's "seemingly erratic" punctuation, omission of initial capitals, etc.; he has understood that Anwar knew these things as integral parts of the poem. "A line," writes Raffel, "that begins with a capital letter has for him a different weight than one beginning with a lower-case letter; a line ending with a period or a comma has a different speed and flow than one ending of its own motion alone." In the process of translation these nuances can rarely be reproduced with validity, but Raffel has written his English versions in the spirit of the original and created equivalent effects, so that the best ones stand on their own feet in the new language, and even those that fall short of that autonomy give one a keen sense of what the tone of the original must be.

AT THE MOSQUE

I shouted at Him
Until He came

We met face to face.

Afterwards He burned in my breast.
All my strength struggles to extinguish Him

My body, which won't be driven, is soaked with sweat

This room
Is the arena where we fight

Destroying each other
One hurling insults, the other gone mad.

Inevitably one is left with many questions. How long did Anwar spend as a guerrilla fighter? How did he live the rest of the time? Which American and English poets, besides those he himself referred to (Dickinson, Eliot, Auden) is he known to have read? (Williams? Cummings? Pound?) Had he made a beginning on the Lorca translations he mentioned in a letter shortly before his death? We don't know. But we have encountered briefly a representative of "the real thing." Fierce, casual, bitter, tender, these are the poems of a man vividly present, careless of order in his living, uncompromisingly engaged in the order and life of the poem.

CHAIRIL ANWAR (1922–1949)

ME

When my time comes
No one's going to cry for me,
And you won't, either

The hell with all those tears!

I'm a wild beast
Driven out of the herd

Bullets may pierce my skin
But I'll keep coming,

Carrying forward my wounds and my pain
Attacking
Attacking
Until suffering disappears

And I won't give a damn

I want to live another thousand years

(translated by Burton Raffel)

AN ORDINARY SONG

On the restaurant terrace, we're face to face
Just introduced. We simply stare
Although we've already dived into the ocean of each
      other's souls

In this first act
We're still only looking
The orchestra plays "Carmen" along with us.

She winks. She laughs
And the dry grass blazes up.
She speaks. Her voice is loud
My blood stops running.

When the orchestra begins the "Ave Maria"
I drag her over there. . . .

(translated by Burton Raffel)

TWILIGHT AT A LITTLE HARBOR

This time no one's looking for love
down between the sheds, the old houses, among the
 twittering
masts and rigging. A boat, a *prau* that will never sail
 again
puffs and snorts, thinking there's something it can catch

The drizzle brings darkness. An eagle's wings flap,
brushing against the gloom; the day whispers,
 swimming silkily
away to meet harbor temptations yet to come. Nothing
 moves
and now the sand and the sea are asleep, the waves gone.

That's all. I'm alone. Walking,
combing the cape, still choking back the hope
of getting to the end and, just once, saying the hell with it
from this fourth beach, embracing the last, the final sob.

(translated by Burton Raffel)

WILLINGNESS

If you like I'll take you back
With all my heart.

I'm still alone.

I know you're not what you were,
Like a flower pulled into parts.

Don't crawl! Stare at me bravely.

If you like I'll take you back
For myself, but

I won't share even with a mirror.

(translated by Burton Raffel)

HEAVEN

Like my mother, and my grandmother too,
plus seven generations before them,
I also seek admission to Heaven
which the Moslem party and the Mohammedan
Union say has rivers of milk
And thousands of houris all over.

But there's a contemplative voice inside me,
stubbornly mocking: Do you really think
the blue sea will go dry
—and what about the sly temptations waiting in
    every port?
Anyway, who can say for sure
that there really are houris there
with voices as rich and husky as Nina's, with eyes
    that flirt like Yati's?

(translated by Burton Raffel)

TUTI'S ICE CREAM

Between present and future happiness the abyss gapes,
My girl is licking happily at her ice cream;
This afternoon you're my love, I adorn you with cake and
	Coca-Cola.
Oh wife-in-training, we've stopped the clocks' ticking.

You kissed skillfully, the scratches still hurt
—when we cycled I took you home—
Your blood was hot, oh you were a woman soon,
And the old man's dreams leaped at the moon.

Every day's whim invited you on, every day's whim was
	different.
Tomorrow we'll fight and turn our backs on each other:
Heaven is this minute's game.

I'm like you, everything ran by,
Me and Tuti and Hreyt and Amoy . . . dilapidated
	hearts.
Love's a danger that quickly fades.

(translated by Burton Raffel)

FOUR MISCELLANEOUS APHORISMS

Living under the Japanese, we had to act—it was doubly nec-
essary, at least to keep our minds and our senses alert, to counter-
act the atmosphere that surrounded us, to keep from losing our
self-respect.

An era of "isms" is a one-sided party for one-sided dancers.
What I admire is the violence, the passion with which they
brawl!

Message for the younger generation: wisdom and insight aren't enough; you've got to work up energy and enthusiasm.

We've got to find our compensations and complexes for ourselves. Compensations and complexes: a huge warehouse, the dark home of our real hidden self.

(translated by Burton Raffel)

32

CHINA

HOW THE "REVOLUTION" OCCURRED IN CHINESE POETRY: A MEMOIR

Bei Dao

Winter, 1978. A snowfall covered Beijing. In the eastern suburbs, a little hamlet of only a few families in size looked across a dirty rivulet toward the embassy district of the capital. Not quite an agricultural village, but not part of the city, either, it was a sort of blind spot in the stifling control system. One of the huts in the village had its windows covered with ragged cloths. Under a dim lamp seven youngsters were bustling around a rickety mimeograph machine. I was one of them. After three days and three nights, we came out with *Today,* the first unofficial literary publication to appear in China since the Communist Party took power in 1949. We bicycled to a restaurant in the city and raised cups in a silent toast.

The next day I went with two friends to paste our harvest up on walls in the city. We changed the numbers on our bicycle license plates in an effort to mislead the police. On December 23, 1978, *Today* could be read outside several government offices and publishing houses, on university campuses, and in Tiananmen Square. We wanted to know how people would react to our works, so we went back later to mix in with the crowds who huddled around them. The poems, in particular, were of a kind that no one had seen in public for thirty years. The response was stronger than we would have imagined.

The original impetus for *Today* came in the late 1960s. That was when Mao Zedong, during his Great Proletarian Cultural Revolution, sought to quell rebellion in the cities by sending high school students to the countryside for "reeducation by the poor and middle peasants." His results, though, were quite the opposite of what he intended. To the young Red Guards, the fall from the heights of society to its depths was a jolt; they were, moreover, severely disillusioned to find a huge disparity between rosy Maoist language about "people's communes" and the harsh realities of village life. They turned to books in search of truth, and to writing as a means to express their perplexity. Each winter, during the agricultural off-season, some of them returned to Beijing, where they exchanged books and writings and met in informal groups.

I can still remember how excited I was, at age twenty, to read the poems of Shi Zhi (literally, "Forefinger"). He started writing in 1967, and must count as the founder of the New Poetry movement that unfolded over the next thirty years. His poems were the first to break with the political didacticism with which we had all grown up, and the first, as well, to express the bewilderment of the Red Guard generation. His fresh images and lilting cadences had an intoxicating effect on young people, who spread his poems widely in hand-copied form. Many years later when I met Forefinger, he had gone insane. He passed his days shuttling between home and the hospital.

I took up writing poetry after reading Forefinger's. I was a construction worker at the time, assigned to an electricity-generating plant about two hundred miles outside of Beijing. It was an isolated environment, and I needed some form of release from the malaise I felt. At the time, probably because of the influence of Mao Zedong as a poet, there was a fad for writing poems in the ancient styles Mao favored. Nearly everybody, it seemed, could recite a few Mao poems. I, too, wrote a few ancient-style poems, but soon found that their formal requirements made it hard to express anything more complex than nostalgia or the parting of friends.

I knew that writing was a forbidden game that could even cost one's life. But prohibition only sweetened the appeal. At the construction site I lived in a dormitory with a few dozen others. In the middle of the night, surrounded by a medley of snores, I would read and write under a table lamp that I had fashioned from a straw hat. Later the propaganda team at the construction site drafted me to work on a photography exhibit, and a darkroom built to my specifications became my cherished hideout. Heavy window shades blocked off the outside world; I finally had my own study. In just a few months I could finish a short novel in addition to many poems.

My friend Zhao Yifan, a collector of underground literary works, was arrested. The police confiscated every scrap of his papers they could find, including my poems and novel. I was ordered back to my original work site for supervised labor. I began to say good-bye to friends, to entrust them with my letters and manuscripts, and to prepare myself for prison whenever the moment might arrive. In the middle of the night the sound of trucks rolling past would startle me awake and leave me unable to reenter sleep. The wait was long and difficult, but in the end the feared event never arrived. Only much later did I learn what had happened: The police could not make head or tail of my poems. They consulted experts from the Literature Research Institute, who also were baffled. Finally the experts came out with a ruling: The poems had been plagiarized from the West. This judgment saved me.

Those were also the days of the banned book. Books were seldom seen in public places. We used to sneak into closed libraries to steal books; or sift through second-hand stores in search of them; or borrow them from other people who were rummaging just as we were. The term *pao shu* "running [around for] books" entered our vocabulary: to find a good book you had to run everywhere, had to be patient and persistent, had to negotiate, to promise, to reciprocate.

The material one reads in youth can be decisive in the rest of life. At first we read omnivorously, hungry for any scrap we could find. But later we grew picky: We set our hearts on the "yellow-covered books." These were a set of about one hundred volumes of literature from the modern West and from the "thaw" period in the Soviet Union and Eastern Europe. They were meant for the eyes of high officials only, and thus had very small print runs and tight restrictions on circulation. Still, in the turmoil of the Cultural Revolution, they leaked down to the general populace. Among the informal literary groups in Beijing, they became the objects of serious treasure hunts. Whenever a group managed to lay its hands on one of these books—sometimes for a negotiated period of only a few days—the group members would draw up a tight schedule for shar-

ing the book around the clock. Reading time was more precious than food
or sleep. My friends and I used to take pills that we knew would make us
ill so that we could get sick leave—that is, reading time—from work.

For underground writers the yellow-covered books not only opened
new vistas for spiritual refuge but exemplified a literary form that was
radically different from the official socialist realism. It was called, at the
time, the "translation style." Certain Chinese writers, including the best
poets of the latter 1940s—Mu Dan, Yuan Kejia, Chen Jingrong, Zheng
Min, and others later known as the Nine Leaves Group—after 1949 had
given up trying to write creatively under the new political guidelines and
had turned instead to work on the translation and research of foreign lit-
erature. The "translation style" of Chinese that they created became, for
my generation, a vehicle for expressing creative impulses and seeking new
linguistic horizons.

In the autumn of 1978 a power struggle at the top of the Communist
Party led to a temporary relaxation of controls on cultural expression.
Underground writing in journals like *Today* could appear in the open,
where, together with unofficial artwork and photography, it posed a major
new challenge to official discourse. *Today* published mostly poetry, intro-
ducing the work of Mang Ke, Gu Cheng, Duoduo, Shu Ting, Yan Li,
Yang Lian, Jiang He, and other important poets. Our printing equipment
was primitive and our "editorial office" little more than a hand-labor
workshop. But quite a few young people pitched in. In two years we pro-
duced nine magazine issues and four books.

We also organized some literary events. Regular monthly sessions to
discuss our recent work attracted a large number of university students. In
the spring of 1979, and once again in the fall, we sponsored outdoor poetry
readings in Beijing's Yuyuantan Park. Chen Kaige, who later directed such
well-known films as *Yellow Earth* and *Farewell, My Concubine,* at that time
was still a student at Beijing Film Academy. He orchestrated some of our
readings for us. The police supervised closely, perhaps puzzled that nearly
a thousand people could listen so intently to our obscure poetic lines.

The Communist Party's brief flirtation with democracy passed quickly,
however. Deng Xiaoping soon ordered the arrest of Wei Jingsheng and
other democracy activists. When *Today* was forced to close in December
1980, the authorities expected me to write a "self-criticism" about my

involvement with the disgraced journal. I had just returned from my honeymoon in Qingdao (Shandong Province) and decided not to do the self-criticism. I was suspended from my job "for reflection." One evening, as I was returning home, a friend darted from behind a tree to tell me he had a reliable report that my name was on an arrest list. Should I flee? My wife and I talked deep into the night and finally decided to stay put but watch closely. Before long the political winds shifted again, and once again I felt I was a lucky survivor.

Today was closed down, but many of its poems began to appear in the official literary magazines under the general heading of "Obscure Poetry"*(menglong shi)*. A nationwide controversy about Obscure Poetry raged for many years. Official critics denounced it as if it were a pestilence or wild beast, but their fulminations served only to deepen interest. Young readers who had felt stifled by official language found in it new air to breathe. There was a spell during which virtually everybody on college campuses was writing poetry, joining poetry clubs, or putting out poetry collections. This lasted through much of the 1980s, until the society-wide rage for commercialism again pushed poetry to the margins.

Eventually *Today* itself became a kind of cloud that hung over a new generation of poets. "The third generation," as they have been called, differ from the *Today* poets because they have grown up after the Cultural Revolution and have enjoyed good educations. To some extent they have been able to lay down the burdens of history, to look more directly at present realities, and to write, as it were, in minor as well as major chords. Important poets in this group include Bai Hua, Zhang Zao, Xi Chuan, Ouyang Jianghe, Song Lin, Zhai Yongming, Han Dong, and Zhang Zhen. Many are from Sichuan. Many, too, have become my friends. We have found that what we share in poetry well exceeds our differences.

In 1990, a year after the guns sounded in Tiananmen Square, a group of Chinese writers met in Oslo, Norway, and decided to revive *Today*. Publication resumed and has continued until now. The twenty-year history of *Today*—from its birth, to its death, to its rebirth—can be viewed as a metaphor for the vitality of all of China's contemporary poetry, whose genies will not go back into bottles.

(translated by Perry Link)

EXQUISITE SWALLOWS AND POETRY QUOTAS: A TUMULTUOUS CENTURY IN CHINESE POETRY

Perry Link and Maghiel van Crevel

Classical Chinese poetry is one of the exquisite inventions of the human mind. Its anatomy is complex: Rhythm, rhyme, and the tones (pitch) of syllables all observe set rules; patterns of antonyms and synonyms are captured in grammatically parallel lines; historical and literary allusion are common. Traditionally written with brush and ink, it appears through the medium of the equally refined art of Chinese calligraphy. Yet for all its demands—and, one might think, constrictions—on the poet, in outward appearance it is as graceful and spontaneous as a swallow that flits in the sunset.

Can such a thing be translated? Of course not. Among the adventurers who have tried, the most successful have themselves been poets. Their method has been to take inspiration (not structure) from a Chinese poem and re-create what they can, knowing that the result will be but a shadow. What about study and analysis? Can a scholar pinpoint all the ins and outs of a classical Chinese poem? Yes. But dissection, while producing a clinical understanding, always kills the swallow, and the innards cannot rival the live bird for beauty.

In the last two centuries, the impact of the technologically advanced Western world had brought China crises and revolutions of several kinds. At the turn of the twentieth century some leading Chinese intellectuals, despairing over their country's weakness, concluded that "new literature" would be a key to reinvigorating the national spirit. The corollary that "old" writing held China back was not far behind: Traditional literary forms should be set aside, if necessary even "knocked down."

After consciously rejecting their classical language and traditional vernacular, the new-style Chinese writers sought to write in "ordinary language," by which they meant the language of the common people. What they actually wrote, though, was a language whose grammar was influenced by Western grammar and whose vocabulary included many

Western-language terms whose Chinese-character equivalents had been invented in Japan. Although this new language did eventually become widespread, in the 1920s and 1930s it was still limited to the elite. New-style writers began to experiment with Western literary forms as well, with some of the pioneers becoming known as "the Chinese Shelley," "the Chinese Goethe," "the Chinese Ibsen," and so on.

The hybridization that resulted was awkward and fruitful at the same time. It affected all genres. The awkwardness was perhaps least for the essay, where traditional forms melded most easily into modern ones. Fiction, especially short fiction, attracted the most attention and had arguably the greatest artistic success, first in the late teens and the twenties, and again in the eighties. A new-style "spoken drama" appeared and existed parallel with the traditional opera during much of the twentieth century, until, in the 1980s and 1990s, television and film gradually displaced stage performances of all kinds.

Of all artistic genres, poetry has had perhaps the most difficult modern passage (unless we count the obliteration that the word-processing revolution appears likely to bring to the art of calligraphy). The first "new style" poems in the late 1910s were either childlike clanking rhymes or a free verse that seemed somewhat artificial and bland by comparison to classical poetry. But these were experiments and were meant as little else: Their point was more to show that "new poetry" could be done at all than that it could be done well. Later experiments included mimicry of the Western sonnet, which had moderate success, and of the limerick, which had less. The best poetry in the first half of the twentieth century, such as that of Wen Yiduo, still owed much to classical style, or, as in Lu Xun's, still used classical form entirely.

China's Maoist interlude at midcentury affected all aspects of life, including poetry. For the three decades from the late 1940s to the late 1970s, only one mainland Chinese poet, Mao himself, could publish poems that sprang from personal inspiration. Everyone else had to "serve politics," which meant giving priority to prescribed guidelines. "Poems" did appear, to be sure; during Mao's "Great Leap Forward" in the late 1950s, when the Chinese people were told to produce everything from rice to iron "more, faster, better, and cheaper," some communes instituted production quotas for poems as well. Here is one:

> Big character posters
> Big character posters
> They are like stars
> And also like cannon

If we count works such as these, the number of Chinese poems written during 1958–1959 probably exceeds all poems written in Chinese history until then.

Underground, however, another tradition was beginning. In the essay that preceded this one, the poet Bei Dao recalls the origins of his radically non-Maoist publication, *Today*. As Bei Dao notes, he and his friends felt a literary continuity with those poets who after the revolution in 1949 gave up creative writing in favor of translating foreign verse into Chinese. In later years critics made the controversial claim that some Chinese poets in the 1980s and 1990s wrote in Chinese as if getting translated into Western languages and earning international reputations were their goal. Such claims are hard to evaluate; they may be true in some cases. But in the 1970s the importance of the "translation style"—which was as far from Maoism as published poetry could then get—was quite the opposite: it was an external source of inspiration for Chinese poets writing in Chinese, not a conduit to a foreign readership.

In its broadest sense, the term "foreign-influenced" is one that could apply to the work of Duoduo (the pen name of Li Shizheng [1951–   ]), who was one of the original group of *Today* poets. Duoduo grew up in Beijing, experienced the turmoil of Mao Zedong's Cultural Revolution in the late 1960s, and first published in *Today*. Invited to participate in the Poetry International Festival in Rotterdam, he left China in 1989 on the day of the Beijing massacre. He has lived in exile in Europe and Canada ever since. He currently lives in Leiden, the Netherlands.

Duoduo's career reflects the history of avant-garde poetry in the People's Republic: From underground scenes in the sixties and seventies, he rose to prominence in the 1980s and gained a significant non-Chinese audience after 1989. His work shows connections with various styles in Chinese poetry since the 1970s, and illustrates a shift from collective activism in the 1980s to individualist approaches in the 1990s.

Duoduo was one of the first in his generation to prize artistic impulses over social and moral ones. His highly original—and sometimes shocking—imagery is powerful enough to preempt the need for explanation or paraphrase, and yet does not conceal the grounding of his concerns. His work exudes an enraged disillusionment, a humanist kind of nihilism. At times his headstrong, idiosyncratic word choice tests the limits of language and engages the paradox of poetry: saying the unsayable. His poems from the 1990s show how far modern Chinese poetry has traveled from one end to the other of a tumultuous century.

DUODUO (1951–)*

IN ENGLAND

after church spires and city chimneys have sunk below
  the horizon
England's skies are gloomier than lovers' whispers
two blind accordion players walk by, heads bowed

without peasants, there'd be no evening prayers
without tombstones, there'd be no declaimers
two rows of newly planted apple trees sting my heart

it's my wings that bring me fame, it's England
that makes me reach the place where I was lost
memories, but no longer leaving furrows

shame is my address
in all of England, there's not one woman who will not
  kiss
all of England is too small for my pride

in mud hidden in the cracks of my nails, I
recognize my native land—mother
has been packed in a small parcel, and sent far away . . .

(translated by Maghiel van Crevel)

*A note on the selection: Bei Dao, who is shortlisted for the Nobel Prize each year, may seem a more obvious choice for the Chinese poet—perhaps too obvious. As his translator, David Hinton, observed, "There seems to be room in the American consciousness for one living Chinese poet, and that poet is Bei Dao." To make room for a second Chinese poet, Bei Dao (a sample of whose work is found on pages 482–483) has written the introduction in order to present his fellow poet Duoduo to American readers.

NONE

there is no bidding me farewell
there is no bidding anyone farewell
there is no bidding the dead farewell, when this morning
    begins

there is no limit to it

except for language, facing the limits where the soil is
    lost
except for the tulip's blossoming flesh, facing a window
    not closed at night
except for my window, facing language I no longer
    understand

there is no language

only the light that never stops to torture, to torture
the saw that never stops pulling back and forth across
    the dawn
only the tulip that is restless, until it is restless no more

there is no tulip

only the light, bogged down in the dawn
starlight, sprinkled in the speeding train's luggage
    compartment, fast asleep
the last light flows down from infants' faces

there is no light

I cleave meat with an ax, I hear the herdsman's scream at
    dawn
I open the window, I hear light and ice shout at one
    another

it is their shout which makes shackles of fog fall apart

there is no shout

only the soil
only the soil and those who carry millet know
only at midnight calls the bird that has seen the dawn

there is no dawn

(translated by Maghiel van Crevel)

HANDICRAFT — AFTER MARINA TSVETAEVA

I write the poetry of degenerate youth
(Unchaste poetry)
I write poetry that is ravished by the poet
In a long narrow room
And is tossed in the street by a café
My indifferent
Remorseless poetry
(Herself a story)
My poetry that no one reads
Like the history of a tale
She who has lost her pride
Her love
(My aristocratic poetry)
Will eventually be married off to a peasant
She is my wasted days

(translated by Michelle Yeh)

MORNING

in the morning or at any time, in the morning
you dream you wake up, you're afraid of waking up
so you say: you're afraid of the rope, afraid of the face
of a bird on a woman, so you dream of your father
speaking birdwords, drinking birdmilk
you dream your father is by himself
and by chance, not in the dream
had you, you dream the dream your father dreamed
you dream your father says: this is a dream a dead man
    dreamed.

you don't believe but you're inclined to believe
this is a dream, but a dream, your dream:
once, it was the handlebar on a bicycle
in the shape it was squeezed into by a hand
now, it droops from your father's belly
once it was a foetus refusing birth
now it is you crawling back to the handlebar
you've dreamed all the details in your dream
like the teeth your father left on the ground, flashing
and laughing at you, so you are not death
but a mere case of death: you've dreamed your dream's
    death.

(translated by Maghiel van Crevel)

NO MORE THAN ONE ALLOWED

    no more than one memory allowed
stretched to where the tracks are powerless to go—
    teaches you
to use millet to measure your prospects, cloth to lay out
    a road

no more than one season allowed
the time for sowing wheat—when sunlight in May
above a naked back flings soil to all sides
no more than one hand allowed
teaches you to bow your head and look—there are
furrows in your palm
thoughts of the soil have slowly been flattened by
another hand
no more than one horse allowed
paralyzed by the glance of a woman at five pm
teaches your temper to bear with your body
no more than one man allowed
the man who taught you to die had died
the wind teaches you to be familiar with that death
no more than one death allowed
every word is a bird with its head crushed
and the sea keeps overflowing from a shattered jar . . .

(translated by Maghiel van Crevel)

NIGHT

In the night, awash with symbols,
the moon seems like the ashen face of an invalid,
like delusive, fleeting time,
like death, like a doctor at a bedside.

A few tired emotions,
a few awful moments of uncertainty.

Moonlight coughs in the dooryard.
Moonlight, oh, sharp intimation of exile.

(translated by Donald Finkel)

FROM DEATH'S POINT OF VIEW

Looking from death's point of view
you'll see people you'd
never see in your life.

For a time you'll wander,
sniffing here and there.
Then you'll bury yourself
at the very heart of their hatred.

They'll shovel dust in your face.
You should be grateful—
doubly grateful.

You'll never see your enemies again,
nor hear again
those malevolent screams
those screams that freeze your spine.

(translated by Donald Finkel)

33

JAPAN

AFTER THE TEA CEREMONY, BEYOND THE GEISHA'S CHARMS: MODERN JAPANESE LITERATURE

Donald Keene

The beginning of modern Japanese literature, like the beginning of everything else that is modern in Japan, is usually traced back to 1868, the first year of the reign of the Emperor Meiji. This political event did not in itself lead to the creation of a new literature, but the oath sworn by the young emperor that "uncivilized" customs of the past would be abolished and knowledge sought throughout the world signified that unprecedented changes would be initiated. The past had always been considered to be the model for the present, even for contemporary literature. The two hundred and more years of isolation from which Japan emerged at this time had at first promoted the development of distinctive forms of literary expression as Japanese writers mined their own past; but by the middle of the nineteenth century they seemed to have exhausted the possibilities of further development of native traditions.

When Emperor Meiji spoke of seeking knowledge from abroad, he probably meant that Japan would borrow from the West its superior scientific knowledge. During the hectic early days of the new regime little consideration was given to the possibility of enriching Japan with the fruits of Western intellectual or artistic progress. The widely accepted formula of "Eastern morality and Western techniques" conveyed instead the hope that Japan would manage to retain its traditional morality even as it borrowed the material achievements of the West. The proposed dichotomy proved to be illusory. Japanese who became familiar with the material culture of the West were often attracted also to its literature, religion, and arts. Again and again stern advocates of purely Japanese traditions rebuked Japanese for their excessive respect for the West; but the voices of reaction could not long change the course of Japanese culture as it moved toward a juncture with the rest of the modern world.

The most conspicuous feature of the change in Japanese poetry and prose after the events of 1868 was the translation and imitation of European and American works of literature. The volume and variety of translations since then has been phenomenal. It has been said that if you could read only one language, you could read more of the world's literature in Japanese than in any other language. It is undeniable, for example, that French writers who are scarcely known in the English-speaking world have not only been translated into Japanese but have exerted influence over twentieth-century writers.

This fact has sometimes earned the Japanese not praise but the derision of critics in the West whenever they detect the influence of Keats or Verlaine or Eliot in a Japanese poem. Japanese authors are aware of this attitude, and some share it. Yasunari Kawabata, who won the Nobel Prize for literature in 1968, once remarked that the enemy of "pure literature" (as opposed to popular fiction) in Japan was the section of the Iwanami Library devoted to translations of European literature. He felt that it was impossible for the Japanese to rival the great European masters. But this modesty was excessive: Kawabata's own novels, even in translation, are not only affecting but highly individual, as anyone who has read them knows.

Kenzaburo Oë, who in 1994 was the second Japanese author to receive the Nobel Prize, contrasted his novels with those of the authors best known abroad—Jun'ichiro Tanizaki, Yasunari Kawabata, and Yukio Mishima. These writers, he said, were admired for their "Japanese" qualities and in particular for their evocations of traditional Japan, whereas he (and the writers with whom he associated himself) were concerned with specifically modern problems and displayed little or no interest in preserving the Japanese heritage. Kobo Abe, often mentioned as a likely winner of the Nobel Prize, when asked what he owed to Japanese tradition, replied, "Nothing."

Of course, even a writer who banishes from his books all mention of conventionally admired sights of nature, the tea ceremony, the charms of the geisha, and similar features of the writings of traditionalists is obliged to obey the stylistic requirements of the Japanese language, and short of writing in another language, cannot be totally cosmopolitan. Attempts have been made to create a more modern Japanese that, for example, supplies the subject of every sentence, does not rely on unspoken overtones, and tries to be as plain-spoken as basic English, but such experiments have been short-lived.

Poets, of course, are even more deeply involved with language than writers of prose. The traditional verse forms—the *tanka* in thirty-one syllables and the *haiku* in seventeen—are still practiced not only by professional poets but by millions of amateurs who attend monthly meetings at which they display their compositions and receive criticism from a professional who is the leader of the group. Most *tanka* poets write in classical Japanese, a language closely related to modern Japanese but with distinctive grammatical features and vocabulary. The conciseness of the classical language appeals to poets with so few syllables at their disposal, but poets in any case tend to be more conscious of literary traditions than are novelists. (Novels were written in classical Japanese up until the end of the nineteenth century but would now be an oddity.)

Although the production of *tanka* and *haiku* is enormous, and some of it may withstand the test of time, the most important poets of the twentieth century have written what was formerly called *shintaishi,* poems in the new style, meaning poems of indeterminate length that usually do not observe traditional metrical rules. Such poems began, not surprisingly, with the introduction and absorption of European poetry. At first Wordsworth, Keats, and Shelley were of the greatest influence, largely because English was the first foreign language of most Japanese. But within a decade or so the poets had moved from Wordsworth to the French symbolists, partly because an affinity was felt between traditional Japanese poetic expression and the poetry of the symbolists. Verlaine went easily into Japanese, and the translations are more beautiful than any English translation of Verlaine with which I am familiar.

The progress of modern Japanese poetry did not, of course, come to a halt with the symbolists. Almost every subsequent movement in Europe or America has had Japanese adherents, ranging from the dadaists to the poets of the Wasteland. Influences on poetry were not always literary: During World War II, poets were among the most enthusiastic supporters of Japanese aggression, but others, both before and after the war, were committed to left-wing causes.

The influence of foreign examples on modern Japanese literature should not obscure its intrinsic excellence. Regardless of the degree of received influence, from abroad or from the literary heritage of its own past, it has emerged as one of the most important literatures of the world.

A Man on a Child's Swing: Contemporary Japanese Poetry

Garrett Hongo

Let me start with an image from Japanese cinema—it is of a man singing, the old bureaucrat played by Takashi Shimura in Akira Kurosawa's *Ikiru,* a drama of contemporary life. The man's name is Watanabe, and he sings something desperate, poignant, and off-key as he sits in a child's swing in a small park somewhere in the gray ruin of postwar Tokyo. We know from the film's narrative that Watanabe has been diagnosed with terminal cancer and that none of his coworkers or family is able to give a damn. He's spent a few nights prowling Tokyo's nightlife for its dizzying myriad of cheap distractions—until he meets a sweet bar girl who has a child in whom he takes an interest. Their relationship is chaste but then begins to convulse. Empowered by fear and a newly aroused compassion, Watanabe comes up with a plan to influence his moribund municipal office to build a playground. He struggles to build human connections, to redeem a life without relationships, without meaning. Finally, through a twist, he succeeds, and, in a scene late in the movie, we find him, still dressed in his long coat and business clothes, seated happily on a child's swing during a snowfall. Kurosawa's 35 mm black-and-white film captures the flurry as amulets of insight falling on the somewhat outsize hat and mortal shoulders of man suddenly made joyous. Watanabe will have his park! He has transformed his own dedicated, incremental misery into a site for the temporal amusement of children.

This is the story of modern Japanese poetry too. It rises from the spiritual, dehumanizing torpor of lives confused and ruined through the long century of Japan's Westernization, industrialization, and militarization since Commodore Perry's black ships forced the opening of Yokohama Bay to foreign trade in 1866. Nearly a century later, by the time of Kurosawa's film, so much social change and cultural displacement, so much true upheaval had called all that had been traditional into question. It was thus with traditional Japanese poetry as well. The old forms of *tanka* and *haiku* spoke for other times, in languages which were fairly restrictive, not only in terms of diction and grammar, but even in vocabulary. A *tanka* or *haiku* poet could not mention all the new things—a steam locomotive, an iron bridge, foreign sailors on liberty gathering at Tokyo Station, an atom bomb. The old literary practices, for all their fabled charm, were almost exclusively bucolic and came couched in a language all too literary—a language that had quickly become a "foreign" one.

The new poets initially responded by revamping traditional forms like the *haiku* and the *tanka,* incorporating not only new vocabularies but the new, angst-ridden moods, and a more libertarian view of personal identities and appropriate poetic subjects. Shiki Masaoka (1867–1902) wrote *haiku* about drying socks as well as wisteria blossoms. Akiko Yosano (1878–1942) wrote vivid *tanka* about her own erotic life, mentioning breasts and thighs and the sated tenderness after lovemaking. And Takuboku Ishikawa (1886–1912) brought into the stately *tanka* the sounds of tubercular breathing and the footfalls of wandering drunks. The overall difference was an embracing of spleen, eroticism, and the humbler items of modern life in exchange for the sweet chorus of pond frogs and images of a silvery snow falling on the thatched rooflines of a far-off village glimpsed at sunset.

Yet the largest revolution was the complete abandonment of traditional forms altogether and the invention of a Japanese free verse reflective of some tradition but responsive to contemporary life. Called *jiyuritsushi,* or literally "free-style poetry," this new form had, to my mind, three important early practitioners, each with their own stylistically recognizable way of handling the problem of creating a vernacular poetry out of the modern Japanese language—two secular intellectuals, Sakutaro Hagiwara and Junzaburo Nishiwaki, and a supremely religious one, Kenji Miyazawa.

When Sakutaro Hagiwara (1886–1942) published *Howling at the Moon* in 1917, the new poetry finally had its first, full-fledged champion. Modern spoken Japanese, full of Western neologisms and the unromanticized cares of harried, newly urbanized lives, at last arrived as a poetic language in Hagiwara. The work is entirely in the free style, almost exclusively in the modern language, yet there are shades of archaism, unexpected twists of syntax, and a deep melancholy about modern life. One of my favorite poems of his was written after he separated from his wife and retreated to his parents' village, bringing his two young daughters on the long train trip from Tokyo to the provinces. Other poems take howling dogs and the corpse of a cat as fitting subjects for poetry, like John Donne's flea and Alan Dugan's mouse caught in a trap, which then occasion metaphysical flight and existential reflection.

That Junzaburo Nishiwaki (1894–1982) published his first volume of poetry, *Spectrum,* in English and not Japanese tells us how ambitious, cosmopolitan, and erudite a poet he was. Nishiwaki was also an editor, a professor of English literature, and a noted theorist on poetics. He went on to publish (in Japanese) about twenty volumes of poetry, several works of translation (Chaucer, Shakespeare, Eliot, and so on), a history of modern English literature, and yet another book of poems in English. Ezra Pound said in 1956, after reading Nishiwaki's English poem "January in Kyoto," that "Junzaburo has a more vital english than any I have seen for some time." In translation, his work has that sense of being a kind of "freed verse" close to Eliot's in "Preludes." His sentences scroll out, somewhat Latinate, with a dazzling rhetorical finish, references to literature and foreign travel, and precise botanical descriptions. Yet it is a fulsome poetry, not unlike Pablo Neruda's of the *Residencias* period, exhilarated with human potential, a surrealist's sense of drama, and a deep, gigantic loneliness.

In Japan today Kenji Miyazawa (1896–1933) is perhaps the most commonly read of the three I've cited, but he was far from well known during his own lifetime. The son of a pawnbroker in Iwate, then a fairly remote prefecture in northern Japan, Miyazawa was formally educated in Buddhism and agriculture. He taught literature, English, and science at various schools during his early professional life, but later turned mainly to farming and a life as a kind of volunteer field agent/adviser to the peasants in the district where he was born. He published *Spring and the Ashura* in 1924 with his own money. He continued writing what he called "image sketches" in various notebooks until 1933, when he succumbed to an illness made fatal by his refusal to leave his work in the fields. Three unpublished volumes of poetry were found among his papers, each with the same title as his first book. The modern vernacular of his verse, full of agrarian life and a deep concern for the farmers among whom he worked, reflects both his personal humility and a devout Buddhist philosophy. Although highly accessible, a provocative Buddhist and scientific vocabulary adds weight and majesty to this sublimely humane life's work.

After these three, Japanese poetry had accomplished its vernacular style, but had yet to respond to the emotionally bleak and economically arduous period following World War II. The militarism and state-sponsored industrial optimism that made up so much of the zeitgeist of prewar Japan had been discredited and abandoned, but not yet replaced. There was a "lost" period, filled by the cultural work of novelists and filmmakers who concentrated on the efforts of Japanese society, through its individuals, to reconstruct itself. Films by Yasujiro Ozu portrayed the new instabilities confronting the Japanese family. Kurosawa made other movies (like *Ikiru*) that placed a lost individual at the center. Novels by Michio Takeyama *(Harp of Burma),* Masuji Ibuse *(Black Rain),* and Shohei Ooka *(Fires on the Plain)* took close, hard looks at the material and spiritual costs of war. Eventually a kind of "consensus of pain" had developed, centering around the works of novelists like Osamu Dazai *(The Setting Sun),* champion of the narrative of suicide.

This was the situation that confronted the new, postwar generation of modern Japanese poets. They did not have to invent a vernacular style but to counteract the circumstances of a bleak, fragmenting society and an exploded traditional culture. Like the Americans of the Beat Generation, their response was a poetry of vigor and newborn innocence that celebrated mundanities as if they were miracles, that raised the rude and humble to the level of a provisional splendor. I have chosen to focus, among the many talented and prolific poets of this group, on Shuntaro Tanikawa.

Tanikawa was born in an intellectual family in Tokyo in 1931, the son of a philosopher and a pianist. He began publishing in magazines when he was twenty. In 1952, by the time he was twenty-two, he published his first collection, *The Loneliness of Twenty Million Light Years.* Encouraged by a group of poets around the magazine *Kai* ("Oar"), he went on to write libretti, radio plays, scripts for television and films, and several more volumes of poetry. He is perhaps the best-known poet of the postwar generation.

Overall Tanikawa concerns himself with strongly humanitarian themes expressed in rhythmic, highly accessible common language. "Nero," an early poem, takes up the topic of the death of his pet dog and lifts this humble consideration toward a real amplitude of thought and feeling. Yet humor and surprise are important features throughout his work, and his poems have a kind of "lightness" akin to that of contemporary tragicomic writers like the Czech novelist Milan Kundera, the Polish poet Zbigniew Herbert, and the American poet Charles Simic. Tanikawa mocks exaggerated pathos, sneezes at literary tragedies, and reviles familiar sanctities.

"After the defeat," he writes, speaking of the postwar period, "all the values that the Japanese had believed in were completely destroyed. It was a period of vacuum for us and nobody knew what to believe." What Tanikawa accomplished, along with others of his generation, is a poetry that urges the disconsolate, postwar sensibility to begin again through its affinities for the first, simplest things—a land, animals, a partner and children under a blue sky, and a place for children to play. His work, like that of any singer's caught out in the rain, like that of *Ikiru*'s once-dour Watanabe exalted by a self-born vision into joy, has been no less a task than the reconstruction of a humane cosmos.

SHUNTARO TANIKAWA (1931–)

GROWTH

age three
there was no past for me

age five
my past went back to yesterday

age seven
my past went back to topknotted samurai

age eleven
my past went back to dinosaurs

age fourteen
my past agreed with the texts at school

age sixteen
I look at the infinity of my past with fear

age eighteen
I know not a thing about time

(translated by Harold Wright)

PORNO-BACH

Are those fingers, the ones playing Bach just now,
and these fingers really the same?
This thing of mine, getting long and getting short,
and not resembling a piano at all,
must be called a comical tool;

so how does this conventional thing
and the great Bach, by your soft fingers,
get joined together?
I, myself, have no idea!
Yet, that thing of yours and this of mine,
now the color of the naked heart,
feel so warm, so smooth
in endless surrender much like death,
and when in this transparent blood filled darkness
I unexpectedly seem to meet Bach face to face.

(translated by Harold Wright)

LANDSCAPE WITH YELLOW BIRDS

there are birds
so there is sky
there is sky
so there are balloons
there are balloons
so children are running
children are running
so there is laughter
there is laughter
so there is sadness
so there is prayer
and ground for kneeling
there is ground
so water is flowing
and there's today and tomorrow
there is a yellow bird
so with all colors forms and movements
there is the world

(translated by Harold Wright)

NERO

(to a loved little dog)

Nero
another summer is coming soon
your tongue
your eyes
your napping in the afternoon
now clearly live again before me.

You knew but about two summers
I already know eighteen summers
and now I can remember various summers
    both of my own and not my own:
the summer of Maisons-Lafitte
the summer of Yodo
the summer of the Williamsburg Bridge
the summer of Oran
so I am wondering
about the number of summers
    that humanity has known.

Nero
another summer is coming soon
but it's not a summer when you were here
a different summer
a completely different summer.
A new summer is coming
I'll be learning various new things
beautiful things   ugly things
things to cheer me   things to sadden me
and so I ask—
what is it?
why is it?
what must be done?

Nero
you have died
without anyone being aware
    you have gone far away alone
your voice
your touch
and even your feelings
now clearly live again before me.

But Nero
another summer is coming soon
a new infinitely vast summer is coming
and then
I'll probably be walking on
to meet the new summer
    to meet autumn
     to meet winter
to meet spring   and
    to expect a new summer again
in order to know all the new things
and
in order to answer
    all my questions
     myself.

(translated by Harold Wright)

PICNIC TO THE EARTH

here let's jump rope together   here
here let's eat balls of rice together
here let me love you
your eyes reflect the blueness of sky
your back will be stained a wormwood green
here let's learn the constellations together

from here let's dream of every distant thing
here let's gather low-tide shells,
from the sea of sky at dawn
let's bring back little starfish
at breakfast we will toss them out
let the night be drawn away
here I'll keep saying, "I am back"
while you repeat, "Welcome home"
here let's come again and again
here let's drink hot tea
here let's sit together for awhile
let's be blown by the cooling breeze.

(translated by Harold Wright)

TWO TOKYOS

Withdrawing all his postal savings
and putting on his only suit,
he packed a bag with old newspapers
and went to a hotel with a foreign name.
He slept in a fluffy bed (alone).
In the morning he ate oatmeal and melon,
in the afternoon he took three showers,
at night he took a sightseeing bus
     with a man from Peru.
TOKYO was noisy.
TOKYO was huge.
TOKYO was fancy.
He wanted to send a picture postcard somewhere,
but there was nowhere to send one.
So he wrote one to himself,
     addressing it to his rooming house,
saying, "Tokyo has everything."

When he returned to his rooming house
the postcard was glittering on his bed.

(translated by Harold Wright)

RAIN PLEASE FALL

Rain please fall
over an unloved woman
rain please fall
in place of unflowing tears
rain please fall   secretly.

Rain please fall
over the cracked fields
rain please fall
over dried-up wells
rain please fall   and soon.

Rain please fall
over the napalm flames
rain please fall
over the burning villages
rain please fall   furiously.

Rain please fall
over the endless desert
rain please fall
over hidden seeds
rain please fall   gently.

Rain please fall
over the reviving green

(translated by Harold Wright)

ZOO

Bathed by tree filtered sun,
    my little girl rides a "monkey train"
when she comes closer I feel happy
when she goes away I feel sad
every third time around I failed pressing the shutter.

There are lots of families just like us
I don't feel happier than them
I don't feel less happy than them
yet, my mood slowly darkens.

The elephant raises and lowers its trunk
the crocodile continues to quietly exist
the deer leaps
what kind of animal can I be called?

(translated by Harold Wright)

DUSK

Once more drifting clouds gather in the western sky
while we, being sustained over and over by things over
        and over,
are still driven toward a tomorrow;
old melodies sung in faint memories are revived,
condolences for the dead deepen in the dimming
        afterglow,
is there anything that needs to be added to our world?
Comets depart for distances without attaining a single
        glance
along with many books and much music people grow
        old,

once more puppies snuggle to a mother dog's breast,
while we, being soothed over and over by things over
    and over,
still walk toward something which returns no more.

(translated by Harold Wright)

TWENTY BILLION LIGHT YEARS OF LONELINESS

Mankind on a little globe
Sleeps, awakes and works
Wishing at times to be friends with Mars.

Martians on a little globe
Are probably doing something; I don't know what
(Maybe *sleep-sleeping, wear-wearing,* or *fret-fretting*)
While wishing at times to be friends with Earth
This is a fact I'm sure of.

This thing called universal gravitation
Is the power of loneliness pulling together.

The universe is distorted
So all join in desire.

The universe goes on expanding
So all feel uneasy.

At the loneliness of twenty billion light years
Without thinking, I sneeze.

(translated by Harold Wright)

34

A SAMPLING OF OTHER ASIAN POETS

NAZIM HIKMET (TURKEY)

ON LIVING

I

Living is no laughing matter:
 you must live with great seriousness
  like a squirrel, for example—
 I mean without looking for something beyond and
  above living,
  I mean living must be your whole occupation.
Living is no laughing matter:
you must take it seriously,
 so much so and to such a degree
 that, for example, your hands tied behind your back,
   your back to the wall,
 or else in a laboratory
 in your white coat and safety glasses,
 you can die for people—
even for people whose faces you've never seen,
even though you know living
 is the most real, most beautiful thing.

I mean, you must take living so seriously
    that even at seventy, for example, you'll plant olive
        trees—
    and not for your children, either,
    but because although you fear death you don't
        believe it,
    because living, I mean, weighs heavier.

    II
Let's say we're seriously ill, need surgery—
which is to say we might not get up
        from the white table.
Even though it's impossible not to feel sad
        about going a little too soon,
we'll still laugh at the jokes being told,
we'll look out the window to see if it's raining,
or still wait anxiously
        for the latest newscast . . .
Let's say we're at the front—
    for something worth fighting for, say,
There, in the first offensive, on that very day,
    we might fall on our face, dead.
We'll know this with a curious anger,
    but we'll still worry ourselves to death
    about the outcome of the war, which could last
        years.
Let's say we're in prison
and close to fifty,
and we have eighteen more years, say,
        before the iron doors will open.
We'll still live with the outside,
with its people and animals, struggle and wind—
        I mean with the outside beyond the walls.
I mean, however and wherever we are,
    we must live as if we will never die.

III

This earth will grow cold,
a star among stars
        and one of the smallest,
a gilded mote on blue velvet—
        I mean *this,* our great earth.
This earth will grow cold one day,
not like a block of ice
or a dead cloud even
but like an empty walnut it will roll along
        in pitch-black space . . .

You must grieve for this right now
—you have to feel the sorrow now—
for the world must be loved this much
        if you're going to say "I've lived" . . .

                (translated by Randy Blasing and Mutlu Konuk)

YEHUDA AMICHAI (ISRAEL)

SEVEN LAMENTS FOR THE WAR-DEAD

I

Mr. Beringer, whose son
fell at the Canal that strangers dug
so ships could cross the desert,
crosses my path at Jaffa Gate:

He has grown very thin, has lost
the weight of his son.
That's why he floats so lightly in the alleys,
and gets caught in my heart like little twigs
that drift away.

2

As a child he would mash his potatoes
to a golden mush.
And then you die.

A living child must be cleaned
when he comes home from playing.
But for a dead man
earth and sand are clear water, in which
his body goes on being bathed and purified
forever.

3

The Tomb of the Unknown Soldier,
across there. On the enemy's side. A good landmark
for gunners of the future.

Or the war monument in London
at Hyde Park Corner, decorated
like a magnificent cake: yet another soldier
lifting head and rifle,
another cannon, another eagle, another
stone angel.

And the whipped cream of a huge marble flag
poured over it all
with an expert hand.

But the candied, much-too-red cherries
were already gobbled up
by the glutton of hearts. Amen.

4

I came upon an old zoology textbook,
Brehm, Volume II, *Birds:*

in sweet phrases, an account of the life of the starling,
swallow, and thrush. Full of mistakes in an antiquated
Gothic typeface, but full of love, too. "Our feathered
friends." "Migrate from us to the warmer climes."
Nest, speckled egg, soft plumage, nightingale,
stork. "The harbingers of spring." The robin,
red-breasted.

Year of publication 1913: Germany,
on the eve of the war that was to be
the eve of all *my* wars.

My good friend, who died in my arms, in
his blood,
on the sands of Ashdod, 1948, June.

Oh my friend,
red-breasted.

5
Dicky was hit,
like the water tower at Yad Mordecai.
Hit. A hole in the belly. Everything
came flooding out.

But he remained standing like that
in the landscape of my memory,
like the water tower at Yad Mordecai.

He fell not far from there,
a little to the north, near Huleikat.

6
Is all of this
sorrow? I don't know.

I stood in the cemetery, dressed in
the camouflage clothes of a living man: brown pants
and a shirt yellow as the sun.

Cemeteries are cheap; they don't ask for much.
Even wastebaskets are small, made for holding
tissue paper
that wrapped flowers from the store.
Cemeteries are a polite and disciplined thing.
"I shall never forget you," in French
on a little ceramic plaque.
I don't know who it is that won't ever forget:
he's more anonymous than the one who died.

Is all of this sorrow? I guess so.
"May ye find consolation in the building
of the homeland." But how long
can you go on building the homeland
and not fall behind in the terrible
three-sided race
between consolation and building and death?

Yes, all of this is sorrow. But leave
a little love burning always
like the small bulb in the room of a sleeping baby
that gives him a bit of security and quiet love
though he doesn't know what the light is
or where it comes from.

7

Memorial day for the war-dead: go tack on
the grief of all your losses—
including a woman who left you—
the grief of losing them; go mix
one sorrow with another, like history,

that in its economical way
heaps pain and feast and sacrifice
onto a single day for easy reference.

Oh sweet world, soaked like bread,
in sweet milk for the terrible
toothless God. "Behind all this
some great happiness is hiding." No use
crying inside and screaming outside.
Behind all this, some great happiness may
be hiding.

Memorial day. Bitter salt, dressed up as
as a little girl with flowers.
Ropes are strung out the whole length of the route
for a joint parade: the living and the dead together.
Children move with the footsteps of someone else's grief
as if picking their way through broken glass.

The flautist's mouth will stay pursed for many days.
A dead soldier swims among the small heads
with the swimming motions of the dead,
with the ancient error the dead have
about the place of the living water.

A flag loses contact with reality and flies away.
A store window decked out with beautiful dresses for
        women
in blue and white. And everything
in three languages: Hebrew, Arabic, and Death.

A great royal beast has been dying all night long
under the jasmine
with a fixed stare at the world.
A man whose son died in the war
walks up the street

like a woman with a dead fetus in her womb.
"Behind all this, some great happiness is hiding."

(translated by Chana Bloch)

ADONIS (SYRIA/LEBANON)

THE DIARY OF BEIRUT UNDER SIEGE, 1982

1.

The cities break up
The land is a train of dust
Only poetry knows how to marry this space.

2.

No road to this house—the siege.
And the streets are graveyards;
     Far away a stunned moon
     Hangs on threads of dust
     Over his house.

3.

I said: This street leads to our house. He said: No.
     You won't pass. And pointed his bullets at me.

Fine, in every street
     I have homes and friends.

4.

Roads of blood,
     The blood a boy was talking about
     And whispering to his friends:

Only some holes known as stars
Remain in the sky.

5.

The voice of the city is soft
The face of the city glows
Like a little boy telling his dreams to the night
And offering his chair to the morning.

6.

They found people in sacks:
One without a head
One without a tongue or hands
One strangled
The rest without shape or names.
Have you gone mad? Please,
        Don't write about these things.
. . . .
From the palm wine to the calmness of the desert . . .
    etc.
From the morning that smuggles its stomach and sleeps
    on the corpses
of the refugees . . . etc.
From the streets, army vehicles, concentration of troops
    . . . etc.
From the shadows, men, women . . . etc.
From the bombs stuffed with the prayers of Muslims and
    infidels . . . .
etc.
From the castles walling our bodies and bombarding us
    with darkness . . . etc.
From the myths of the dead which speak of life, express
    life . . . etc.
From the speech which is the slaughter, the slaughtered
    and the

slaughterers . . . etc.

From the dark dark dark

I breathe, feel my body, search for you and him, myself
    and others,

And hang my death

Between my face and these bleeding words . . . etc.

. . . .

Anything rejected by other eyes will be looked after by
    my eyes.

This is my friendship's promise to destruction.

. . . .

All the certainty I have lived slips away

All the torches of my desire slip away

All that was between the faces that lit my exile and me
    slips away

I have to start from the beginning

To reach my limbs to reach my future,

To talk, to climb, to descend from the beginning

In the sky of beginnings, in the abyss of the alphabet.

They are falling, the land is a thread of smoke

    Time a train

      Traveling along a track of smoke . . .

My obsession is here now, loss.

My concern is the end

    Is not over.

They are falling, I am not looking for a new beginning.

—from *The Desert*

MAHMOUD DARWISH (PALESTINE)

ON OUR LAST EVENING ON THIS LAND

On our last evening on this land we chop our days
from our young trees, count the ribs we'll take with us
and the ribs we'll leave behind . . . On the last evening
we bid nothing farewell, nor find the time to end . . .
Everything remains as it is, it is the place that changes
        our dreams
and its visitors. Suddenly, we're incapable of irony,
this land will now host atoms of dust . . . Here, on our
        last evening,
we look closely at the mountains besieging the clouds: a
        conquest . . . and a counter conquest,
and an old time handing this new time the keys to our
        doors.
So enter our houses, conquerors, and drink the wine
of our mellifluous *Mouwashah*.* We are the night at
        midnight,
and no horseman will bring dawn from the sanctuary of
        the last Call to Prayer . . .
Our tea is green and hot; drink it. Our pistachios are
        fresh; eat them.
The beds are of green cedar, fall on them,
following this long siege, lie down on the feathers of our
        dreams.
The sheets are crisp, perfumes are ready by the door, and
        there are plenty of mirrors:
enter them so we may exit completely. Soon we will
        search

Mouwashah: the characteristic form of Andalusian poetry, recited and sung, and still
performed throughout the Arab world.

in the margins of your history, in distant countries,
for what was once *our* history. And in the end we will ask
    ourselves:
Was Andalusia here or there? On the land . . . or in this
    poem?

—from *Eleven Stars over Andalusia*

(translated by Agha Shahid Ali, with Mona Anis, Ahmad
Dallal, and Nigel Ryan)

BALAKRISHNA SAMA (NEPAL)

THE SONG

Krishna played on the charmingly juicy flute.
In the town of Mathura,
In every house
In every room
In every fold of the heart
The air began to tremble in concord with the flute.
Krishna played on the charmingly juicy flute.

The grasses fell down from the chewing mouth of the
    cows,
The fishes came out of water.
The peacocks were lost in meditation,
So they dropped down their feathers on the Lord,
And the cuckoos and the nightingales,
Tearing off their breasts with their own nails
Fell down on the branches of the trees in concord
    with the flute.
Krishna played on the charmingly juicy flute.

The milkmaids began to weep bitterly in happiness,
After sometime like the golden images they remained
    motionless,
The river of adoration was profusely flowing,
And Krishna began to smile,
The whole universe dozed in ecstasy,
The Heaven and the Earth kissed each other,
The eyelashes of the milkmaids began to be entangled
    in concord with the flute,
Krishna played on the charmingly juicy flute.

CECIL RAJENDRA (MALAYSIA)

MY MESSAGE

And now you ask
what is my message
i say with Nabokov
i am a poet
not a postman
i have no message.

but i want the cadences
of my verse to crack
the carapace of indifference
prise open torpid eyelids
thick-coated with silver.

i want syllables
that will dance, pirouette
in the fantasies of nymphets
i want vowels that float
into the dreams of old men.

i want my consonants
to project kaleidoscopic visions
on the screens of the blind
& on the eardrums of the deaf
i want pentameters that sing
like ten thousand mandolins.

i want such rhythms
as will shake pine
angsana, oak & meranti
out of their pacific
slumber, uproot them-
selves, hurdle over
buzz-saw & bull-dozer
and rush to crush
with long heavy toes
merchants of defoliants.

i want stanzas
that will put a sten-gun
in the paw of polar-bear & tiger
a harpoon under the fin
of every seal, whale & dolphin
arm them to stem
the massacre of their number.

i want every punctuation—
full-stop, comma & semi-colon
to turn into a grain of barley
millet, maize, wheat or rice
in the mouths of our hungry;
i want each & every metaphor
to metamorphose into a rooftop
over the heads of our homeless.

i want the assonances
of my songs to put smiles
on the faces of the sick
the destitute & the lonely
pump adrenaline into the veins
of every farmer & worker
the battle-scarred & the weary.

and yes, yes, i want my poems
to leap out from the page
rip off the covers of my books
and march forthrightly to
that sea of somnolent humanity
lay bare the verbs, vowels
syllables, consonants . . . & say
"these are my sores, my wounds:
this is my distended belly:
here i went ragged and hungry:
in that place i bled, was tortured;
and on this electric cross i died.
Brothers, sisters, HERE I AM."

HO CHI MINH (VIETNAM)

TWO PRISON POEMS

WATER-DOLE

Half a basin:
Have a bath, have tea.
Have tea but no bath.
Have a bath and no tea.

FESTIVAL OF TSING MING

Tsing Ming, and it
Drizzles on.
"Freedom, where's freedom?" The jailer points
To the governor's house, far, far away.

(translated by Burton Raffel)

BEI DAO (CHINA)

ANSWER

The scoundrel carries his baseness around like an ID
     card.
The honest man bears his honor like an epitaph.
Look—the gilded sky is swimming
with undulant reflections of the dead.

They say the ice age ended years ago.
Why are there icicles everywhere?
The Cape of Good Hope has already been found.
Why should all those sails contend on the Dead Sea?

I came into this world with nothing
but paper, rope, and shadow.
Now I come to be judged,
and I've nothing to say but this:

Listen. *I don't believe!*
OK. You've trampled
a thousand enemies underfoot. Call me
a thousand and one.

I don't believe the sky is blue.
I don't believe what the thunder says.
I don't believe dreams aren't real.
that beyond death there is no reprisal.

If the sea should break through the sea-wall,
let its brackish water fill my heart.
If the land should rise from the sea again,
we'll choose again to live in the heights.

The earth revolves. A glittering constellation
pricks the vast defenseless sky.
Can you see it there? that ancient ideogram—
the eye of the future, gazing back.

(translated by Donald Finkel)

CHO PYONG-HWA (KOREA)

ONE WINTRY DAY

Between the boughs of a tall tree the sun rises like a
persimmon in the gray sky.

I will rise before sunrise and wait for the persimmon sun
to climb up the eastern sky below my window.

My room is perched up high like a magpie's nest.

Cold winds steal into my room, where I live through the
chilly winter.

The thermometer shows around 37 degrees.

I live on the warmth of the sun.

I look down on the rising sun from my bed perched like
a magpie's nest, wrapped in a soft quilt.

Like a crayon painting the beautiful persimmon sun
mounts the gray sky between the tall boughs,
pouring its warmth on my body.

(translated by Peter H. Lee)

THE EDITORS

Jeffery Paine is the author of *Father India: Westerners Under the Spell of an Ancient Culture,* and contributes to *The New York Times, The Washington Post,* the *Los Angeles Times,* and various literary periodicals. He is contributing editor and was for many years literary editor of *The Wilson Quarterly* and has served as vice president of the National Book Critics Circle and a judge of the Pulitzer Prize. He has taught at Princeton University, the New School for Social Research, and the Volksuniversiteit Amsterdam.

Kwame Anthony Appiah is the author of *In My Father's House: Africa in the Philosophy of Culture* and *The Dictionary of Global Culture* (with Henry Louis Gates, Jr.) and is currently editing *The Oxford Book of African Literature.* He is a professor of philosophy and African-American studies at Harvard University.

Sven Birkerts is the author of several works of criticism, among them *The Electric Life: Essays on Modern Poetry, An Artificial Wilderness,* and *The Gutenberg Elegies.* He won the National Book Critics Circle Award for Criticism and lives in Arlington, Massachusetts.

Joseph Brodsky emigrated from the Soviet Union to the United States in 1972 and won the Nobel Prize for Literature in 1987. He and Jeffery Paine conceived the idea for this anthology when they were co-editors of a magazine.

Carolyn Forché won the Yale Series of Younger Poets Award for her first volume of poetry, *Gathering the Tribes;* her second collection, *The Country Between Us*, received the Lamont Award of the Academy of American Poets. She is also the author of the poetry collection *The Angel of History*. She edited *Against Forgetting: Twentieth-Century Poetry of Witness* and teaches at George Mason University.

Helen Vendler, widely regarded as America's leading critic of contemporary poetry, is A. Kingsley Porter University Professor at Harvard University. Her numerous works include *On Extended Wings: Wallace Stevens's Longer Poems, The Art of Shakespeare's Sonnets,* and *Part of Nature, Part of Us,* which won the National Book Critics Circle Award.

Agha Shahid Ali, whose poetry includes *A Nostalgist's Map of America* and *The Country Without a Post Office*, directs the creative writing program at the University of Massachusetts.

Bei Dao, considered the leading Chinese dissident writer living in exile, has written both poetry *(The August Sleepwalkers)* and fiction *(The Waves)* and teaches at the University of California—Davis.

Anita Desai, who teaches in the writing program at MIT, had two of her novels—*Clear Light of Day* and *In Custody*—shortlisted for the Booker Prize.

Edward C. Dimock, Distinguished Service Professor at the University of Chicago and past president of the American Association of Indian Studies, is the author of, most recently, *Mr. Dimock Explores the Mystery of the East*.

Edward Hirsch, whose works include *Wild Gratitude, On Love,* and *How to Read a Poem,* has won the National Book Critics Circle Award and the Rome Prize, as well as a MacArthur "genius" award.

Garrett Hongo, director of the creative writing program at the University of Oregon, is the author of *Yellow Light, The River of Heaven, and Volcano*.

Donald Keene, the dean of American critics of Japanese literature, has authored dozens of books in both English and Japanese.

Denise Levertov, who taught English at Stanford University, published fifteen volumes of poetry during her lifetime.

Perry Link, professor of Chinese literature at Princeton University, is the author of *Mandarin Ducks and Butterflies* and *Evening Chats in Beijing*.

Burton Raffel, Distinguished Professor of Humanities at the University of Southwestern Louisiana, has published translations from more than a dozen languages, including Indonesian, Chinese, and Vietnamese.

PERMISSIONS

of April '43," "Memory I," "Memory II," "Euripedes the Athenian," "The Last Day," "Narration," from *George Seferis: Collected Poems* (revised edition), translated by Edmund Keeley and Philip Sherrard. Reprinted by permission of Princeton University Press.

Léopold Sédar Senghor: "In Memoriam," "Porte Dorée," "All Day Long . . . ," "Totem," "Camp 1940," "To New York," "Suddenly Startled," "I Am Alone" from *Léopold Sédar Senghor: The Collected Poetry*, translated by Melvin Dixon. Reprinted by the University Press of Virginia.

Wole Soyinka: "Ikeja, Friday, Four O'Clock," "Post Mortem," "Telephone Conversation," "Isara, the Ancestral Village," "Civilian and Soldier," "A Man's First Duties," "Abiku," and from "Funeral in Soweto." Reprinted by permission of Wole Soyinka.

Shuntaro Tanikawa: "Growth," "Porno-Bach," "Landscape with Yellow Birds," "Nero," "Picnic to the Earth," "Two Tokyos," "Rain Please Fall," "Zoo," "Dusk," and "Twenty Billion Light Years of Loneliness," from the *Selected Poems of Shuntaro Tanikawa*, translated by Harold Wright. Reprinted by permission of Harold Wright.

César Vallejo: "To My Brother Miguel," "The Eternal Dice," and "Have You Anything to Say in Your Defense?" translated by James Wright, in *Neruda and Vallejo*, published by Beacon Press, edited by Robert Bly. Reprinted by permission of Robert Bly. "Good Sense," "I am going to speak of hope," "Intensity and Height," and "A Man Walks by with a Loaf of Bread on His Shoulder," from the *Complete Posthumous Poetry* by César Vallejo, translated by Clayton Eshleman. Reprinted by permission of the University of California Press.

Derek Walcott: excerpt from "The Divided Child," "The Gulf," excerpt from *Midsummer,* "Nights in the Gardens of Port of Spain," "Sea Grapes," "The Season of Phantasmal Peace," and "I, Adios, Carenage" from "The Schooner Flight," from *Collected Poems 1948–1984.* "Tomorrow, Tomorrow" from *The Arkansas Testament.* Reprinted by permission of Farrar, Straus & Giroux.

A Sampling of Other African Poets: "Nightsong: City" by Dennis Brutus from *Sirens, Knuckles, Boots.* Reprinted by permission of Dennis Brutus. "Letter from a Contract Worker" by Antonio Jacinto from *Poems from Angola*, edited and translated by Michael Wolfers. Reprinted by permission of Michael Wolfers. "Isatou Died," by Lenrie Peters. Reprinted by permission of Dr. Lenrie Peters. "One Night at Victoria Beach" by Gabriel Okara from *West African Verse* (Donatus I. Nwoga, ed.). Reprinted by permission of Gabriel Okara. "Elegy for My Friend E. Galo," by Mazisi Kunene from *Zulu Poems* (Africana Publishing House). Reprinted by permission of the publisher. "On the New Year" by Christopher Okigbo from *Christopher Okigbo.* Reprinted by permission of Heinemann.

A Sampling of Other Asian Poets: "On Living" from *Poems of Nazim Hikmet* translated by Randy Blasing and Mutlu Konuk. Reprinted by Permisson of Persea Books, Inc. "Seven Laments for the War-Dead," from *The Selected Poetry of Yehuda Amichai,* translated by Chana Bloch and Stephen Mitchell. Reprinted by permission of Chana Bloch. "On Our Last Evening on This Land," from *Eleven Stars Over Andalusia,* by Mahmoud Darwish, translated by Agha Shahid Ali. Reprinted by permission of Agha Shahid Ali. "My Message" from *Hour of Assassins and Other Poems* by Cecil Rajendra. Reprinted by permission of Cecil Rajendra. "Two Prison Poems" by Ho Chi Minh from *From the Vietnamese: Ten Centuries of Poetry*, translated by Burton Raffel. Reprinted by permission of Burton Raffel. "Answer" by Bei Dao from *A Splintered Mirror*, translated by Donald Finkel. Reprinted by permission from North Point Press/Farrar, Straus & Giroux.

A Sampling of Other English-Language Poets: "Easter Morning" from *The Selected Poems: Expanded Edition* by A. R. Ammons. Reprinted by permission of W. W. Norton and Company, Inc. "Soonest Mended" by John Ashbery from *The Double Dream of Spring*. Reprinted by permission of Georges Borchardt, Inc., for the author. "Four Small Elegies" from *Selected Poems* by Margaret Atwood. Reprinted by permission of Houghton Mifflin and Oxford University Press Canada. "Dream Song 14" from the *Dream Songs* by John Berryman. Reprinted by permission of Farrar, Straus & Giroux. "LV" from *The Triumph of Love* by Geoffrey Hill. Reprinted by permission of Houghton Mifflin. "Milkweed and Monarch" from the *Annals of Chile* by Paul Muldoon. Reprinted by permission of Farrar, Straus & Giroux. "Cotton Flannelette" from *Subhuman Redneck Poems* by Les Murray. Reprinted by permission of Farrar, Straus & Giroux. "Lady Lazarus" from the *Collected Poems* by Sylvia Plath. Reprinted by permission of HarperCollins. "Between" from *Between* by C. K. Stead. Reprinted by permission of Auckland University Press. "The Calling" from *Laboratories of the Spirit* by R. S. Thomas. Reprinted by permission of David R. Godine, Publisher.

A Sampling of Other European Poets: "Blue" by Raphael Alberti, translated by Mark Strand. Reprinted by permission of Mark Strand. "A Kind of Loss" from *In the Storm of Roses* by Ingeborg Bachmann, translated by Mark Anderson. Reprinted by permission of Mark Anderson. "The Book, for Growing Old" from *New and Selected Poems* by Yves Bonnefoy, translated by Emily Grosholz. Reprinted by permission of University of Chicago Press. "Letters from the Ming Dynasty" from a *Part of Speech* by Joseph Brodsky. Reprinted by permission of Farrar, Straus & Giroux. "Avignon" by Remco Campert, translated by Jeffery Paine. Reprinted by permission of Jeffery Paine. "The Fly" from *Selected Poems* by Miroslav Holub, translated by Ian Milner and George Theiner. Reprinted by permission of Penguin UK. "Encounter" from *Bells in Winter* by Czeslaw Milosz, translated by the author and Lillian Vallee. Reprinted by permission of Ecco Press. "O the Chimneys" from *O the Chimneys* by Nelly Sachs, translated by Michael Roloff. Reprinted by permission of Farrar, Straus & Giroux.

TITLE INDEX

GENERAL INDEX

Page numbers in **bold type** refer to the anthologized poems and appear after the names of the poets and translators.